THE BRAND GPA

THE BRAND GPA

MAKING THE GRADE WITH YOUR CUSTOMERS

JOSH GRAU

FC
FAST
COMPANY
Press

Fast Company Press
New York, New York
www.fastcompanypress.com

Distributed by Greenleaf Book Group

For ordering information or special discounts for bulk purchases, please contact Greenleaf Book Group at PO Box 91869, Austin, TX 78709, 512.891.6100.

Design and composition by Greenleaf Book Group and Brian Phillips
Cover design by Greenleaf Book Group and Brian Phillips

Publisher's Cataloging-in-Publication data is available.

Print ISBN: 978-1-63908-192-9

eBook ISBN: 978-1-63908-193-6

To offset the number of trees consumed in the printing of our books, Greenleaf donates a portion of the proceeds from each printing to the Arbor Day Foundation. Greenleaf Book Group has replaced over 50,000 trees since 2007.

Printed in the United States of America on acid-free paper

26 27 28 29 30 31 32 33 10 9 8 7 6 5 4 3 2 1

To my late father, Henry—
the Valedictorian of dads—
who taught me the importance
of listening to customers.

CONTENTS

INTRODUCTION

TO BRAND OR NOT TO BRAND

ASK ANY CEO OR FOUNDER IF THEY WANT a great brand, and they'll universally say yes. Yet the concept of "brand" remains plagued by misperceptions. Too often it's reduced to expensive Super Bowl ads (brand advertising) or updating fonts and colors (branding), which explains why CMOs feel like they're walking the plank whenever brand conversations arise, especially in tech.

There's data that backs up that feeling. According to Gartner, more than 40 percent of CMOs who push for larger brand budgets will lose influence with the C-suite by 2027.[1] And 84 percent of companies are already caught in what Gartner calls a "doom loop"—meaning underfunded brand measurement leads to unclear impact, which leads to C-suite skepticism, which leads to tighter budgets, which leads to further diminishment of brand.

I speak from experience—and have the PTSD to prove it. I have been a CMO four times, and at the beginning of the journey, the message was the same: We want our brand to win. But inevitably, the story changes, and *brand* becomes a four-letter word. One founder/CEO told me, "We don't do 'brand' here," and literally banned the term from meetings. Another insisted that focusing on brand means you're not focusing on growth (hoo boy). And nearly every conversation with executive recruiters begins with that dreaded and oh-so-reductive "Are you more brand or performance?" question.

I can hear the eye rolls from those who've endured these same conversations. Ask any loyal customer why they keep coming back to a brand, and you'll never hear someone say, "Well, it's these great performance ads I keep seeing on Facebook!"

Think about the brands you personally love. How do you talk about them? I doubt last-click attribution is how you sell a friend on why Claude is so much better than ChatGPT or why bubly tastes so much better than LaCroix. Yet inside an organization, the customer's "why" gets lost in the lead gen dashboards and KPI decks.

Don't get me wrong, data is critically important. This book is *all* about using data. But to build a winning brand, you have to zoom out and look at every touchpoint. Think about brands that have been winning with their customers for what seems like forever—Apple, Patagonia, Costco. These companies have become indispensable because they are consistent, anticipate what their customers need next, and have built exceptional brand moats. Meanwhile, past darlings like Allbirds, Peloton, and WeWork have faded mightily compared to their bolder former selves because they lost the brand plot—and their customers.

Having worked in both B2C and B2B in my career, the philosophical divide—brand vs. performance—is almost as intense as the heated rivalry between Steve Jobs and Bill Gates. More often than not, B2B companies believe they somehow operate by different rules than consumer brands. But in the eyes of the customer, *everything is a consumer brand.* Whether you're selling enterprise software to millennial CTOs or '90s jeans to Gen Z college students, you are being evaluated by your customers using the same fundamental criteria: Can you solve my problem? Do you understand my ongoing needs? Are you worth it? If the answers are yes, you probably have a pretty strong brand.

As a marketing leader, you can bombard your CEO and board with data about why brand drives growth, retention, and renewal. Yet the result remains predictable: Brand becomes something shiny you slap onto a business when things are going well. When headwinds appear? Brand gets shoved back into cold storage. And in today's AI frenzy, brand faces even greater risk of being misunderstood. The integration of AI into search engines is changing how users interact with search results, often reducing the need to click through to individual websites. On that, media mogul and entrepreneur Barry Diller recently said, "So long as we invest in [our brand], that is our best defense against AI."[2] In other words, investing in having a strong brand means people will come directly to you rather than finding you through search mechanisms. He went on to say that anything without brand potential is worthless.

Preach, Barry! And while he is speaking about the importance of brand in the media context, this perspective is applicable across all industries, from consumer to enterprise. Visionaries like Bezos, Branson, Jobs, and Schultz have long extolled the virtues of brand and its critical importance in building trust and long-lasting relationships with customers. But despite a quote book full of validating statements from the would-be experts on the topic, brand still remains at the kids' table.

We can bang our fists and say that's not fair, or we can be grown-ups and be honest about what's really going on: Brand has a brand perception problem.

There, I said it.

THE "PROBLEM" WITH BRAND

Recently, I came across a LinkedIn "hot take" by a well-known founder of a popular clothing company that captured this dynamic perfectly. In a fictional dialogue between a CEO and CMO, the author has the CMO declare: "I think brand marketing is bullshit." The CEO's confusion is immediate—wait, what?—until the CMO clarifies: "When CFOs and CEOs hear 'brand marketing,' they think: unaccountable, expensive, and money wasting. The vocab's gotta change."

He's not wrong about the problem. Brand has become toxic vocabulary because it's been reduced to expensive vanity projects that never ladder up to business outcomes. It's a self-fulfilling prophecy: Teams get budget for a brand campaign, hire a creative agency, build a killer media plan, launch it, and then—crickets. When nothing immediately moves the needle on leads or inventory, it's chalked up as a colossal failure, and brand gets written off as a pointless endeavor.

But here's what makes posts like this so damaging: They diagnose the problem while embodying it. A founder cosplaying as a CMO in a fictional dialogue to rack up engagement isn't solving the brand measurement crisis—it's performing it. Well, dear author—and to paraphrase Anheuser-Busch—this book's for you.

Even the research meant to sound the alarm misses the point. The Gartner doom loop study frames this as a measurement challenge—get better at proving brand's ROI and CMOs will regain influence.[3] That's not wrong, but it still perpetuates the same definitional problem. By "brand," Gartner means brand marketing—advertising, campaigns, awareness spend. So the implicit prescription is this: Figure out how to better measure brand advertising, or it's curtains. But the bigger and more important issue isn't measurement of a narrow set of marketing metrics—it's that brand has been reduced to a cost center rather than the entire basis of why customers value your business.

The perception worsens when we conflate creative and industry accolades with brand performance. For instance, every year, Cannes Lions celebrates ad campaigns, and LinkedIn is all a twitter (so to speak) with marketers taking a victory lap. If your customers are churning like crazy, a trophy doesn't help with that. Meanwhile, "Most Innovative CMO" lists often spotlight leaders of brands that are objectively not so hot when it comes to end-to-end brand performance. Don't get me wrong, I love being creative. In fact, I think the most successful brands take a creative approach to every part of the customer journey. But when the industry celebrates the wrong metrics, it's no wonder CEOs and CFOs remain skeptical of brand investment.

FROM HOT TAKES TO HOT POTATOES

Not everyone gets it wrong. Product growth expert Elena Verna recently made waves with a blog post provocatively titled "Brand . . . a Product Job Now?"[4] Her argument is compelling: People don't trust marketing claims—they trust the experience. As she memorably puts it, "Utility gets usage. Emotion gets loyalty." Spot on! But I'll take it one step further:

UTILITY + EMOTION = BRAND

Verna is onto something crucial: Product teams can't hide behind velocity charts and feature road maps. They have to care about how the product makes people feel. But here's where the thinking stops short: Brand is not a hot potato that gets tossed from marketing to product to whomever else when the heat gets too high. In fact, brand isn't just the potato—it's the whole damn meal.

Verna says, "Marketing can shout, but product has to deserve to be talked about." Indeed, the product creates a feeling. But so does the support team. If they resolve an issue right away, the customer feels great. If it takes a week to get a response, they feel ignored. The same is true with the sales team, the finance team, the engineering team, and, of course, the marketing team. Anyone interacting with customers or informing their experience creates a feeling. So the solution isn't about reassigning ownership—it's about shared accountability.

IT'S NOT US, IT'S YOU

If you've ever been a CMO, you know this script by heart. When a brand is struggling, it's often attributed to "marketing issues." Budgets get slashed, head count gets frozen, and the chief marketer likely exits the business shortly thereafter. And brand priorities? Forget it! Brand is frivolous, a luxury. Brand is what you talk about during peacetime. But wartime? Brand goes into the bunker.

Here's the irony: Things get rocky *because* of brand. Growth is slowing? That's a brand problem. Engagement drops? That's a brand problem. Customers no longer see the value, and churn increases? That's a brand problem. It may seem like I'm beating up on the marketing team, who I just said get enough heat, but the reality is brand is everyone's problem. When you have a high-functioning brand, it's because all parts of the customer experience are working harmoniously, and that requires all areas of an organization. But if one part of that experience weakens, then you risk the whole house of cards falling. So rather than unfairly asking marketing to hold all the cards, it's time to rally around brand as a full-funnel, all-hands-on-(the)-deck (pun intended) priority.

But that's not the only problem. There's an equally big issue with how we grade ourselves. Companies spend a lot of time hustling to develop KPIs for the next quarter, and from my experience, it's always a scramble. As a functional leader, I've found myself frantically grading our previous quarter's KPIs (some of which were no longer relevant and were long abandoned) and swiftly conjuring up some new goals to meet the internal deadline. Those bottom-up submissions were then merged with all the other departments' goals and shared at an all-hands. Mission accomplished! But what did we actually accomplish?

Each department was essentially grading their own exams.

Marketing celebrates a 40 percent email open rate. Product high-fives shipping twelve new features. Customer success rings the bell for 85 percent satisfaction. Yes, these are wins, but they are wins in isolation—and often self-serving. The result? A bunch of green lights on individual dashboards while the brand is blinking red.

THE KPI PROBLEM: WHY TRADITIONAL MEASUREMENT FALLS SHORT

Most companies rely on crude KPI scoring systems that would make any high school teacher cringe:

- **Traffic light/RAG (red-amber-green) system:** Red = bad, yellow = caution, green = good
- **Binary goal systems:** Either you hit your target or you don't
- **Percentage thresholds:** Green if within 5 percent of target, red if exceeding 10 percent

The problem? These systems suffer from "departmental myopia." Each functional leader grades their own homework using subjective criteria that often bear little resemblance to what customers actually care about. While your CMO might celebrate hitting "green" on customer acquisition, what does that actually tell you? That you're not failing?

Traditional KPIs also create defensive behavior where people avoid "red" ratings at all costs, making performance reporting meaningless. When was the last time you saw a department voluntarily report a red score?

We grade ourselves inside a company all the time, but our customers are grading us on completely different criteria. And guess what? How customers measure you is a lot more meaningful to your future prospects than how you score yourself.

In a business context, customers are the teachers, and they determine if you'll pass or fail. To put it bluntly, when they give your brand a bad score, it's definitely your fault.

What Companies Study vs. What Customers Grade

What Companies Study	What Customers Grade
Campaign performance	Product fit
Creative cleverness	Speed + clarity
Margin protection	Value delivered
Feature lists	Emotional connection
Brand safety	Values alignment

IT'S TIME FOR A REFRAME

But what if you stopped cramming for that doomsday quarterly KPI exam and took a fresh approach? What if you stopped spinning in circles, swimming upstream, and beating your head against the wall (the triathlon of a typical chief marketer)? What if you reframed brand measurement to better align with how customers measure a brand—and made it a full-company exercise along the way? What if you could get a brand score that gave you an accurate grade so you knew how much to re-source—and how much to worry?

I can hear many of you saying, "That *sounds* nice, but organizational change is so hard." I get it. It's easy to have "measurement senioritis" when these systems are essentially cemented into companies. But when your KPI dashboard is green but your brand is in the red, Houston, we have a problem.

In this book, we'll get you off that KPI launchpad and show you a new way of measuring your brand's health that gathers inputs from every customer touchpoint. This framework takes the stress and opacity out of the tired KPI process and makes understanding how well your brand is doing (or not) more familiar and—importantly—more collaborative. You'll also see this framework in action, as we look at a number of brands across multiple verticals that are leading the way—and those that are falling behind. And you'll get to apply the methodology to your own brand at the end of several chapters with pop quizzes designed to give you a high-level diagnosis you can act on immediately.

If you're a long-suffering CMO, you're in the right place. If you work in another customer-facing part of the organization, like product, engineering, sales, or customer success, you have a big role to play in making sure your brand is firing on all cylinders, so definitely pull up a chair and dig in. And if you're a founder or CEO who has a love-hate relationship with the word *brand*, this book is definitely for you.

But no matter who picks this up, I promise that you'll walk away with a clear understanding that brand isn't just a topping you sprinkle on top—it's the whole enchilada.

You're now ready for the Brand GPA—a fresh approach to measuring how great, or not great—your brand actually is.

PART ONE

THE CURRICULUM

BEFORE WE CAN GIVE YOUR BRAND A GRADE, we need to establish the grading criteria. The Brand GPA framework evaluates across five core thematic subjects: Chemistry, Communications, Psychology, Sociology, and Economics. Each one represents a distinct dimension of how customers actually experience your brand—and each subject is weighted based on its impact on the customer experience.

Now that you've learned the overall framework, the core subjects are broken down into three measurable sub-subjects grounded in real industry benchmarks. You'll learn the grading rubric, and Making the Grade and Missing the Mark case studies will bring things to life.

Brands will be put under the microscope—some earning top marks, others in serious need of academic intervention. Sometimes a sub-brand will be represented, but that's only in cases where the parent company is massive and the sub-brand could easily be its own stand-alone company.

At the end of each subject chapter there is a grid highlighting twelve industries and the best- and worst-performing brands within those verticals. Finally, you'll find a pop quiz at the end of each chapter so you can start sizing up your own brand along the way.

Are you ready to make the grade with your customers? Let's go!

CHAPTER 1

THE BRAND GPA

WE'VE ALL EXPERIENCED THE HIGHS AND LOWS (literally) of maintaining a grade point average (GPA) in school. In fact, the majority of opportunities you get after completing school—college admissions and job interviews—are based heavily (and in some cases, solely) on your GPA.

In high school, the weighted GPA is fairly common. Rather than treating all courses as equal, your ability to challenge yourself with honors, advanced placement (AP), or international baccalaureate courses tends to give you an edge because they carry more weight than standard versions or electives. Skeptics may think of this as padding, but it clearly provides a more nuanced view of a student's academic achievements because it considers the rigor of their coursework. This same logic applies to brands: Not all customer touchpoints carry equal weight in determining your brand's overall performance.

Maintaining a strong GPA takes dedication, discipline, and determination. But to err is human, and we've all bombed a quiz or a test. While that hurts in the moment, odds are you can recover. However, there are those classes that just don't click, and if that subject carries a lot of weight, you could be in trouble. You can suffer through it, or you can seek out assistance to help boost your grade, such as a tutor or a study buddy.

The same is true for a brand.

Just like teachers grade students, customers are constantly grading brands, and they expect an A experience every time they engage. So when an experience is a C or a D (or, dare I say, an F), it can have a direct impact on your company's growth. And when growth starts to falter, a business is at risk of failure. Yet, just like bombing a single quiz or a test in school doesn't necessarily mean your overall GPA is going to plummet, a bad customer experience doesn't mean your business will collapse. However, when there are consistent issues that affect loads of customers, you can kiss the dean's list goodbye.

In terms of weight, there are definitely parts of the customer experience that carry more influence. For instance, if your customers aren't aligned to your product or service, that can lead to fast failure. Meanwhile, just because you post an ill-timed or tone-deaf tweet doesn't mean total expulsion (maybe just a trip to the principal's office).

If you've ever wondered whether your brand is making the grade or needs serious help, the first step is understanding the curriculum and how to master each subject.

THE FIVE CORE SUBJECTS OF THE BRAND GPA

Like in school, a brand's GPA is made up of performance across multiple subjects—each one representing a critical area where brands and customers often operate with completely different assumptions. Some carry more weight than others, but all are essential if you want to graduate top of your class (or in this case, in your business vertical).

But here's the fundamental disconnect: Companies measure what's easy to track internally, while customers judge based on what actually affects their experience. For example, a B2B SaaS company might celebrate hitting its new logo targets for the quarter, not realizing that customer success is scrambling to figure out why

40 percent of the previous quarter's cohort quietly stopped logging in. The acquisition KPIs are flashing green, but the retention dashboard is a code red.

The Brand GPA framework takes into account what businesses often look at and what customers most often care about and frames it in an academic context across five subjects: Chemistry, Communications, Psychology, Sociology, and Economics.

Chemistry measures your customer–brand fit through Activity, Affinity, and Retention. Communications evaluates how clearly and consistently you tell your brand story across channels. Psychology captures how your brand makes people feel. Sociology assesses how your brand engages with the world. Finally, Economics looks at perceived and actual value, from initial purchase to lifetime value.

Each subject contains three measurable components (called sub-subjects), which we'll dive into in their respective chapters. But first, let's talk about why some subjects carry more weight than others.

THE WEIGHTING (IS THE HARDEST PART)

Just as AP classes carry more weight than electives, not all brand touchpoints are created equal. Getting the weights wrong means you'll either over-invest in activities that don't move the needle or under-invest in the things that actually drive customer decisions. These subjects also map to distinct business functions, like product, customer experience, marketing, and operations, while maintaining a focus on what customers actually use to make decisions. The weightings were determined by triangulating multiple sources of research on customer behavior, retention drivers, and business impact across industries.

Chemistry holds a 30 percent weight overall. This subject gets the highest weight because Retention is the single greatest predictor of long-term profitability. According to Bain & Company's latest research, a 5 percent increase in Retention can boost profits by 25–95 percent depending on industry. Companies with 85 percent+ retention rates consistently grow 2–7x faster than their peers across categories.[1]

Communications carries a 20 percent weight. While not as heavily weighted as Chemistry, this subject maintains a significant weight because poor communication is a primary cause of churn and erosion of trust. McKinsey's 2021 study of 2,000+ consumers found that 71 percent expect personalized interactions and 76 percent get frustrated when this doesn't happen.[2] According to PwC's Consumer Intelligence Series, 32 percent of customers would stop doing business with a brand they loved after just one bad experience.[3]

Psychology comes in at 15 percent. This subject receives a slightly more moderate weighting, but that doesn't diminish its importance. While functional benefits get customers to try a brand, emotional connection keeps them choosing it over time—and that can significantly impact customer lifetime value and loyalty.

Sociology also carries a 15 percent weight. This subject might feel more like an "elective," but it's absolutely core to the customer experience, as values Alignment increasingly shapes purchase decisions. Edelman's 2024 Trust Barometer of 32,000+ respondents found that 63 percent of consumers will buy or boycott based on a brand's stance on social and political issues.[4]

Economics rounds out the framework at 20 percent. This subject carries substantial weight because perceived value drives renewal and expansion decisions. Industry research consistently shows that customers will pay premium prices for superior experiences but will churn quickly when the value equation feels unbalanced. Further, Economics comes last because the other subjects can have a direct impact on economic value—and the bottom line.

The Brand GPA Framework

Core Subject	Weight	What It Measures
Chemistry	30%	Customer–brand fit through Activity, Affinity, Retention
Communications	20%	Clarity and consistency across all channels
Psychology	15%	Emotional connection and how the brand makes people feel
Sociology	15%	Values Alignment and cultural engagement
Economics	20%	Perceived and actual value from purchase to lifetime value

To get the Brand GPA metric, the math is pretty simple:

Brand GPA = (Chemistry grade × 30%) + (Communications grade × 20%) + (Psychology grade × 15%) + (Sociology grade × 15%) + (Economics grade × 20%)

The same principle that works across each subject applies *within* them—the three sub-subjects carry their own internal weights, which combine to produce each subject's overall grade.

THE BRAND GPA GRADING SCALE

Where traditional KPI systems give you just two to three vague signals regarding performance, the Brand GPA framework provides five distinct levels—or grades—with clear, universally understood definitions. There's no ambiguity like "Is a yellow KPI result bad or just cautious?" Everyone knows what a B grade means versus a C.

This isn't just about measuring performance—it's about measuring the *right* performance through the lens of what matters most to your customers, not your internal departments. But unlike school, there's no curve here—a poor performance with your customers doesn't get rounded up. And sorry, no extra credit.

The Brand GPA Grading Scale Table

Grade	Performance Level	Key Indicators
A (3.8)	Category leadership	85%+ retention rates, industry-leading margins, top quartile NPS
B (3.0)	Above average	70–84% retention, healthy growth, positive sentiment
C (2.0)	Average/concerning	55–69% retention, flat margins, mixed sentiment
D (1.0)	Severe dysfunction	<55% retention, declining performance, low trust
F (0.0)	Existential crisis	Business survival at risk, massive losses, brand toxicity

Perfection in business—and life, really—isn't practical. Whether you have hundreds or thousands or millions of customers, it's statistically impossible for everyone to have a flawless experience with your brand every single time. So a 3.8 keeps it real—and gives you two-tenths of a point to go the extra mile.

At the same time, if you see a brand with a D, don't think they have a lot of breathing room. In the Brand GPA framework, a D means *severe* dysfunction—customers are leaving, trust is eroding, and the business is showing real signs of distress. An F in the Brand GPA means existential crisis: bankruptcy risk, complete customer exodus, a brand so toxic it threatens the survival of the business itself. But the difference between a D and an F is not a wide chasm—it's a short cliff. Think of a D as an "F in motion"—one bad quarter, one viral controversy, one regulatory action, one competitor disruption at a time can be the brand death knell. So a D is a warning with a very short leash because an F-bomb is just around the corner.

THE GRADING PERIOD

In the following chapters, I will evaluate brand examples using the five subject chapters—Chemistry, Communications, Psychology, Sociology, and Economics—based on their performance during the ten-quarter period from Q1 2023 through Q2 2025. This window provides sufficient time to assess sustained performance rather than momentary spikes, while remaining recent enough to reflect current market conditions at the time of publication. And that's important to remember—this is a snapshot in time. Depending on when you are reading this book, any brand that is a standout student could have fallen from grace. Likewise, a borderline dropout could be crushing it.

Brands that earned a Making the Grade distinction demonstrated strong performance throughout this period, while Missing the Mark examples showed consistent struggles or measurable decline. The Top Scholar and Bottom Dweller selections represent excellence or failure across an entire subject during this evaluation window. Think of the Top Scholar as the book award winner for the subject—and the Bottom Dweller as the one who needs to hit the books.

YOUR ASSIGNMENT

Getting good grades matters, but learning something matters more. In fact, the GPA has a double meaning in this context. Yes, the framework uses grades, but its premise is to help you make your brand great. In other words, it's measuring your *great* point average.

But the Brand GPA isn't just about measuring differently—it's about measuring smarter so that you can understand what *actually* matters for the long-term success, or "greatness," of your brand. To achieve that, the framework provides an outside-in view that cuts through departmental myopia and gives you a clear read on where your brand actually stands so you know how much to resource—and how much to worry.

So dive in, take good mental notes, and get ready to change the way you think about brand—forever.

NEXT UP . . .

We'll take a deep dive into each of the core subjects, starting with Chemistry. You'll learn about each subject's "sub-subjects," what they measure, and how they are weighted to determine each subject's grade. And spoiler alert: Each section has a pop quiz so you can get an early read on whether your own brand is doing great—or if it's greatly missing the mark.

CHAPTER 2

CHEMISTRY

NO, NOT LAB COATS AND TEST TUBES. We're talking about that special spark between your brand and your customers. Get it right and you have the potential for true love always. But if there isn't a fit, they'll probably swipe left and move on to one of your competitors. Just because someone is initially attracted to your product or service doesn't mean they will automatically stick around.

WHY THIS MATTERS

Just like when two people have great chemistry, a strong bond between a brand and a customer can lead to a deeper emotional bond, affinity, and a long-lasting relationship (aka stickiness). To achieve this, you have to focus on aligning what your brand delivers with what your customers actually want and value. And just like relationships, you have to keep working on it.

Brands and customers can hit it off initially, but that spark can fizzle quickly if there isn't material value, meaning your product or service needs to solve a real, recurring problem. Think of a meal kit service that wows on the first delivery. But if new customers aren't reordering by month three, then you're stuck on first base. In other words, your brand isn't a firestarter. But if that same meal kit brand has the majority of customers signing up for their sixth consecutive box, trying new recipes, and gifting subscriptions to friends, that's not just getting to third base—that's some serious chemistry. However, if there's a gradual (or worse, sudden) drop in Retention, then you won't be scoring a run. The good news is there are early signals so you won't get caught stealing home—declines in key metrics like Net Promoter Score (NPS) and review sentiment, such as Trustpilot scores, are important signals that there is trouble in paradise.

You might be thinking this sounds like product-market fit (PMF), and you're not entirely wrong. If you think about it, PMF is sort of like business dating: Everyone's looking for "the one," but there's no definitive moment when you know you've found your soulmate. Things can start hot and heavy, but then they can dissipate quickly.

Why does this matter so much? According to Twilio Segment's 2022 *State of Personalization* report, 62 percent of consumers say a brand will lose their loyalty if their experience is not personalized.[1] And according to Pew, about half of US adults say they have stopped doing business with a company because of poor customer service.[2]

Further, external or environmental factors can completely change how your customer feels about you. That's called product-market fit collapse (PMFC), a term coined by Brian Balfour, founder and CEO of Reforge, to describe what happens when evolving customer needs outpace your product's relevance.[3] On the flip side, Bain & Company's landmark research shows that increasing Retention by just 5 percent can boost profits by 25–95 percent, depending on industry.[4]

WHAT WE MEASURE

Chemistry is evaluated across three key, measurable sub-subjects (with all examples in this chapter assessed from Q1 2023 through Q2 2025). These were selected based on the most important—and quantifiable—criteria to determine if there is a real love connection between you and your customers:

- **Activity:** Are customers actively using your product or service?
- **Affinity:** Does your product or service forge a lasting bond with your target audience?
- **Retention:** Are customers sticking around and increasing their engagement over time?

When a brand is succeeding across all of those sub-subjects, the Chemistry grade will be higher. And with a GPA weight of 30 percent, that has a substantial impact on the near- and long-term success of your business.

One thing you won't see here that you might be expecting is Net Promoter Score (NPS). Don't get me wrong—NPS has value, and it's something we relied on even before it was officially a thing. (Remember those four out of five dentists who were always recommending a certain toothpaste or sugar-free gum?) But in the Brand GPA context, NPS is like the CliffsNotes of Chemistry. It offers a fast one-question snapshot that hints at how a customer feels, but it doesn't tell the whole story. Sure, it can be useful—but relying solely on NPS is like basing a semester's grade on a single quiz.

To achieve real chemistry, you have to look at a collection of signals, so it's less about one answer and more about the holy trinity of customer engagement: Activity (i.e., usage), Affinity (i.e., popularity), and Retention (i.e., stickiness).

HOW WE GRADE

The three sub-subjects are weighted to determine a brand's overall Chemistry grade, which, as we've seen, accounts for 30 percent of the overall Brand GPA. To calculate a brand's Chemistry grade, apply the internal sub-subject weightings: 40 percent Activity, 20 percent Affinity, 40 percent Retention. The grading criteria for each sub-subject is explained further in their respective sections.

BRINGING IT ALL TOGETHER

Sub-Subject Weighting: Chemistry

Sub-Subject	Weighting	Primary Metric	A-Level Standard Description
Activity	40%	Active users vs. goal	At or above goal, high DAU/MAU, strong referrals, clear value
Affinity	20%	Share of voice (SOV)	Top quartile SOV, strong cultural presence, high brand engagement
Retention	40%	Retention/repurchase	At or above category benchmark retention or repeat rate, healthy cohorts, expanding usage

Industry benchmark note: Benchmarks vary by industry. Examples include—streaming/entertainment: 40–50 percent DAU/MAU for elite performance; B2B SaaS/productivity: 40 percent+ DAU/MAU, 85 percent+ annual retention; consumer goods: 60+ NPS, 25 percent+ SOV; meal kit/food delivery: 60–70 percent monthly repeat rates, 20 percent+ annual retention

THE SUB-SUBJECTS: ACTIVITY

"If you build it, they will come" worked on the silver screen, but in the real world, just launching a brand doesn't guarantee success. If we assume you have great positioning, a clear understanding of your audience and where to find them, and a seamless onboarding process (note: not easy to achieve!), then the real question is this: Are the dogs merely eating the dog food, or are they savoring every morsel?

Depending on the company, looking at things like daily or monthly active users (or, more specifically, daily and monthly monetized users) or subscribers vs. the goals that have been set can give a real sense of how well your customers are responding to what you've built—or if your field of dreams is sort of a nightmare. For the Brand GPA framework, Activity is determined by the following.

WHAT WE MEASURE

Primary Metric: Daily/Monthly Active Users or Subscriber Engagement

Track how many customers are actively using your product or service on a daily, weekly, or monthly basis. For subscription businesses, monitor engaged subscribers versus dormant accounts. The key is measuring actual usage against your goals: Are you hitting 100 percent+ of your active user targets or falling short?

Secondary Indicators

- **Trial-to-conversion rate:** Percentage of trial users who convert to paying customers
- **Average session length:** How long users spend in your product per session
- **DAU/MAU ratio:** Daily active users (DAU) divided by monthly active users (MAU), showing stickiness and habit formation

GRADING RUBRIC

The rubric provides guidance on whether you're at the head of the class—or in desperate need of some extra help.

For A-level Activity performance, DAU/MAU benchmarks vary significantly by category and business model. Social and gaming platforms operate at structurally higher ratios due to frequent, habit-driven usage, while transactional or episodic-use products like fintech and health care see lower daily engagement tied to specific user needs. E-commerce platforms typically exhibit lower daily ratios but offset this with high-intent purchase behavior. Activity performance should be evaluated relative to category-specific usage patterns, not a universal threshold.

Grading Rubric: Activity

Grade	Description	Key Metric
A	Product-market fit achieved, high-frequency usage	Top quartile DAU/MAU for category, rapid organic growth
B	Strong adoption with consistent engagement	Above category median DAU/MAU, steady growth
C	Moderate adoption with inconsistent usage	At or just below category median, inconsistent growth
D	Poor adoption, declining usage and engagement	Bottom quartile DAU/MAU, negative growth trends
F	Product-market fit failure, user abandonment	Sustained DAU/MAU collapse, mass user exodus

Important note: DAU/MAU benchmarks vary significantly by category and business model. For category-specific benchmarks, refer to Amplitude, CleverTap, or Adjust industry reports. Transactional and episodic-use products naturally operate at lower DAU/MAU ratios than social or gaming platforms and should be evaluated accordingly.

MAKING THE GRADE: NETFLIX (GRADE: A)

While many streaming services' business models are like a house of cards, Netflix is a steel fortress. Netflix ended 2023 with 260.28 million global paid memberships and surged to 301.63 million by year-end 2024—adding 41.36 million paid memberships across the year, including 18.91 million in Q4 alone.[5] Engagement averaged two hours per day per member in Q3 2024.[6]

The Retention metrics reinforce the standout Activity. Antenna estimated Netflix's churn at 1.8 percent gross and 1.0 percent net as of September 2024—dramatically outperforming the streaming industry average.[7] With hundreds of millions of global subscribers and consistent engagement growth even among mature user bases, Netflix proves that a massive library of unique and exclusive content—from squid gaming to cake guessing—paired with frictionless discovery creates the sticky, habit-forming behavior that defines A-level Activity. Entering 2025, analyst estimates still placed Netflix's churn well under 4 percent, firmly maintaining its lead as the stickiest subscription product in streaming.[8]

MISSING THE MARK: PELOTON (GRADE: D)

Peloton's meteoric rise during the pandemic made it one of the most talked-about brands in the world. But when gyms reopened and people started leaving the house, Peloton got out of shape quickly. Paid Connected Fitness Subscriptions declined from 3.13 million in Q3 fiscal 2023 to 2.879 million by Q2 fiscal 2025—a sustained multiquarter backpedal that reflected a fundamental shift in customer behavior rather than a momentary blip.[9]

But Peloton didn't just lose subscribers; instead, the brand lost the daily ritual that made it a one-time Chemistry superstar. Despite having a strong cast of cool-kid influencer instructors with their own cult following, the brand fell in with the loser crowd of equipment-cum-clothing-rack brands like BowFlex and NordicTrack.

THE SUB-SUBJECTS: AFFINITY

When a brand has strong Affinity, it has that "X factor," meaning it's recognized for being relatable and reliable. But if those qualities fade, then it quickly turns into the "ex-factor."

Unlike Activity, which is rooted in utility and usage, Affinity leans into identity. When a customer feels like a brand truly gets them, they're no longer just a user—they're a loyalist. But when that relationship erodes, their willingness to engage (or even be associated) dwindles. And once the love fades, so does the buzz.

While Affinity may seem like a "soft" metric, it's surprisingly measurable when viewed through the lens of how often your brand is in the conversation. Do you get a lot of positive mentions on social media? Are you consistently referenced in the media? Are creators organically featuring your product? Being part of the zeitgeist is what every brand aspires to, but you have to walk before you run. Share of voice (SOV) across your competitive set is a great starting point, especially when benchmarked year over year. If people consistently talk about you over the long haul, then you're officially on the main menu and not just a flash in the pan.

WHAT WE MEASURE

Primary Metric: Share of Voice (SOV)

This is your brand's percentage of total conversation within your category compared to competitors. Track mentions across social media, news outlets, podcasts, creator content, and customer conversations. A rising SOV means you're gaining cultural relevance; declining SOV signals you're losing mindshare to competitors.

Secondary Indicators

- **Branded search volume:** Number of people searching for your brand name specifically (not just category terms)
- **Social mentions:** Volume and sentiment of organic brand mentions across platforms
- **Creator features:** Frequency of unpaid mentions or features from influencers, creators, and media
- **Net promoter score (NPS):** Percentage of customers willing to recommend you minus detractors

GRADING RUBRIC

For A-level Affinity performance, top-performing technology companies often achieve NPS scores of 70+ for category leadership, while traditional service industries benchmark lower due to operational complexity. Airlines typically operate with lower NPS scores (often in the 10–30 range), retail sees 30–50 as solid performance, while SaaS platforms often target 50–70+ for strong customer Advocacy. Within Affinity, NPS serves a specific purpose: measuring emotional advocacy and cultural resonance—not as the CliffsNotes shorthand for the whole Chemistry grade but as one targeted signal among three.

Grading Rubric: Affinity[10]

Grade	Description	Key Metric
A	Strong emotional connection and active Advocacy	NPS 70+, strong referral rates
B	Positive sentiment with good loyalty signals	NPS 30–69, moderate Advocacy
C	Neutral Affinity, transactional relationship	NPS 0–29, minimal Advocacy
D	Weak connection, passive dissatisfaction	NPS −30 to −1, few referrals
F	Negative sentiment, active detraction	NPS below −30, negative word of mouth

MAKING THE GRADE: YETI (GRADE: A)

YETI's brand Affinity cup runneth over, exceeding outdoor and consumer goods benchmarks by turning coolers and drinkware into lifestyle statements. Direct-to-consumer sales grew 11 percent to $344.9 million in Q4 2023, representing approximately 66 percent of total Q4 revenue—a clear sign that customers actively seek out YETI rather than randomly discovering it through retail channels.[11]

What makes YETI's Affinity particularly impressive is sustained social proof across the evaluation period. RivalIQ's *2023 Social Media Industry Benchmark Report* confirmed YETI's Instagram engagement rate placed it among the strongest performers in the consumer goods category—more than double the CPG category median.[12] Customers routinely share unprompted content featuring

YETI products as badges of outdoor honor, cementing the brand's status as the defining lifestyle marker of the outdoor enthusiast.

MISSING THE MARK: ALLBIRDS (GRADE: D)

Once the darling of casual (and sustainable) footwear, Allbirds' Affinity metrics show a nosedive across multiple indicators—an alarm call for how quickly cultural relevance can fade. Financials for Q1 2025 show net revenue down 18.3 percent year over year.[13] The buzz that once surrounded Allbirds—celebrity endorsements, sustainability awards, tech industry obsession—has largely dissipated as competitors matched their sustainability claims with lower price points.

The physical footprint tells an even starker story. The company contracted sharply from sixty stores at year-end 2023 to just twenty-four by mid-2025, including the closure of their flagship San Francisco location—signaling weakening brand desire in the markets that made Allbirds fly.[14] Its struggles reflect a common Affinity trap: Early buzz doesn't automatically translate into sustained cultural relevance, and without continuous innovation or deepening emotional connection, customers will fly south—many never to return.

THE SUB-SUBJECTS: RETENTION

Are you and your customers as intertwined as Baucis and Philemon, or is your brand Carrie dealing with a sea of noncommittal Mr. Bigs? Strong Activity and Affinity show that your customers are enamored of you, but Retention tells you if it's true love always—or if they're just not that into you. Like Activity, Retention has a heavier weight of 40 percent since usage and Retention are the stronger signals of great chemistry. For the GPA framework, Retention is determined by the following.

WHAT WE MEASURE

Primary Metric: Twelve-Month Retention Rate or Repeat Purchase Rate

For subscription businesses, track the percentage of customers who remain active after twelve months. For transactional businesses, measure how many customers make a repeat purchase within a year. This is your clearest signal of whether customers see ongoing value in your brand.

Secondary Indicators

- **Churn rate:** Percentage of customers who cancel or stop using your product each month or quarter
- **Cohort stickiness:** Whether newer customer cohorts retain at equal or better rates than earlier cohorts
- **Return frequency:** How often customers come back to use your product or make purchases

GRADING RUBRIC

For A-level Retention performance, enterprise SaaS companies consistently outperform small business–focused software, which faces structurally higher churn due to smaller contract sizes and shorter customer life cycles. Consumer subscription services and e-commerce businesses benchmark lower still, with repeat behavior varying significantly by category and purchase frequency. Retention benchmarks are inherently category specific—and should be evaluated relative to industry norms rather than a single universal threshold.[15]

Grading Rubric: Retention

Grade	Description	Key Metric
A	Excellent Retention with sustained usage	Top quartile Retention for category, expanding engagement over time
B	Strong Retention with healthy trends	Above category median Retention, stable engagement
C	Average Retention with early warning signs	At or just below category median, flat engagement
D	Poor Retention with significant churn	Bottom quartile Retention, declining engagement
F	Retention crisis, mass customer exodus	Sustained cohort decay, widespread churn and disengagement

Important note: Retention benchmarks vary significantly by category and business model. Enterprise SaaS companies typically exhibit higher Retention than small business–focused software, while consumer subscription and e-commerce businesses operate with lower repeat rates. Evaluate Retention relative to category-specific norms rather than a universal threshold.

MAKING THE GRADE: MONDAY.COM (GRADE: A)

Somebody doesn't have a case of the Mondays when it comes to sharp Retention. Across the full grading period, net dollar retention (NDR) for monday.com never dipped below 110 percent, meaning existing customers didn't just stick around—they consistently spent more.[16] Enterprise cohorts performed even stronger: NDR for customers with more than $50,000 in annual recurring revenue (ARR) held above 115 percent through Q1 2025, while that same customer segment grew from 1,683 accounts in Q1 2023 to 3,444 by Q1 2025—more than doubling in two years.[17]

The expansion behavior tells the real story. In Q2 2024, monday.com closed the largest deal in company history, expanding its largest customer to 80,000 seats. By Q3 2024, its second-largest customer had more than doubled seat count to 60,000.[18] Since customers keep finding more reasons to go deeper into the platform seven days a week, monday.com is the teacher's pet of Retention.

MISSING THE MARK: HELLOFRESH (GRADE: D)

HelloFresh was made for the pandemic—a captive audience of homebound, home-cooking converts who needed dinner delivered said hello to the brand many times over. Then the world opened back up, and it was a firm goodbye.

Active customers declined from 7.11 million in Q1 2023 to 6.64 million by Q4 2024—a steady, multiquarter bleed that no amount of creative recipes could help.[19] HelloFresh's own March 2024 guidance disclosure confirmed that meal kits were experiencing "negative revenue growth in the high single digits" and that the company's previously announced midterm ambitions were unlikely to be reached—not exactly a ringing endorsement of a sticky brand.[20] HelloFresh's Q1 2024 earnings release told the same story in plain numbers: Orders fell 2.6 percent year over year, meals delivered dropped 2.0 percent, and meal kit revenue declined 6.9 percent—which, in plain English, means the customers who stayed were ordering less.[21] A shrinking base plus shrinking engagement meant that the good times had long spoiled. HelloFresh thought they had a recipe for a rocket ship; instead, they cooked up some turbulence.

TOP AND BOTTOM OF THEIR CLASS: CHEMISTRY

There are fortunately countless examples of brands that have achieved great chemistry with their customers—and, unfortunately, there are plenty of stinkers out there. So as this class session comes to an end, we'll highlight brands that are leading their respective verticals when it comes to Chemistry and point out those that have sadly lost that lovin' feeling.

As a reminder, the Chemistry score in the Brand GPA framework reflects how strongly a brand connects with its customers across usage, resonance, and loyalty. Brands earning the summa cum laude distinction scored at or near the top of their class in Activity, Affinity, and Retention, demonstrating high customer engagement, dominant SOV, and consistent repeat behavior. In contrast, Flunking Out brands underperformed across the board, often suffering from significant customer churn due to a degraded product experience, failing to deliver on value, or being rendered less relevant by external factors.

TO QUALIFY AS A "BEST IN CHEMISTRY" BRAND, WE LOOKED FOR THESE QUALITIES:

- ≥100 percent of goal attainment for active users*
- Top quartile SOV (or clear cultural leadership)**
- Retention rates above 85 percent or strong repeat behaviors***

BRANDS THAT FLUNKED CHEMISTRY TYPICALLY HAD THESE QUALITIES:

- Fell short on core user engagement targets*
- Lost relevance in the public conversation**
- Struggled to retain users post-acquisition or post-onboarding***

*Based on DAU/MAU and cohort Retention benchmarks from Amplitude and Adjust, category-specific analysis (2023–2024)

**Based on SOV and brand-tracking data from Kantar, Sprout Social, and Edelman (2023–2024)

***Based on Retention benchmarks from Recurly and Bain & Company, category-specific analysis (2023–2024)

Here's the full honor roll—and the list of those who need to repeat the class.

Top and Bottom of Their Class: Chemistry

Vertical	Summa Cum Laude	Why They Excel	Flunking Out	Why They Fail
Apparel and footwear	Lululemon[22]	Company-operated store revenue increased 14% and e-commerce revenue increased 6% in FY2024; FY2024 revenue grew 10% to $10.6B, with Q1 fiscal 2025 revenue up 7%; China Mainland net revenue increased 21% in Q1 2025, reflecting sustained global demand and broadening international reach	Allbirds[23]	FY2024 revenue declined 25.3% to $189.8M, including a 22.4% YoY drop in Q4; 2024 Form 10-K warned that failure to attract new customers or drive repeat purchases could materially harm business prospects, underscoring weakening consumer engagement
Consumer goods	YETI[24]	DTC sales grew 11% to $344.9M in Q4 2023; full-year 2024 net sales up 10%; strong repeat customer engagement and sustained category leadership in outdoor lifestyle	Tupperware[25]	Filed Chapter 11 on September 17, 2024; Reuters reported six consecutive quarters of declining sales; headline said it all—"Tupperware files for bankruptcy as its colorful containers lose relevance"
Media and entertainment	Netflix[26]	Antenna estimated 1.8% gross churn and 1.0% net churn as of September 2024 vs. premium SVOD average of 5.3% gross and 3.1% net; approximately two hours of daily engagement per paid membership; personalization infrastructure sustains habitual viewing at scale	Luminary[27]	Bloomberg reported in April 2023 that Luminary cut marquee shows including Lena Dunham's *The C-Word* and *Snap Judgment Presents: Spooked*—content retrenchment signaling failure to build habitual subscriber engagement in a crowded podcast market

continued →

Fitness and wellness	Equinox[28]	Revenues up 27% in 2023; January 2024 gym visits up 12% YoY per Bloomberg; sustained premium member engagement throughout the grading period	Weight Watchers (WW)[29]	Subscribers fell from 4.0M to 3.4M YoY as GLP-1 drug popularity undercut demand for traditional weight loss services; subscription revenue down 7.2% in Q4 2024 (constant currency); Chapter 11 filed May 2025 with ~$1.6B in debt
Healthcare	Cleveland Clinic[30]	15.7M outpatient encounters in 2024—largest in history; ranked #2 globally by *Newsweek's World's Best Hospitals 2024*; longitudinal patient loyalty across digital and physical touchpoints	CVS MinuteClinic[31]	Location count fell from ~1,150 to 875 between May 2023 and December 2024—a nearly 24% reduction; systematic network retrenchment reflects sustained patient attrition across the urgent care category
Consumer tech	Canva[32]	Grew from 135M MAUs to 220M+ MAUs; 9.2M weekly active users in Q4 2024 with rising download velocity; consumer pull and repeat engagement signal elite product-market fit	Evernote[33]	Free plan capped at 50 notes in late 2023 to force paid upgrades—a Retention-friction move that signaled product desperation; trade press called it a "zombie app" defined by years of stagnation, leadership churn, and declining UX
B2B tech	Notion[34]	100M+ users by August 2024; 4.8/5 App Store (79K ratings); organic expansion from notes to databases, wikis, and workflows signals deep, compounding product-market fit	Freshworks[35]	NDR declined from 108% to 103% across Q4 2023–Q4 2024 per SEC earnings releases; company cited lower expansion within existing customers and macroeconomic pressure on upsell as primary drivers; five consecutive quarters of net Retention deterioration
Education	Duolingo[36]	DAUs reached 37.2M in Q3 2024, up 54% YoY; DAU/MAU ratio hit 34.7% in Q4 2024—well above education app benchmarks; habitual daily usage and exceptional Retention defining the category	Chegg[37]	Nonsubscriber traffic down 49% YoY in January 2025; subscribers fell 31% to 3.2M in Q1 2025; revenue dropped 30% to $121M—AI substitution rendered the core product irrelevant

Food service	Sweetgreen[38]	4.9/5 App Store rating (166,000+ ratings); digital revenue represented 56% of total sales in fiscal year 2024, up from prior year, reflecting sustained repeat digital engagement and loyalty program stickiness	Red Lobster[39]	Visits fell ~30% YoY in 2024 prior to bankruptcy filing; Chapter 11 filed May 19, 2024; ~100 locations shuttered in a single month; Endless Shrimp promotion generated $11M in losses and became a viral brand-damage moment—a multiquarter customer exodus that ended in existential collapse
Travel	Airbnb[40]	448.2M nights and experiences booked in 2023, growing to 491.5M in 2024; active listings exceeded 7.7M at year-end 2023 and 8M+ at end-2024; platform growth driven by new customers and repeat guests increasing activity YoY	Southwest[41]	16,900 flight cancellations; 2M+ passengers stranded; $140M DOT civil penalty—largest consumer protection penalty in DOT history; $600M+ refunded or reimbursed to affected passengers
On-demand	DoorDash[42]	22M combined DashPass and Wolt+ subscribers as of Q1 2025; subscription loyalty and repeat order frequency define durable on-demand Chemistry	GoPuff[43]	Eliminated 6% of its workforce in May 2024 in a bid to reach cash flow positivity; habitual usage never materialized beyond initial acquisition, reflecting persistent failure to convert convenience into a recurring customer habit
Financial services	American Express[44]	Record $1.551T in worldwide billed business in FY2024; record 13M new card acquisitions; ranked #1 in *JD Power 2023–2024 US Credit Card Satisfaction Study*	Robinhood[45]	Monthly active users fell 16% YoY to 10.3M in Q3 2023; sustained engagement erosion reflecting failure to retain core retail investors beyond initial acquisition

TOP SCHOLAR AND BOTTOM DWELLER

Like in every class, there is always that one pupil who stands out—and that one who brings down the curve. While Netflix dominates media streaming and Apple rules hardware ecosystems, we chose Canva as our Valedictorian. As the new darling of creative tools, Canva has developed a sticky product that just keeps getting better while also mastering the rare feat of winning both consumer and enterprise hearts (which ain't easy!). For our cautionary tale, we picked (on?) Chegg as our "failedictorian" since they represent the ultimate in a Chemistry collapse. The public company was a long-standing leader in education until they became an AI casualty and lost their spark with students in record time.

TOP SCHOLAR: CANVA

Canva earns the top honor in Chemistry, but its product is a case study in alchemy, helping anyone perform like a professional designer. The platform grew from 135 million monthly active users to more than 220 million—tremendous growth reflecting pixel-perfect product-market fit across both B2C and B2B, from weekend hobbyists to the marketing departments of some of the world's most iconic brands.[46]

Users aren't just signing up and moving on—they're returning regularly thanks to the range of projects they can create, from logos to social graphics to videos to mega presentations. The freemium model creates frictionless entry but then delivers so much value that conversion to paid is a no-brainer.

Great Chemistry leads to growth, and the brand is raking it in. Canva generated approximately $1.7 billion in annualized recurring revenue in late 2023, surging to more than $2.5 billion by early 2025.[47] What makes Canva so unique from typical SaaS success stories is the rare achievement of winning both consumer and enterprise hearts. That's because the brand understands that no matter the context—a home project or a huge business pitch—customers have faced the same barriers when trying to produce designer-level work without the skills, training, or resources. As such, the platform has become one of the most widely used design tools on the internet—and one of the most beloved brands globally.

Top Scholar Report Card: Canva

Sub-Subject	Grade	Metrics
Activity	A	Grew from 135M MAUs (June 2023) to 220M+ MAUs (early 2025); 9.2M weekly active users in Q4 2024; rising download velocity signals sustained consumer repeat engagement
Affinity	A	Freemium model drives viral adoption; strong brand recognition across consumer and enterprise; "empowering design" is a clear value proposition
Retention	A	Net revenue retention >100% consistently; template ecosystem drives stickiness; word-of-mouth growth demonstrates loyalty

BOTTOM DWELLER: CHEGG

Irony isn't dead: Chegg, the online education platform, may help students ace Chemistry in school, but it has failed the subject in our Brand GPA terms. The once-dominant player in homework help and textbook rentals saw nonsubscriber traffic plunge 49 percent year over year in January 2025—compared to just an 8 percent decline in Q2 2024—while global subscription counts tumbled 31 percent to just 3.2 million in Q1 2025, performance that falls well below the typical 40+ NPS and 25 percent SOV benchmarks for edtech leaders.[48] Unlike Canva, which uses AI to make their platform even better, Chegg succumbed to the technology, losing its previously sticky user base to the many free tools and services, like ChatGPT, that have won over students and their cost-conscious parents. Ouch.

That's the ultimate—and unfortunate—product-market fit collapse, and the growth story is more like a horror story. Q1 2025 revenue crashed nearly 30 percent to $121 million, with subscription revenue down 30 percent to $108 million and the company posting a net loss of approximately $17.5 million.[49] The brand's operational response confirmed the crisis—Chegg announced it would lay off approximately 22 percent of its workforce (about 248 employees) and shut down US and Canadian offices by year-end, aggressively cutting costs in response to traffic collapse driven by AI tools and Google's AI Overviews.[50] The company explored strategic alternatives, including a potential sale or going private, as its stock—once a marker of edtech dominance—became a marker of distress, falling from a 2021 high of around $113 per share to nearly penny stock territory at approximately $1 by early 2025.[51] Ouch, indeed.

Bottom Dweller Report Card: Chegg

Sub-Subject	Grade	Metrics
Activity	F	Nonsubscriber traffic down 49% YoY in January 2025; users migrating to free AI alternatives; platform engagement in freefall
Affinity	F	Trustpilot 2.0/5 from 6,692 reviews; lost relevance in student conversation as ChatGPT became the default homework tool
Retention	F	Subscription count down 31% to 3.2M in Q1 2025; Q1 2025 revenue down 30% to $121M; no cohort recovery signal within the grading period

NEXT UP . . .

Establishing strong Chemistry is like successfully completing all the prerequisites—it gives your brand a strong foundation for everything that follows. But even brands with top marks in Chemistry can stumble in the next critical phase: Communications. In other words, are you just a bunch of pillow talk, or are you fluent in delighting your customers?

POP QUIZ: CHEMISTRY

You can't run a comprehensive brand diagnostic overnight, but this short Chemistry quiz can give you a directional sense of how your brand is doing in this subject. Answer each question with a checkmark (✓) for yes or leave blank for no. Then apply the weighting formula to calculate your back-of-the-envelope Chemistry score.

ACTIVITY (40 PERCENT)

- Are at least 100 percent of your monthly or quarterly active user goals being met?
- Is your DAU/WAU ratio in the top quartile for your category (or improving quarter over quarter)?
- Are you seeing ≥25 percent of new users arrive via referral or word of mouth?
- Do ≥60 percent of new users demonstrate activation within seven days (e.g., reach "aha" moment)?

Industry benchmarks: Streaming 40–50 percent, SaaS 40 percent +, design tools 30–40 percent

AFFINITY (20 PERCENT)

- Does your SOV exceed industry benchmark compared to key category competitors?

- Is branded search volume up ≥10 percent year over year?
- Are you seeing at least 1x weekly organic mentions on top social platforms?
- Does your brand track in the top quartile for customer sentiment or recall in your industry?

Industry benchmarks: Consumer goods 25 percent + SOV, outdoor/B2B 15 percent +, NPS thresholds vary by category

RETENTION (40 PERCENT)

- Is your twelve-month Retention rate above industry benchmark (or repeat purchase rate above category standard)?
- Is churn stable or decreasing for at least two consecutive quarters?
- Are newer cohorts retaining or expanding usage at equal or better rates than earlier cohorts?
- Do ≥30 percent of customers return to use your product/service ≥3x/month (or your frequency goal)?

Industry benchmarks: SaaS 85 percent +, subscription learning 35 percent +, meal kits 20 percent+

SCORING METHOD

Count your total "yes" answers in each section, then multiply your Activity score by 0.4, your Affinity score by 0.2, and your Retention score by 0.4. Add all three adjusted scores together to get your final Chemistry score. See the next page for the scoring rubric (and sorry, there's no extra credit).

Pop Quiz Scoring Table: Chemistry

Weighted Score Total	Chemistry Grade	Interpretation
10–12	A	Top performance—your brand chemistry is working across all dimensions
8–9	B	Strong foundation but room for optimization in weaker areas
6–7	C	Mixed signals—you've got work to do; focus on lowest-scoring sub-subject
4–5	D	Trouble ahead—customer connection is weak; prioritize Retention and Activity
<4	F	Chemistry crisis—urgent course correction required across all areas

Important note: Scoring should be interpreted within your industry context. Retention benchmarks vary significantly by category—what qualifies as strong performance for a meal kit service would fall short of expectations for a SaaS platform. Evaluate your results against your category peers, not the universal scale.

CHAPTER 3

COMMUNICATIONS

BEFORE YOU CHUCK THIS OVER TO YOUR PR TEAM to deal with, remember that Communications isn't just a press release or media hit. In the Brand GPA context, success in this subject depends on how well your brand shows up across all customer touchpoints. From the home page to a customer service chat, consistency is key—otherwise your brand will feel disjointed at best and inauthentic at worst.

WHY THIS MATTERS

We live in a world of rapid-fire content consumption, shorter attention spans, and information overload. According to a 2021 McKinsey report, 71 percent of consumers expect companies to deliver personalized interactions—and 76 percent get frustrated when this doesn't happen. McKinsey's findings were based on a multi-industry survey supported by over 2,000 consumer diary entries, making it one of the most authoritative sources on Personalization to date.[1]

But Personalization without consistency is just noise. Your brand's ability to cut through depends on unifying what you say, how you say it, and where you show up.

Communications isn't just marketing output—it's the connective tissue between your positioning and your presence. Misaligned or unclear communication can lead to brand confusion, reputational damage, or churn. Get it right and you don't just earn attention—you earn trust, traction, and long-term business.

WHAT WE MEASURE

Communications is evaluated across three key measurable sub-subjects. These were selected based on the most important and measurable signals that influence whether your brand message resonates and sticks:

- **Clarity:** Can customers quickly understand what your product does and how to get started?
- **Engagement:** Are your communications driving action, interaction, or amplification?
- **Responsiveness:** Are you listening to customers and responding clearly, quickly, and helpfully?

When a brand succeeds across all three of these sub-subjects, the Communications grade will be higher. And with a GPA weight of 20 percent, Communications plays a meaningful supporting role in brand success.

One common misconception is that marketing owns Communications. In reality, it's cross-functional. Product, support, brand, sales, and legal teams all influence the message a customer receives. Inconsistent copy, broken onboarding, or unclear support responses can each chip away at consumer trust. When Communications is working, customers don't notice it. When it's broken, it's all they notice.

HOW WE GRADE

The three sub-subjects are weighted to determine a brand's overall Communications grade, which accounts for 20 percent of the overall Brand GPA. To calculate a brand's Communications grade, apply the internal sub-subject weightings (35 percent Clarity, 30 percent Engagement, 35 percent Responsiveness) and then factor Communications as 20 percent of the overall GPA. The grading criteria for each sub-subject is explained further in their respective sections.

Sub-Subject Weighting: Communications

Sub-Subject	Weighting	Primary Metric	A-Level Standard Description
Clarity	35%	First-time user task success	Top quartile task success for category, low bounce, clear onboarding
Engagement	30%	Content engagement rate (OR/CTR)	Top 25% for category, organic sharing, active feedback
Responsiveness	35%	CSAT/response time	Top quartile CSAT for category, fast support replies, public transparency

Industry benchmark note: Benchmarks vary by industry. For email engagement, ACSI industry scores, and task success rates, benchmarks differ significantly by category and should be evaluated relative to category norms. For current benchmarks refer to Nielsen Norman Group (www.nngroup.com), Baymard Institute (www.baymard.com), and ACSI (www.theacsi.org).

THE SUB-SUBJECTS: CLARITY

This is the baseline. Can customers easily understand what you offer and how to get started? Brands that nail Clarity reduce drop-off, boost trial and conversion, and build initial trust. Clarity spans home page copy, onboarding flows, in-app tooltips, customer support answers, and more.

WHAT WE MEASURE

Primary Metric: First-Time User Task Success

Measured through usability testing or clickstream data, this tracks whether new users can complete critical tasks (sign up, make a purchase, find information) without help. Task success thresholds are shaped by product complexity and user context—filing your taxes online is a fundamentally different challenge than reordering your favorite sneakers. So while 80 percent task success signals strong Clarity for most categories, what counts as "excellent" varies significantly by industry. It's true—some customers are really tough graders.

Secondary Indicators

- **Bounce rate:** Percentage of visitors who leave after viewing only one page
- **Home page task completion:** Whether users successfully complete intended actions from your home page
- **Customer support inquiry volume:** Declining support tickets often signal improving Clarity

GRADING RUBRIC

For A-level Clarity performance, task success benchmarks vary significantly by category and complexity. SaaS, finance, and retail tools operate at higher thresholds due to simpler user flows, while health care, government, and high-complexity tools naturally benchmark lower given inherent friction. Bounce rate standards similarly vary by category and traffic source. Clarity performance should be evaluated relative to category-specific norms rather than a universal threshold.

Grading Rubric: Clarity[2]

Grade	Description	Key Metric
A	Crystal clear UX and messaging, intuitive navigation, seamless onboarding	Top quartile task success for category, low bounce rate, clear value proposition
B	Mostly clear experience, minor friction points, generally intuitive	Above category median task success, moderate bounce rate, good user flow
C	Some confusion present, requires occasional support, mixed signals	At or just below category median task success, average bounce rate, unclear messaging
D	High drop-off rates, unclear CTAs, frequent user confusion	Bottom quartile task success, high bounce rate, poor onboarding
F	Confusing interface, frustrating experience, inconsistent messaging throughout	Sustained task failure, excessive bounce rate, major user abandonment

MAKING THE GRADE: AIRBNB (GRADE: A)

Airbnb gets a five-star review for platform Clarity, earning Baymard Institute's recognition as a top 1 percent desktop UX performer within the travel accommodations industry for 2024. That sounds like a lot of lofty jargon, but it isn't—fewer than 2 percent of evaluated platforms make the cut. And it's not an arbitrary rating—platforms are graded across 550+ UX guidelines spanning booking flows, search functionality, and mobile experience. When benchmarked against fifty-plus travel platforms, including other big dogs like Expedia, Booking.com, and Vrbo, Airbnb consistently ranked in the top one to two performers per critical user flow.[3]

In addition, according to SimilarWeb platform data, Airbnb's home page maintains a bounce rate of approximately 30 percent—well below the travel industry average of 45–50 percent—in a category where checkout abandonment rates consistently rank among the highest in e-commerce.[4]

With Airbnb, Clarity extends across all major touchpoints and devices. Baymard's travel accommodations research specifically highlights the importance of a clear path to booking, minimal checkout friction, and simplified navigation—criteria on which Airbnb consistently performs at the top of their evaluations.[5] The platform's filtering and search functionality reduces cognitive load through consistent iconography and in-line guidance, while pricing breakdowns and cancellation policies remain transparent throughout the booking process. Translation: They've made it remarkably dummy proof.

This integrated approach to Clarity, spanning desktop, mobile, and in-app experiences, demonstrates how exceptional UX design translates directly into meaningful (and measurable!) business performance. Or put another way, it's high time Airbnb gave their design team a raise!

MISSING THE MARK: GRUBHUB (GRADE: D)

Grubhub's checkout flow had one job: tell customers what their order actually costs. But it didn't—and that seemed to be a feature, not a bug. The Clarity failures weren't buried in fine print—they were baked into the core ordering flow, where pricing, subscription benefits, and account access are the table stakes of Customer Communications 101. Instead, the brand was enrolled in 301-level deceit.

The jig was up when the FTC and Illinois attorney general found that Grubhub hid fees until the last minute, misled Grubhub+ subscribers into believing they could avoid fees altogether, and blocked some customers from accessing their own gift card balances.[6] Regulators created quite a hubbub for Grubhub, initially seeking a $140 million judgment before settling for $25 million based on the company's ability to pay.[7] In a category where DoorDash and Uber Eats have invested heavily in transparent pricing and clear subscription communication because it's the right thing to do, Grubhub's regulatory settlement is a clear signal that Clarity was only a priority when it had to be.

THE SUB-SUBJECTS: ENGAGEMENT

If Clarity is about understanding, Engagement is about interest. Are your customers actually paying attention to what you're saying—and acting on it? Great Engagement means your content is relevant, is well timed, and resonates enough to drive interaction, not just impressions.

WHAT WE MEASURE

Primary Metric: Content Engagement Rate

This varies by format but measures whether customers are actually interacting with your communications. For email, track open rates and click-through rates (CTRs). For content, measure dwell time or scroll depth. For social, track shares and meaningful interactions beyond passive likes.

Secondary Indicators

- **Unsubscribe rate:** Percentage of email recipients opting out
- **Social shares:** Organic amplification of your content
- **UGC activity:** User-generated content (UGC) featuring or discussing your brand
- **Post-click engagement:** Whether email traffic translates into meaningful onsite behavior

GRADING RUBRIC

For A-level Engagement performance, email marketing benchmarks vary significantly by industry. A retailer blasting daily promotions is held to different standards than a B2B SaaS company sending a monthly product update. That said, outstanding performers consistently land in the top quartile for their category, while baseline performance sits at or below the category median. The bottom line: Engagement levels vary by business model, audience, and communication strategy, so performance is best evaluated relative to category-specific norms.

Grading Rubric: Engagement[8]

Grade	Description	Key Metric
A	Exceptional Engagement, content drives action and amplification	Top quartile open/CTR for category, strong organic sharing
B	Strong Engagement with consistent interaction patterns	Above category median open/CTR, steady social amplification
C	Moderate Engagement, inconsistent interaction	At or just below category median, limited organic sharing
D	Low Engagement, content rarely drives action	Bottom quartile open/CTR, high unsubscribe rates
F	Engagement failure, content ignored or actively rejected	Sustained disengagement, mass opt-outs, no amplification

MAKING THE GRADE: CHATGPT (GRADE: A)

The fastest-growing consumer application in history according to a UBS analysis cited by Reuters, ChatGPT has redefined Engagement in the AI space (and beyond), achieving massive scale through viral user-generated content and off-the-charts daily usage.[9] With approximately 100 million weekly active users as of late 2023, ChatGPT blows traditional Engagement benchmarks out of the AI-generated water.[10]

What sets ChatGPT apart is its organic amplification through prompt sharing and user-generated tutorials across social platforms. The platform's viral "prompt engineering" community has created an entire ecosystem of shared content, with users regularly posting creative use cases on Reddit, Twitter, and LinkedIn in droves. This user-driven content strategy has sustained ChatGPT's cultural relevance far beyond its initial launch hype, proving that when users become your marketing team, authentic Engagement drives exponential growth—and helps your brand climb the ranks.

MISSING THE MARK: WENDY'S (GRADE: D)

When your Communications strategy becomes the news instead of your burgers, there's trouble in fast-food paradise. In February 2024, Wendy's CEO Kirk Tanner announced the chain would begin testing "dynamic pricing and daypart offerings"—and the internet got a little . . . frosty.[11] Sir, is this a Wendy's?

Reuters reported the brand got blown up on social media within hours of the announcement, forcing Wendy's to publicly reverse course and tell Reuters directly it "would not raise prices when our customers are visiting us most."[12] Restaurant Dive documented the "widespread consumer backlash" and same-week retreat, making it one of the most self-inflicted Communications failures in quick service restaurants (QSRs) during the grading period—when it was probably intended to be a compelling message to drive traffic.[13]

Au contraire. Placer.ai data cited by Reuters showed Wendy's visits declined in all three months of Q4 2023, meaning the brand added insult to injury with the comms faux pas.[14] Subpar ACSI scores of 76 in 2024 and 75 in 2025 against a QSR average of 79 confirm Wendy's story is sadder than a side of soggy fries.[15]

THE SUB-SUBJECTS: RESPONSIVENESS

Responsiveness is where your brand proves it's actually listening. Whether it's replying to a support ticket, acknowledging feedback on social, or communicating during a crisis, Responsiveness shows customers that their voices matter. It's not just about speed—it's about empathy, helpfulness, and tone.

WHAT WE MEASURE

Primary Metric: CSAT (Customer Satisfaction) or Median Response Time

For CSAT, track the percentage of customers rating their support interaction as "satisfied" or "very satisfied." For response time, measure median time from initial inquiry to first meaningful response. CSAT performance varies by industry complexity and operational constraints—categories like travel and hospitality face unique challenges related to real-time service disruptions, while e-commerce, SaaS, and finance often operate in more controlled environments.

Secondary Indicators

- **First-contact resolution (FCR):** Percentage of issues resolved in the first interaction
- **SLA compliance:** Percentage of inquiries responded to within your committed time frame
- **Social support responsiveness:** Speed and quality of responses on public channels like Twitter/X

GRADING RUBRIC

For A-level Responsiveness performance, CSAT benchmarks vary by industry complexity and customer expectations. Response time expectations similarly differ by context—consumer-facing brands are held to faster standards than B2B environments. We're all impatient consumers, but Responsiveness should be evaluated relative to category-specific norms rather than a universal threshold.[16]

Grading Rubric: Responsiveness[17]

Grade	Description	Key Metric
A	Exceptionally responsive and helpful	Top quartile CSAT for category, fast response time
B	Generally responsive, occasional delays	Above category median CSAT, reasonable response time
C	Adequate but inconsistent	At or just below category median CSAT, slow responses
D	Slow or unhelpful responses	Bottom quartile CSAT, frequent delays
F	Poor or no response	Sustained CSAT failure, ignored customer needs

MAKING THE GRADE: ALASKA AIRLINES (GRADE: A)

Alaska Airlines sits comfortably in first class for Responsiveness, setting a standard in the travel sector. Alaska ranked #1 among traditional carriers in the *JD Power 2024 North America Airline Satisfaction Study*, measuring top marks across staff, digital tools, and trust—while the American Customer Satisfaction Index scored Alaska at 80 in 2024, soaring near the top of the industry.[18]

Plus, they are just pleasant to deal with. The DOT's *Air Travel Consumer Report* consistently places Alaska among the lowest complaint rates of any major US carrier—and passengers notice.[19]

Proactive communication is a key differentiator. During weather disruptions or system delays, Alaska uses in-app alerts, SMS updates, and social posts to keep customers informed in near real time. The airline also proactively monitors social sentiment and customer feedback to inform messaging updates and UX improvements across its digital touchpoints. In a category notorious for frustrating (and often absent) customer service, Alaska demonstrates that transparent communications and timely support are the best way to avoid turbulent customers and keep their brand aiming high.

MISSING THE MARK: TICKETMASTER (GRADE: D)

Ticketmaster's customer communication consistently ranks among the worst in the category—and consumers are noticing. Nearly nine thousand Better Business Bureau complaints over three years cite delayed or nonexistent responses, bot-based interactions, and a lack of transparency around refunds or cancellations.[20] Customer service issues aren't rare—they're the norm. Following the Taylor Swift Eras Tour presale meltdown, thousands of consumers reported unresolved ticket issues and radio silence from Ticketmaster support—a failure so widespread it triggered a US Senate Judiciary Committee hearing and eventually a full DOJ monopolization suit joined by thirty state and district attorneys general.[21]

Chatbots are the default, and customers report difficulty escalating to a human—especially when resolving refund or transfer issues. The Taylor Swift presale was the canary in the coal mine—and Ticketmaster didn't hear it singing. To make matters worse, fee transparency was so broken it took both a White House junk-fee initiative in June 2023 and an FTC rule in December 2024 to force the company to show customers what tickets actually cost up front.[22] Talk about tone deaf. The viral backlash sparked congressional hearings and led to lasting brand damage that was, um, "unprecedented."

TOP AND BOTTOM OF THEIR CLASS: COMMUNICATIONS

Great brands don't just talk *at*—they connect *with*. So when Communications fails, you've not only lost the plot; you've lost business. Joan Jett might not give a damn about her bad reputation—but a brand aspiring to be best in class certainly should.

Here's the brutal truth: When your home page confuses visitors, your emails land with a thud, and your support team is MIA, you're not just failing Communications—you're failing your customers.

In this section, we'll spotlight the brands leading their categories in Communications, along with those who struggle mightily.

The Communications score measures whether brands can actually connect with humans across every touchpoint, not just check boxes. Brands earning the summa cum laude distinction scored at or near the top of their class in Clarity, Engagement, and Responsiveness, showing strength in everything from UX copy to proactive, helpful customer interactions. In contrast, Flunking Out brands typically suffer from broken handoffs, misaligned tone, and reactive or missing communication during critical moments.

To qualify as a "Best in Communications" brand, we looked for the following:

- Top quartile task success and low bounce rates for category
- Email or content Engagement in the top 25 percent of their industry
- Top quartile CSAT or response times for category

Brands that flunked Communications typically exhibited the following:

- Fell short on core task success and home page Engagement targets
- Had email or content Engagement in the bottom quartile of their sector
- Received poor CSAT scores and failed to respond during critical moments[23]

You may notice some familiar faces in this grid. Yes, you *are* seeing double—and that's the point. Just like the brainy classmate in school who excelled at multiple subjects (or maybe that was you?), there are some brands that turn in top scores across multiple subjects.

At the same time, there are some who struggle across the board. Spoiler alert: DoorDash, Duolingo, Lululemon, and Sweetgreen are those brainiac brands. Meanwhile, Robinhood returns to brand detention, revealing even more cracks in its foundation.

Top and Bottom of Their Class: Communications

Vertical	Summa Cum Laude	Why They Excel	Flunking Out	Why They Fail
Apparel and footwear	Lululemon[24]	Company-operated store net revenue increased 14% and e-commerce net revenue increased 6% in FY2024; comparable sales remained positive through the year, including a 3% increase in Q4 and 4% in Q3; sustained demand across both physical and digital channels reflects consistent brand-to-customer communication	Old Navy[25]	Reuters reported in April 2024 that Coach sued Gap over Old Navy's sale of "Coach"-branded T-shirts, alleging the shirts were likely to confuse consumers about brand affiliation; Trustpilot reviews within the grading window cite nonfunctional customer service chat and website usability problems
Consumer goods	Dove[26]	"Real Beauty Redefined for the AI Era" won the Media Lions Grand Prix at Cannes Lions 2025; 4Bearned impressions and 500M views globally—sustained, measurable communications excellence across channels	Keurig[27]	SEC charged Keurig on September 10, 2024, with inaccurate recyclability claims for K-Cup pods; failed to disclose that two of the largest US recycling companies had expressed significant concerns and had no plans to accept them; $1.5M civil penalty
Media and entertainment	Spotify[28]	Wrapped 2024 engaged 245 million users—surpassing 2023's record within seven days—with millions sharing results on X; CEO Daniel Ek cited Wrapped as "a massive cultural moment" and "a significant driver" of MAU and subscriber growth	Clubhouse[29]	September 2023 relaunch as an asynchronous "chats" format—described by *TechCrunch* as a "Hail Mary" for relevance—confirmed a platform that had "faded from public discourse almost as quickly" as it rose; unclear product road map left users and creators with no reason to stay

Fitness and wellness	Strava[30]	4.8/5 on the Apple App Store with Apple Editors' Choice designation; 4.6/5 across 1.08M Google Play reviews with 100M+ downloads—category-leading app performance across both major platforms	BetterHelp[31]	FTC charged BetterHelp in March 2023 with sharing sensitive mental health data for advertising while promising privacy; $7.8M settlement with refunds to approximately 800K consumers
Health care	Mayo Clinic[32]	4.8/5 App Store (70K+ reviews); 120–150M monthly visits to mayoclinic.org; ranked #1 globally by *Newsweek*'s *World's Best Hospitals 2024*—Clarity, Engagement, and trust at a scale no health-care brand matches	Cigna[33]	$1.4M in Texas penalties across two 2024 consent orders for 14K+ IDR failures; Virginia market conduct exam found 111 violations for written claim denial and benefit determination failures
Consumer tech	Apple[34]	Ranked #1 in *Laptop Mag*'s 2023 Tech Support Showdown and #1 in ACSI's Personal Computer category in 2024, while also co-leading ACSI's Cell Phone rankings in 2024 and 2025—consistent top-tier performance across support and satisfaction benchmarks	Ticketmaster[35]	DOJ and 30 state attorneys general sued for monopolistic practices harming fans through higher prices and restricted competition in May 2024; fee transparency so broken it required White House pressure and a formal regulatory mandate to show customers what tickets actually cost
B2B tech	HubSpot[36]	In G2's 2024 Best Software Awards, HubSpot's Sales Hub ranked #1 in Sales Products, Marketing Hub ranked #1 in Marketing & Digital Advertising Products; high review volume and ratings signal consistent communications quality across the enterprise software category	Oracle NetSuite[37]	2024 federal lawsuit (*Realscape v. Oracle*, N.D. Oh. 2024) alleges brand was marketed as "off the shelf" ready and allegedly failed to deliver functioning software; product-positioning Clarity failure documented in federal court filing
Education	Duolingo[38]	DAUs grew from 21.4M (Q2 2023) to 37.2M (Q3 2024); 17M TikTok followers with posts regularly exceeding 1M views; category standard across all three Communications sub-subjects	Grand Canyon University[39]	FTC complaint alleged deceptive doctoral program communications around cost, course requirements, and nonprofit status; documented abusive telemarketing practices

continued →

Food service	Sweetgreen[40]	4.9/5 App Store rating (166K+ ratings); Apple editorial description specifically cites reordering ease, rewards Clarity, and customization transparency as standout features reflecting best-in-class digital communication and UX Clarity	Subway[41]	ACSI score of 74 against a quick-service industry average of 79; franchisee meeting in August 2024 amid same-store sales declines of 5–10% and unresolved communications conflicts between corporate and operators; persistent app complaints citing inconsistent options, unclear pricing, and buggy ordering experience throughout the grading period
Travel	Delta Airlines[42]	Named Best Airline Website in *Global Traveler*'s 2024 GT Tested Reader Survey Awards; loyalty program generated $3.8B+ in revenue in 2024, up 11% YoY; ranked #1 among traditional carriers in *JD Power 2024 North America Airline Satisfaction Study*; CEO customer update published within hours of July 2024 CrowdStrike outage with live disruption hub, travel waivers, and reimbursement guidance throughout recovery	Spirit Airlines[43]	Consistently ranked among the most complained about US carriers in DOT *Air Travel Consumer Report*; ACSI scores placed Spirit near the bottom of airline satisfaction rankings, well below industry average; Trustpilot rating of 1.2/5 across 12K+ reviews reflects widespread frustration with delays, cancellations, and support interactions
On-demand	DoorDash[44]	4.8/5 across 17.3M App Store ratings with Editors' Choice designation; consistent push notification reliability and delivery issue resolution performance above category benchmarks	Grubhub[45]	FTC and Illinois attorney general announced a $25M settlement in December 2024 over deceptive fee disclosures, misleading subscription benefits, and false delivery guarantees—textbook Communications failure
Financial services	Capital One[46]	Ranked #1 among national banks in *JD Power 2024 National Banking Satisfaction Study*—for consecutive years; #1 in online banking satisfaction among national banks (JD Power 2025)	Robinhood[47]	$10.2M multistate settlement (April 2023) for platform outages that prevented customer account access; $29.75M FINRA settlement (March 2025) citing failure to supervise, AML deficiencies, and delayed trade processing

TOP SCHOLAR AND BOTTOM DWELLER

Like we saw in Chemistry, every subject has its star student as well as the one hiding in the back of the class. For Communications, we chose Duolingo as our best communicator, a great brand that actually makes talking to customers look effortless (and fun!) while nailing Clarity, Engagement, and Responsiveness across every single touchpoint. Our fail is Spirit Airlines, which is a cautionary tale that "no frills" doesn't have to mean "no clue." When your Communications strategy makes customers feel like they're being pranked, you clearly didn't understand the assignment.

TOP SCHOLAR: DUOLINGO

It's more like *Triolingo*—because Duolingo aces all three Communications sub-subjects: Clarity, Engagement, and Responsiveness. From the moment a new user lands on their home page or downloads the app, the brand's value proposition is instantly clear. The UX is streamlined, multilingual, and delightfully gamified, helping Duolingo stand out as a best-practice case in onboarding Clarity. The brand's value proposition is clear, and users move seamlessly into the core learning experience. Along the way, learning streaks, progress feedback, and other reinforcements keep engagement climbing.

Duolingo's Engagement prowess comes from treating every touchpoint like a conversation, not a transaction. Their email nudges don't guilt-trip—they charm. Push notifications feel like a friend checking in, not a robot nagging. And their TikTok presence (over sixteen million followers with posts regularly crossing one million views) has turned Duo, the neon green owl, into an icon that people actually want to engage with.[48] With more than twenty-one million daily active users and over ninety-five million monthly active users by 2024, Duolingo ranks among the most widely used educational apps on the planet.[49] The results prove it works: Their 2024 shareholder letter revealed 50 percent year-over-year growth in paid subscribers, record-high free-to-paid conversion rates, and a content Engagement strategy that has earned widespread industry recognition, including an in-depth feature in *Adweek* praising the brand's social-first approach as a model for modern marketing.[50]

Duolingo's Responsiveness is just as strong—as indicated by a 4.7-star rating on Apple's App Store across more than one million reviews and a 4.7-star rating from more than forty-three million reviews on Google Play.[51] Their help center, user forums, and social media replies reflect both tone and empathy, and several product features (like the revamp of leaderboards and the launch of Duolingo Max) were developed in direct response to user feedback on Reddit and Twitter. In short, Duolingo listens—and when it comes to Communications, it leads.

Top Scholar Report Card: Duolingo

Sub-Subject	Grade	Metrics
Clarity	A	Cited as UX best-practice by CXL; intuitive onboarding; value proposition is obvious; streamlined, multilingual, gamified UX
Engagement	A	21.4M daily active users; 16.8M TikTok followers with viral content; 38% retention rate (3–4x education app average)
Responsiveness	A	4.7/5 App Store from 5M ratings; 4.7/5 Google Play from 43.9M reviews; community-driven product development documented by *Adweek*

BOTTOM DWELLER: SPIRIT AIRLINES

If you want your blood pressure to rise, try communicating with Spirit Airlines. Across all three Communications sub-subjects, Spirit struggles to meet even the baseline expectations. Its brand promise of "low fares, no frills" sounds great—until you realize that a carry-on bag, seat selection, or even a cup of water is considered a "frill." The model became so confusing that by July 2024, Spirit had overhauled it entirely—launching four new ticket bundles (Go, Go Savvy, Go Comfy, and Go Big) to replace a fragmented à la carte structure that had been alienating customers for years.[52] When your Clarity fix is a complete product restructure, that's not a communications tweak—that's an admission.

Engagement metrics are equally turbulent. Spirit's loyalty program failed to drive enough customer pull that the airline announced plans to redesign it specifically "to attract customers" as part of its post-bankruptcy turnaround.[53] A loyalty program that has to be rebuilt from scratch to attract the customers it was supposed to be retaining isn't a loyalty program—it's a placeholder. Even social media offers little value; despite an active presence, Engagement rates lag far behind peers like Delta and Southwest, both of whom have leaned into humor, service tips, and travel storytelling to actually humanize their brands.

But it's in Responsiveness where the wheels really come off. Spirit's DOT complaint rate consistently ranked among the highest of any major US carrier in 2023 and 2024—clocking in at 12.8 complaints per 100,000 passengers, second worst among all US carriers.[54] Customers frequently cite opaque chatbot loops and difficulty accessing live agents. On Reddit and X/Twitter, customer complaints often go unanswered—or worse, are met with canned replies days later. And even after reported service improvements, the American Customer Satisfaction Index still scored Spirit at just 69 in 2025—near the bottom of the entire airline industry.[55] In fact, these issues became so problematic that on May 2, 2026, Spirit Airlines officially ceased operations. When tone, transparency, and timeliness are treated as "frills," you can't be surprised when customers check out—before they even check in.

Bottom Dweller Report Card: Spirit Airlines

Sub-Subject	Grade	Metrics
Clarity	F	À la carte model so confusing it required complete overhaul; four new bundles launched July 2024 to replace fragmented add-on structure
Engagement	F	Loyalty program required redesign "to attract customers"; social Engagement lags peers; promos over personalization
Responsiveness	F	12.8 DOT complaints per 100,000 passengers, second worst among US carriers; ACSI score of 69, near bottom of industry

NEXT UP . . .

Having great Communications means you know how to attract, hook, and keep your customers. But just because you're a smooth talker doesn't mean you really get the gist of *why* they stay—or go. The next subject helps get into the mind of your customers. Fair warning: Things might get a little heady as we move on to the next subject—Psychology.

POP QUIZ: COMMUNICATIONS

You can't run a comprehensive brand diagnostic overnight, but this short Communications quiz can give you a sense of how your brand is doing in this subject. Answer each question with a checkmark (✓) for yes or leave blank for no. Then apply the weighting formula to calculate your back-of-the-envelope Communications score.

CLARITY (35 PERCENT)

- Can a first-time visitor complete a key task in under two minutes?

- Are fewer than 40 percent of your home page visits bouncing?
- Are your onboarding flows or tooltips successfully used by >75 percent of new users?
- Is the support team reporting fewer clarification tickets over time?

Industry benchmarks: SaaS/finance 80 percent+ task success, health care/complex tools 70 percent+

ENGAGEMENT (30 PERCENT)

- Do your top five content pieces achieve open or click rates in the top 25 percent of your category?
- Are social shares or comments steadily increasing over the past six months?
- Are unsubscribe rates below your industry's average?
- Are customers replying, sharing, or interacting with life cycle emails or help content?

Industry benchmarks: Email engagement varies from 30 percent baseline to 50 percent+ outstanding

RESPONSIVENESS (35 PERCENT)

- Is your median support response time under one hour?
- Are ≥85 percent of CSAT responses marked satisfied or very satisfied?
- Do users report feeling "heard" in surveys or support reviews?
- Do you offer real-time or near-real-time updates during high-stress moments (e.g., outages, delays)?

Industry benchmarks: Travel 76 percent+ CSAT, SaaS/finance 80 percent+ CSAT

SCORING METHOD

Count your total "yes" answers in each section, then multiply your Clarity score by 0.35, your Engagement score by 0.30, and your Responsiveness score by 0.35. Add all three adjusted scores together to get your final Communications score. See the following scoring rubric (and sorry, there's no extra credit).

Pop Quiz Scoring Table: Communications

Weighted Score Total	Communications Grade	Interpretation
10–12	A	Top performance—your Communications are working across all dimensions
8–9	B	Strong foundation but room for optimization in weaker areas
6–7	C	Mixed signals—focus on lowest-scoring sub-subject
4–5	D	Trouble ahead—Communications Clarity and Responsiveness need attention
<4	F	Communications crisis—urgent course correction required across all areas

Important note: Scoring should be interpreted within your industry context. Task success and response time benchmarks vary significantly by category—what qualifies as strong performance for a health-care company would fall short of expectations for a SaaS platform. Evaluate your results against your category peers, not the universal scale.

CHAPTER 4

PSYCHOLOGY

I PROMISE THIS ISN'T GOING TO BE PSYCHOBABBLE. Psychology in the Brand GPA framework focuses on the customer and their motivations, their preferences, and their beliefs. In other words, it's the "why" behind consumer decision-making. Psychological triggers move people toward action—or inaction—often without them even realizing it. As Nobel laureate Daniel Kahneman notes in *Thinking, Fast and Slow*, most decisions are made using "System 1" thinking, defined as fast, intuitive, and emotional.[1] Great brands understand this and design experiences accordingly, reducing barriers to entry and delighting customers so they can build deeper connections.

WHY THIS MATTERS

While Chemistry explores what fans the flames between brands and customers, Psychology dives into why people actually decide to play with fire in the first place. For instance, customers might be initially intrigued by your product or service, but psychological friction can make an initial spark extinguish forever. So it's imperative that brands understand what makes a customer play hard to get, such as low completion rates with a sign-up flow or an abandoned shopping cart, as well as when the relationship is really on the rocks, such as declining engagement or an increase in complaints. Whether you like it or not, your brand is always in a one-sided state of couples therapy, and the onus is on you to understand what's going wrong (and right!). Fortunately, there are plenty of data sources to give you a quick read so you can take swift action.

For instance, you can give your customers a complex by making things too complex. Research by Iyengar and Lepper found that when customers face more than ten options, purchase likelihood drops significantly, potentially up to 40 percent.[2] Similarly, Dan Ariely's book *Predictably Irrational* shows that increasing complexity raises cognitive friction and often leads to decreased task completion.[3] In other words, keep it simple, stupid. (Nothing personal!)

But speaking of personal, McKinsey's 2021 "Next in Personalization" report showed that companies excelling at Personalization generate 40 percent more revenue from those activities than average players.[4] And it makes sense. After all, Abraham Maslow places "love and belonging" as a fundamental human need, and who doesn't trust that handy pyramid? But seriously, people want to be heard and understood, and nothing is more frustrating than feeling like you're just a number or that after years of loyalty, a brand still doesn't get you.

That sentiment is acutely felt during times of conflict. But here's what customers really need brands to understand: When issues arise, they don't want to work that hard to reach a resolution. In other words, waiting on hold, going through a jungle of decision-tree prompts, or having to tell your entire life story in a complaint field feels like work, and the last thing people want is more work in their lives. On that point, Nielsen Norman Group has documented cases where improving self-service UX reduces support demand and notes that effective self-service supports goals like reducing call-center costs and improving customer satisfaction.[5] The old adage "the customer is always right" can be maddening when you are dealing with an irate Karen or an irrational Todd, but the fastest way to help them cool their jets is a seamless, intuitive, and solutions-oriented customer success engine. Not only will it help empower your customers to solve issues on their own, but you'll also save money (mo' tickets, mo' budget) and reduce employee burnout (customer support agents are people too!) in the process.

So while the notion of Psychology in business can feel "squishy" to some, the risks of not taking it seriously couldn't be more rock solid. Confused, stuck, or misunderstood customers are a fast track to increased churn and leaving revenue on the table—and your brand on the fainting sofa.

WHAT WE MEASURE

Psychology is evaluated across three measurable sub-subjects. These were selected based on behavioral economics research showing the primary psychological drivers of customer action:

- **Motivation:** Do customers feel confident and compelled to act, or are they stalling out due to uncertainty?
- **Personalization:** Does the experience feel tailored, familiar, and emotionally relevant?
- **Control:** Are customers able to complete key actions easily, without friction or reliance on support?

When a brand succeeds across all three sub-subjects, the Psychology grade will be higher. And with a GPA weight of 15 percent, Psychology plays a crucial role in creating the mental conditions for customer action.

HOW WE GRADE

Motivation holds a 35 percent weight overall. This sub-subject gets a higher weight because behavioral economics research, including Kahneman's work on System 1 decision-making, shows that friction at the point of initial engagement can significantly reduce action. Think a pricing page with four nearly identical tiers or a sign-up flow that asks for your credit card before you've seen the product. The first example feels like a mind game, the second like a bait and switch. Both create just enough doubt to make your brand seem questionable.

Personalization carries a 30 percent weight. While Personalization significantly impacts engagement and revenue, Epsilon's 2022 *Power of Me* study shows it primarily enhances experiences after customers have already decided to engage, making it a powerful but secondary psychological factor.[6]

Control rounds out the sub-subjects at 35 percent. This substantial weight reflects self-determination theory research—the widely cited framework holding that humans are driven by autonomy, competence, and relatedness—showing that customer autonomy impacts both initial trust formation and ongoing satisfaction. Gagné and Deci's foundational self-determination theory research confirms that autonomy and perceived control consistently enhance motivation, performance, and well-being.[7]

BRINGING IT ALL TOGETHER

Sub-Subject Weighting: Psychology

Sub-Subject	Weighting	Primary Metric	A-Level Standard Description
Motivation	35%	Task initiation rate	Top quartile initiation rate for category, clear value proposition, minimal psychological barriers
Personalization	30%	Personalized content engagement	Top quartile lift over generic content for category, relevant recommendations, tailored experiences
Control	35%	Self-service resolution rate	Top quartile self-service resolution for category, high FCR, customer autonomy

Industry benchmark note: Benchmarks vary significantly by industry and business model. SaaS, e-commerce, financial services, and health care each operate under different psychological constraints and should be evaluated relative to category-specific norms.

THE SUB-SUBJECTS: MOTIVATION

When customers hit your website, app, or store, they're making split-second judgments: "Is this worth my time? Can I trust this? What happens if I'm wrong?" Motivation is about eliminating those psychological speed bumps that cause people to hesitate, second-guess, or abandon ship entirely.

Unlike Activity in Chemistry (which measures if people actually use your product), Motivation measures the psychological barriers that prevent people from even trying. Think of it as the mental runway customers need before they're willing to take off. Too much friction on that runway and they never get airborne.

WHAT WE MEASURE

Primary Metric: Task Initiation Rate

This tracks the percentage of visitors who start key conversion actions (signing up for a trial, adding items to cart, beginning onboarding). Unlike completion rates, task initiation measures whether customers overcome the initial psychological hurdle to even try. Industry benchmarks vary significantly by business model and funnel stage. For example, task initiation rates for SaaS free trials differ meaningfully from e-commerce add-to-cart behavior, and both should be evaluated relative to category-specific norms.

Secondary Indicators

- **Time to first action:** How quickly users take their first meaningful action after arriving
- **Abandonment at decision points:** Where psychological friction causes users to leave
- **Help-seeking behavior during onboarding:** Whether users need assistance to get started

GRADING RUBRIC

The rubric provides guidance on whether you're creating the psychological conditions for action—or inadvertently building barriers that keep customers on the sidelines.

Grading Rubric: Motivation

Grade	Description	Key Metric
A	Frictionless Motivation and clear value	Top quartile task initiation for category, rapid time to first action
B	Strong Motivation with minor hesitation	Above category median initiation, minimal friction signals
C	Mixed signals, moderate barriers	At or just below category median, notable abandonment at key decision points
D	Unclear value or process friction	Bottom quartile initiation, high abandonment, slow time to action
F	Existential psychological barriers	Sustained initiation failure, complete user abandonment

Industry benchmark note: Task initiation rates and time-to-first-action benchmarks vary significantly by business model, funnel stage, and category. Evaluate performance relative to category-specific norms rather than a universal threshold.

MAKING THE GRADE: FIGMA (GRADE: A)

While many tools boast about their ease of use and collaboration capabilities, those claims are a mere fig leaf compared to Figma, the Motivation MVP. New users click a shared link and start working within seconds—no installation, no admin approval, no IT ticket. The psychological impact is immediate and obvious: You can do the thing before anyone explains how to do the thing. Talk about doing the right thing.

The lack of product friction leads to lots of brand addiction: Forrester Consulting's *Total Economic Impact of Figma Dev Mode* study found that developers saved an average of ninety-eight minutes per week through streamlined design-to-development workflows, with interviewees estimating 20–30 percent higher output from reduced friction and context switching.[8] As such, Reuters reported Figma's annual recurring revenue was expected to grow 40 percent to over $600 million in 2023—not because of hard-charging sales tactics but because of an easygoing product.[9]

MISSING THE MARK: WORKDAY (GRADE: D)

Workday is working it—more than half the Fortune 500 uses it to hire, onboard, and pay their employees. But it's also working many last nerves, punctuated by a mince-no-words headline from *Business Insider*: "Everyone hates Workday."[10]

The piece describes a product that has been "making a mint creating misery where painless processes could be," with users reporting that even simple tasks leave them "scratching their heads" and that getting someone onboarded "is like trying to get water from your sink to your stove using a colander."[11] The data confirms it: G2 Ease of Setup score came in averaging a mediocre 7.6/10 from nearly three hundred enterprise reviews—validating the scathing article and frustrated customers from coast to coast.[12]

THE SUB-SUBJECTS: PERSONALIZATION

Here's where things get personal—literally. Personalization in the Psychology context isn't about calling customers by their first name in emails (though that doesn't hurt)—it's about creating experiences that feel like they were designed specifically for each individual, making customers think, *This brand really gets me.*

The psychological impact is profound. When experiences feel tailored, customers move from feeling like anonymous visitors to feeling understood and valued. McKinsey's research shows this emotional shift translates directly to business results: Companies excelling at Personalization generate 40 percent more revenue from those activities than average players.[13]

But Personalization isn't just recommendation engines and "customers who bought this also bought . . ." It's about understanding customer intent, preferences, and context well enough to reduce cognitive load. When Netflix shows you exactly the content you want to watch, when Spotify creates playlists that match your mood, when Amazon anticipates what you need before you know you need it, that's Personalization creating psychological ease.

The flip side? Generic one-size-fits-all experiences that make customers feel like just another number in the database. Nothing says, "We don't care about you as an individual" quite like irrelevant product recommendations or email content that has nothing to do with your actual interests or purchase history.

WHAT WE MEASURE

Primary Metric: Personalized Content Engagement Rate

This measures how customers interact with personalized versus generic content—tracking clicks, opens, and interactions to determine whether tailored experiences drive meaningfully higher engagement. The benchmark is clear: Personalized email subject lines are 26 percent more likely to be opened than generic versions.[14] Recommendation click-through rates vary significantly by category and should be evaluated relative to industry norms.

Secondary Indicators

- **Recommendation click-through rates:** Percentage of users clicking personalized product or content suggestions
- **Email personalization performance:** Open and click rates for personalized versus broadcast messages
- **Return visitor behavior:** Whether returning customers experience different, tailored interactions
- **Time spent with personalized content:** Engagement depth with customized experiences

GRADING RUBRIC

For A-level Personalization performance, customers should feel like the brand actually knows them—not just their email address. But acing Personalization is easier said than done due to its complexity. For example, personalized content should meaningfully outperform generic alternatives across every channel you measure. Then there are email personalization lifts, recommendation click-through rates, and on-site behavioral targeting—all equally important. And spoiler: Top-performing brands show consistent lift across all three, not just one. So evaluate Personalization relative to your category norms, not a universal standard that treats all industries—and their customers—the same.

Grading Rubric: Personalization

Grade	Description	Key Metrics
A	Highly personalized experiences driving measurable action	Top quartile engagement lift over generic content for category, strong recommendation CTR
B	Strong Personalization with consistent engagement lift	Above category median engagement lift, positive recommendation performance
C	Basic Personalization with inconsistent lift	At or just below category median, limited recommendation impact
D	Minimal Personalization, generic experiences	Bottom quartile engagement lift, low recommendation CTR
F	Generic or irrelevant content causing disengagement and exodus	Sustained negative engagement, increasing unsubscribes, customer complaints about irrelevance

Industry benchmark note: Personalization performance varies significantly by channel, category, and business model. For current category-specific benchmarks, refer to Mailchimp email benchmarks (www.mailchimp.com/resources/email-marketing-benchmarks/) and McKinsey personalization research (www.mckinsey.com).

MAKING THE GRADE: SPOTIFY (GRADE: A)

Spotify rocks when it comes to Personalization, with algorithmic curation that feels handcrafted. Across the grading period, Spotify grew from 602 million to 626 million monthly active users and from 236 million to 246 million premium subscribers—engaged primarily through personalized experiences rather than manual browsing (remember record stores?).[15] Their Discover Weekly playlist exemplifies this psychological mastery. The feature has introduced countless artist discoveries across the platform, demonstrating sustained user engagement at massive scale.

The psychological impact is profound: Instead of feeling overwhelmed by one hundred million tracks, users feel like Spotify knows their taste better than they do. The platform learns from every skip, every replay, every playlist addition. Daily Mix blends familiar favorites with new recommendations. Release Radar surfaces new music from followed artists. When algorithms create experiences that feel more intuitive than manual browsing, things do get personal on Spotify—in a good way.

But Spotify's Personalization extends beyond algorithms. Spotify Wrapped, which earned the brand highest marks in Communications for its engagement impact, does double duty here—not only providing unique personal insights into your musical tastes and consumption habits but also becoming a viral sensation every December. With over 245 million users engaging with Wrapped in 2024 alone—and CEO Daniel Ek explicitly citing it as a significant driver of MAU and subscriber growth—it's also brilliant for retention since it's a motivator for people to listen more—or to potentially less of an embarrassing genre—in the new year.[16]

MISSING THE MARK: STATE FARM (GRADE: D)

State Farm is like a good neighbor—if that neighbor barely knows you. In an era when competitors like Progressive and Allstate tailor pricing to individual driving behavior through telematics programs, State Farm's experience remains largely standardized with broad underwriting tiers, agent-mediated coverage, and mass rate increases applied regardless of individual behavior. The *JD Power 2024 U.S. Auto Insurance Study* is the tell: State Farm scored 657—below the industry average of 672—in a study that explicitly identified personalized guidance and relevant coverage recommendations as primary satisfaction drivers.[17] Reuters also reported State Farm sought a 22 percent rate increase for California homeowners to offset wildfire-related losses—the same rate for everyone, regardless of the circumstance.[18] When the largest insurer in the country treats ninety-one million policyholders like a number rather than a person, that's a claim the insurance brand *should* want to repair.

THE SUB-SUBJECTS: CONTROL

Control is about customer autonomy—the feeling that they're in the driver's seat of their experience with your brand. When customers feel like they can easily accomplish what they want without having to ask for help, trust your self-service options, and navigate your experience on their own terms, they're more likely to engage deeply and return frequently.

The flip side is dependency—when customers constantly need to contact support, can't find what they're looking for, or feel trapped in processes they can't control. That's when frustration builds and Psychology scores plummet.

From a self-determination theory perspective, autonomy is one of three basic psychological needs (along with competence and relatedness). Research shows that perceived autonomy, competence, and relatedness are strong predictors of user adoption intentions. When customers feel in control, they're not just more satisfied—they're more likely to engage, return, and recommend.

WHAT WE MEASURE

Primary Metric: Self-Service Resolution Rate

This tracks the percentage of customer issues resolved without human intervention—a direct measure of whether customers feel empowered to help themselves. World-class support organizations resolve more than 80 percent of issues without escalation, reflecting strong self-service and first-contact resolution capabilities, with industry research showing that every 1 percent increase in first-contact resolution improves customer satisfaction by approximately 1 percent.[19]

Secondary Indicators

- **First-contact resolution (FCR):** Percentage of issues resolved in the first interaction when customers do need help
- **Customer autonomy survey scores:** Direct feedback on whether customers feel in Control of their experience
- **Privacy-control engagement:** How customers use settings to manage their data and preferences

GRADING RUBRIC

For A-level Control performance, customers should never have to talk to you. Well, most of the time at least. They should be able to resolve the vast majority of issues on their own—without picking up the phone, waiting on hold, or submitting a ticket. Self-service benchmarks vary significantly by category and complexity, with enterprise B2B tools naturally requiring more human intervention than consumer apps. Evaluate Control performance relative to your category norms rather than a catchall solution that might be a C in A clothing.

Grading Rubric: Control[20]

Grade	Description	Metrics
A	High autonomy, excellent self-service	Top quartile self-service resolution for category, high FCR
B	Good self-service, occasional assistance needed	Above category median self-service resolution, strong FCR
C	Mixed self-service, moderate dependency	At or just below category median, inconsistent FCR
D	Poor self-service, high support dependency	Bottom quartile self-service resolution, low FCR
F	Broken self-service creating customer crisis	Sustained resolution failure, support overwhelmed, customer exodus

MAKING THE GRADE: STRIPE (GRADE: A)

Stripe has earned its stripes in customer Control by delivering exceptional self-service capabilities that put complete autonomy in users' hands. Their developer-first approach means businesses can manage billing, subscriptions, invoices, and payment settings entirely through their dashboard without ever needing support intervention—and in August 2024, Stripe made that even easier by opening Workbench to everyone, giving developers a dedicated home inside the Dashboard to debug, monitor, and grow their integration independently.[21]

The validation came from an independent source: In February 2025, Forrester named Stripe Billing a "Leader in The Forrester Wave: Recurring Billing Solutions, Q1 2025," with Stripe receiving the highest possible scores in ten criteria.[22] *TechCrunch* noted in April 2024 that Stripe was decoupling payments from the rest of its stack and expanding its developer tools to give builders even more modular Control over their own payment infrastructure.[23] By dialing down technical complexity and turning up user confidence, Stripe is the back-end solution that puts customer Control at the forefront.

MISSING THE MARK: T-MOBILE (GRADE: D)

T-Mobile built its entire brand identity around being the "un-carrier"—the scrappy challenger brand that gave customers more Control and transparency in a category notorious for trapping people in complex contracts with lots of buried fees. For years, it worked. But in May 2024, T-Mobile raised prices on legacy plans that customers had specifically chosen because of the company's "price lock" promise—the explicit guarantee that their rates wouldn't change.[24]

Their customers, who normally bled pink, were seeing red, and the backlash was immediate and well documented.[25] Control is all about user autonomy and the ability to make your own decisions, but T-Mobile's message was clear: Pay more or leave. Talk about "un-control."

TOP AND BOTTOM OF THEIR CLASS: PSYCHOLOGY

Psychology is where brands either become trusted partners in customers' mental lives or annoying obstacles to overcome. The best brands understand that every interaction is an opportunity to reduce friction, increase relevance, and empower customers. The worst create unnecessary complexity, irrelevant experiences, and dependency that makes customers feel helpless.

The Psychology score measures whether brands create the mental conditions for customers to engage confidently and successfully. Brands earning the summa cum laude distinction scored at or near the top of their class in Motivation, Personalization, and Control, demonstrating they understand and optimize for human psychology.

In contrast, Flunking Out brands typically create barriers, deliver irrelevant experiences, and leave customers feeling frustrated or dependent.

To qualify as a "Best in Psychology" brand, we looked for the following:

- Top quartile task initiation for category with minimal psychological friction
- Measurable Personalization lift with relevant, tailored experiences
- Top quartile self-service success rates enabling customer autonomy

Brands that flunked Psychology typically exhibited the following:

- Low task initiation rates due to psychological barriers
- Generic, irrelevant experiences with minimal Personalization impact
- High support dependency reflecting poor self-service performance[26]

One brand in this grid—Drizly—is no longer operating. While the rest of the book features brands still alive and kicking, its inclusion in this chapter is intentional. A brand that fails Psychology doesn't just lose customers; it can lose everything. Drizly's story is a reminder that a subject-level failure is a bellwether for darker days ahead. On the flip side, Peloton earns category-level Psychology props yet was a Missing the Mark example in the Chemistry chapter. That's not your eyes deceiving you—that's the Brand GPA at work. It is possible for brands to shine in one area and struggle in another, which is why a holistic framework matters more than any single metric to show how a brand is truly performing.

Top and Bottom of Their Class: Psychology

Vertical	Summa Cum Laude	Why They Excel	Flunking Out	Why They Fail
Apparel and footwear	Nordstrom[27]	ACSI score of 78 in 2025, above named online apparel peers including Macy's (77), Nike (76), and Gap (72); holiday-quarter comparable sales increased 4.7% in Q4 2024, beating Wall Street consensus of 1.25%, while maintaining customer satisfaction scores above several major apparel peers	Stitch Fix[28]	Active clients fell 15.5% YoY to 2.371M in Q2 FY2025; active clients declined further to 2.353M in Q3 FY2025, down 10.6% YoY; *Retail Dive* reported seven consecutive quarters of YoY sales declines as of January 2024
Consumer goods	Liquid Death[29]	Purchase consideration rose from 2.5% to 5.5% (2022–2024); likely buyers over-index on environmental policy (34% vs. 18%) and ecological responsibility (32% vs. 18%)—canned water as a psychological statement	Bud Light[30]	Sales fell 24.6% in four weeks (June 2023); dropped to #3 behind Modelo and Michelob Ultra by July 2024; YouGov documented reputation score going negative and consideration collapsing to 11% of aware consumers
Media and entertainment	Pinterest[31]	553M MAUs in Q4 2024 (+11% YoY); 4.8/5 App Store rating (5.6M ratings); user-directed board curation and personalized discovery create a high-autonomy, low-friction experience that keeps users engaged and in control	Comcast[32]	Xfinity scored 67 in ACSI 2024, trailing all major non-fiber peers; FCC 24-29 named Comcast for obscuring fees; FTC click-to-cancel rule (2023) triggered by cancellation complaints
Fitness and wellness	Peloton[33]	Average net monthly churn of 1.2% among connected-fitness subscribers; subscribers engaging across two or more disciplines show ~60% lower churn—reflecting deep motivational stickiness and community-driven loyalty across the grading period	BetterHelp[34]	FTC charged BetterHelp in March 2023 with sharing sensitive mental health data for advertising while promising privacy; $7.8M settlement with refunds to approximately 800K consumers

continued →

Health care	Zocdoc[35]	4.9/5 App Store rating (152K reviews); Guided Search delivers tailored provider results based on unique care needs; patients see a doctor within 24–72 hours of booking; real-time insurance filtering and instant self-service booking put full Control in the patients' hands	United Healthcare[36]	2023 class action (D. Minn. 23-cv-03514) alleged AI algorithm systematically denied elderly patients' claims, overriding physician recommendations; 33% of UnitedHealth Group in-network claims denied across marketplace plans
Consumer tech	Grammarly[37]	4.7/5 App Store rating (210K+ ratings); 4.6/5 on Gartner Peer Insights (2,493 ratings); featured in *Fast Company*'s Most Innovative Companies 2024; puts users in command of their own voice through personalization, tone controls, and writing goal setting	Sonos[38]	May 2024 app redesign collapsed to 1.3 stars on Google Play; cost $20–30M to fix; CEO resigned January 2025—a self-inflicted Psychology failure with a paper trail
B2B tech	Asana[39]	Named TrustRadius's Best for Mid-Sized Teams (December 2024); featured in G2's Best Software Products 2025 across four categories; $723.9M revenue FY2025; freemium model and full self-service require zero IT overhead	Microsoft Teams[40]	CSRB report cited Microsoft's 2023 Exchange breach as "preventable"; January 2024 Teams outage peaked at 14,000+ reported incidents, stripping operational Control from millions of dependent users
Education	Khan Academy[41]	4.6/5 App Store (104K ratings), Editors' Choice; 4.2/5 Google Play (172K reviews); peer-reviewed study found users outperformed control groups 61% vs. 31%; Khanmigo praised for step-by-step personalized guidance	Blackboard[42]	At least three universities migrated to Brightspace during the grading period; Phil Hill's February 2025 LMS analysis confirmed accelerating account losses; 3.3/5 Google Play (100K reviews); persistent complaints about navigation and forced login friction

Food service	Domino's[43]	ACSI score of 78; rewards program reached 35.7M active members by end of 2024 following relaunch that added 2M+members; frictionless ordering, real-time delivery tracking, and a personalized rewards system driving repeat purchase behavior at scale	Wendy's[44]	ACSI score of 76, below quick-service industry average of 79; surge pricing announcement in early 2024 triggered immediate consumer backlash, Senate criticism, and boycott calls before Wendy's reversed course—a self-inflicted trust collapse; persistent app complaints about login failures, reward redemption errors, and promotional clutter throughout the grading period
Travel	Booking.com[45]	4.8/5 App Store rating (2M reviews); ACSI category leader at 80 in 2024; YouGov consideration growth from 15.2% to 24.1% between 2019 and 2024; booking experience built around user confidence, Control, and motivated return	American Airlines[46]	ACSI score dropped from 79 to 74 in 2025; loyalty program friction and operational misfires explicitly cited by ACSI; Christmas Eve 2024 ground stop and June 2025 systems failure compounded a year of eroding customer trust and Control
On-demand	Lyft[47]	ACSI category leader at 77 in 2024, surpassing Uber's 75; 4.9/5 App Store rating (17M reviews)	Drizly[48]	FTC data breach order in January 2023, exposing 2.5M consumers, and full platform shutdown announced January 2024 and completed March 2024—a brand that lost consumer trust so thoroughly its parent company pulled the plug entirely

continued →

Financial services	Marcus by Goldman Sachs[49]	Ranked #3 in *JD Power 2025 Direct Banking Satisfaction Study* (score: 735 vs. 705 segment average); 4.9/5 App Store rating (235K+ ratings); frictionless self-service UX drives strong user confidence and control	GEICO[50]	Scored 626 vs. 637 regional average in *JD Power 2024 Auto Insurance Study* (California); 7,701 employees cut in 2023; systematic failures across Motivation, Personalization, and Control undermine a brand built on effortless coverage

TOP SCHOLAR AND BOTTOM DWELLER

Psychology has its overachiever—and its head case. We chose Asana as our clear-headed winner because they've exceled at understanding customer psychology through exceptional user empowerment, perfecting the art and social science of Motivation, Personalization, and Control. In sharp contrast, Comcast is the example setter for a systemic failure to understand customer Psychology, delivering confusion instead of clarity and generic experiences instead of personalized service, leaving customers feeling trapped instead of empowered.

TOP SCHOLAR: ASANA

With a name like Asana, you would expect it to be easy to deal with. The founders chose the name deliberately—it's Sanskrit for "yoga pose," and in the enterprise context, the brand represents focus, flow, and balance in teamwork. As it turns out, that's not just yogababble—those are brand values in fluid motion.

The Motivation case starts with the platform's onboarding. Asana's freemium model removes the single biggest psychological barrier in enterprise software: commitment before value. *Forbes Advisor* called the platform's workflow tools "intuitive" and "suitable for teams old and new," noting the automation builder makes it simple to create complex cross-platform workflows without heavy implementation overhead.[51] There's no lengthy setup, no IT provisioning, and no mental gymnastics required to get started.

Personalization is where Asana separates itself from the field of often rigid, one-size-fits-all enterprise tools. TrustRadius named Asana Best for Mid-Sized Teams in December 2024, specifically citing custom fields that allow teams to tailor the tool to their needs.[52] In other words, it's your practice.

In terms of Control, Asana is all about customer empowerment. G2 named Asana among its Best Software Products for 2025, recognizing it across Best Project Management, Best Global Sellers, Best Mid-Market, and Best Highest Satisfaction categories—in large part because the platform allows teams to configure billing, workflows, permissions, and reporting entirely through self-service.[53] The business results say it all: Asana reported $723.9 million in revenue for fiscal 2025, with 24,062 core customers contributing approximately 72 percent of total revenue and 726 customers spending over $100,000 annually.[54] For a brand that is all about the namaste, it operates like a real warrior.

Top Scholar Report Card: Asana

Sub-Subject	Grade	Metrics
Motivation	A	Freemium model removes commitment barrier before value; *Forbes Advisor* cites intuitive workflow tools suitable for all team types; no IT overhead required to get started
Personaliza-tion	A	TrustRadius's Best for Mid-Sized Teams (Dec. 2, 2024); custom fields and multiple views adapt to cross-functional team needs; 72% of revenue from core customers who've built Asana into daily workflows
Control & Autonomy	A	G2 Best Software Products 2025 across four categories; full self-service configuration; 726 customers spending $100K+ annually; $723.9M revenue reflects sticky, autonomous adoption

BOTTOM DWELLER: COMCAST

Comcast is a masterclass in how to frustrate customers at every turn—and in a truly competitive market, scores like these would earn a straight F. Comcast survives on necessity, not loyalty. In the 2024 American Customer Satisfaction Index for Telecommunications, Comcast's Xfinity internet service scored 67 out of 100, while its pay-TV service scored 69, placing it among the lowest-rated major telecom providers.[55] The FCC's own All-In Pricing proceeding found that Comcast and peer providers routinely obscure company-imposed fees—and actively suggest to customers they have no choice but to pay them.[56] These aren't isolated incidents—they're symptoms of fundamental psychological design failures.

The Motivation problems start immediately, with confusing bundle packages and Byzantine-era sign-up flows. In the 2024 *ACSI Telecommunications Study*, Xfinity trailed every leading non-fiber peer—scoring 67 against AT&T Internet (69), Cox (68), and Spectrum (68)—with call center satisfaction ranking as the worst part of the customer experience across non-fiber providers.[57] The infamous "triple play" bundles require landing a mental triple lutz to understand what you're actually getting and what it will cost after promotional pricing expires—and promotional internet pricing frequently expires after the first year, often leading to substantial increases in monthly bills. On Personalization, Comcast delivers spectacular failure despite sitting on vast troves of customer data. Traditional cable recommendation systems have struggled to match the Personalization capabilities of modern streaming platforms, and Comcast is exhibit A—sports packages pushed to people who never watch sports, movie bundles suggested to cord-cutters who only want internet.

Control is where Comcast teeters into psychological warfare. Comcast has long faced criticism for customer service performance, ranking near the bottom of major internet providers in consumer satisfaction surveys and drawing regulatory scrutiny over billing transparency and cancellation practices—the FTC even proposed new "click-to-cancel" rules in 2023 in direct response to widespread consumer complaints about deliberately difficult cancellation processes.[58] Meanwhile, the FCC's own *2024 Communications Marketplace Report* found that more than a third of Americans have only one provider of high-speed broadband or none at all—and Comcast dominates many of those markets.[59] And in these monopoly/duopoly regions, customers feel less empowered and more imprisoned.

Bottom Dweller Report Card: Comcast

Sub-Subject	Grade	Metrics
Motivation	D	Complex processes; unclear next steps
Personalization	D	Generic communications; poor relevance
Control	D	Limited self-service; dependency-driven

NEXT UP . . .

Psychology creates the mental conditions for customer action, but even brands with great psychological design can stumble when it comes to how they engage with the broader world. Next up: Sociology—because understanding individual psychology is just the beginning of the conversation.

POP QUIZ: PSYCHOLOGY

You can't run a comprehensive brand diagnostic overnight, but this short Psychology quiz can give you a directional sense of how your brand is doing in this subject. Answer each question with a checkmark (✓) for yes or leave blank for no. Then apply the weighting formula to calculate your back-of-the-envelope Psychology score.

MOTIVATION (35 PERCENT)

- Do ≥20 percent of visitors who start your primary conversion flow actually complete the first step?
- Can first-time users understand your value proposition and take meaningful action within ten seconds?
- Are psychological barriers (uncertainty, complexity, risk) actively identified and minimized in your key flows?
- Do users show clear momentum from initial interest to first meaningful action without hesitation?

Industry benchmarks: SaaS 15–25 percent trial initiation; e-commerce 7–11 percent add-to-cart rates; financial services may be lower due to security requirements

PERSONALIZATION (30 PERCENT)

- Do your personalized communications achieve ≥30 percent higher engagement than generic versions?

- Are product/content recommendations driving measurable increases in consumption or conversion?
- Do returning customers experience tailored interactions based on their previous behavior or preferences?
- Are you able to demonstrate revenue lift of ≥15 percent from Personalization efforts?

Industry benchmarks: Personalized emails show 26–29 percent higher open rates; retail recommendations average 11 percent CTR (A-level ≥15 percent); media platforms achieve 70 percent+ consumption from personalized content

CONTROL (35 PERCENT)

- Can customers resolve ≥80 percent of common issues through self-service without contacting support?
- Do users report feeling empowered and autonomous in their interactions with your brand?
- Are key customer actions (account management, preferences, billing) easily controllable by users themselves?
- Does your first-contact resolution rate exceed 80 percent when customers do need human help?

Industry benchmarks: World-class self-service resolution ≥80 percent; FCR benchmarks vary by complexity, but 80 percent represents excellence across most categories.

SCORING METHOD

Count your total "yes" answers in each section, then multiply your Motivation score by 0.35, your Personalization score by 0.30, and your Control score by 0.35. Add all three adjusted scores together to get your final Psychology score. See the following scoring rubric (and sorry, there's no extra credit).

Pop Quiz Scoring Table: Psychology

Weighted Score Total	Psychology Grade	Interpretation
10–12	A	Exceptional psychology—your brand creates ideal mental conditions for customer action
8–9	B	Strong foundation, but opportunities to reduce friction in weaker areas
6–7	C	Mixed signals—focus on lowest-scoring sub-subject for biggest impact
4–5	D	Psychological barriers—customers likely experiencing frustration or confusion
<4	F	Psychology crisis—urgent attention needed across Motivation, Personalization, and Control

Important Note: Scoring should be interpreted within your industry context. Motivation, Personalization, and Control benchmarks vary significantly by category—what qualifies as strong performance for a complex enterprise tool would fall short of expectations for a consumer app. Evaluate your results against your category peers, not the universal scale.

CHAPTER 5

SOCIOLOGY

IF YOU'RE EXPECTING MARXISM, you're in the wrong class. Sociology in the Brand GPA context is about consumerism—specifically. It's about how your brand shows up in society and engages with the world around it. Your customers care about the quality of your product, but they also care about the quality of your brand—what it represents, supports, and shies away from. We live in an era where brand values are scrutinized as intensely as quarterly earnings, so every tweet, every donation, and every endorsement can pull customers closer—or push them away.

WHY THIS MATTERS

According to Ipsos research across twenty-five countries, an average of 70 percent of consumers say they buy from brands they believe reflect their own principles.[1] Harris Poll research commissioned by Google Cloud found that 82 percent of shoppers want a brand's values to align with their own, and three-quarters had parted ways with a brand over a conflict in values.[2] Further, a 2024 Edelman special report puts it even more starkly: 84 percent of consumers say they need to share values with a brand before they'll buy from it at all.[3]

This isn't just feel-good marketing speak. A majority (55 percent) of consumers said they are especially interested in supporting sustainable brands, with 64 percent seeking out eco-friendly companies and 58 percent saying they would pay more for more sustainable products.[4] But here's the kicker: 60 percent of global consumers say they're skeptical of green claims made by brands.[5] Translation? Consumers want authenticity, not activism theater.

The stakes have never been higher. Six in ten consumers globally are buying or boycotting brands to express their politics.[6] And when consumers disagree with a brand's values, the fallout rarely stays private—it spreads through conversations, social feeds, and purchasing decisions. That's negative word of mouth at serious scale.

WHAT WE MEASURE

Sociology is evaluated across three key measurable sub-subjects that capture how well your brand navigates the cultural landscape:

- **Alignment:** Do your brand values authentically match what your customers care about?
- **Advocacy:** Are you actively supporting causes that matter or just paying lip service?
- **Cultural Resonance:** Does your brand feel relevant and connected to the communities you serve?

When a brand succeeds across all three sub-subjects, the Sociology grade will soar. And with a GPA weight of 15 percent, Sociology represents a meaningful component of your overall brand performance—one that's becoming increasingly difficult to ignore.

HOW WE GRADE

To calculate a brand's Sociology grade, apply the internal sub-subject weightings (40 percent Alignment, 30 percent Advocacy, 30 percent Cultural Resonance) and then factor Sociology as 15 percent of the overall GPA. The grading criteria for each sub-subject is explained further in their respective sections.

BRINGING IT ALL TOGETHER

Sub-Subject Weighting: Sociology

Sub-Subject	Weighting	Primary Metric	A-Level Standard Description
Alignment	40%	Values match score	Top quartile customer–brand values Alignment, authentic positioning, consistent messaging
Advocacy	30%	Social impact investment	Above category benchmark revenue to causes, measurable community impact, transparent reporting
Cultural Resonance	30%	Community engagement rate	Top quartile cultural participation, strong local connections, relevant positioning

Industry benchmark note: Benchmarks vary by industry. Examples include—B2B/enterprise: values Alignment 60 percent+, ESG investment 0.5 percent+, professional community engagement; consumer goods: values Alignment 70 percent+, cause marketing 1 percent+, lifestyle community integration; fashion/lifestyle: values Alignment 75 percent+, social causes 1.5 percent+, cultural trendsetting leadership; food/beverage: values Alignment 65 percent+, sustainability focus 1 percent+, local community partnerships

THE SUB-SUBJECTS: ALIGNMENT

Think of Alignment as your brand's compatibility test with society. It's not enough to slap a rainbow logo on your social media during Pride Month and call it a day. Authentic Alignment means your brand values genuinely match what your customers care about—and more importantly, that your actions back up your words.

According to Edelman Trust Barometer 2024, 76 percent of consumers say they buy brands that align with their values, while 67 percent say they would boycott brands that stay silent on social issues important to them.[7] But here's the challenge: Modern consumers are savvy. Ipsos Global Trends 2023–24 shows that 74 percent believe "brands pretend to care more than they do."[8]

WHAT WE MEASURE

Primary Metric: Values Match Score

This is the percentage of surveyed customers who believe your brand's values align with their own. You can use existing brand trackers like Morning Consult, Harris Brand Platform, or Ipsos Navigator or run a direct question: "To what extent do you agree: [Brand] shares my personal values." Calculate the percentage who select "agree" or "strongly agree." Simple question, revealing answer.

Secondary Indicators

- **Message consistency index:** Percentage of audited brand materials showing aligned values language across marketing, digital, product, and customer experience touchpoints
- **Authenticity score:** Composite measurement of sentiment, trust, and perceived integrity in how you actually act on stated values (pulled from social listening and sentiment tools)
- **Purpose-driven purchase intent:** Percentage of customers who cite your brand mission or values as a factor in their purchase decision

GRADING RUBRIC

For A-level Alignment performance, benchmarks vary meaningfully by industry—and for good reason. Categories where customers make identity-driven purchases, like fashion, lifestyle, and outdoor gear, often demand the highest values match scores (80 percent or higher) because the brand *is* the statement. Apparel, footwear, and fitness brands operate just below that threshold (75 percent or higher) for similar reasons. Food, beverage, and consumer goods brands sit in the midrange, where purchase decisions blend values with habit and convenience. B2B and enterprise brands benchmark lower given the more rational, outcome-driven nature of those buying decisions—values matter, but ROI matters more (cue Gordon Gekko). Finance and insurance brands get a little latitude—customers may not expect their bank to share their worldview, but they absolutely expect it not to contradict it.

Grading Rubric: Alignment[9]

Grade	Description	Key Metric
A	Authentic values integration, brand actions consistently match stated positioning	Top quartile values match score for category, high purpose-driven purchase intent
B	Strong Alignment with occasional inconsistencies, generally trusted positioning	Above category median values match score, positive authenticity sentiment
C	Mixed signals, some values messaging contradicted by brand actions	At or just below category median, inconsistent message audit results
D	Weak Alignment, growing skepticism about brand authenticity	Bottom quartile values match score, low purpose-driven purchase intent
F	Fundamental misalignment, brand actions contradict stated values	Category floor values match score, active consumer backlash documented

MAKING THE GRADE: REI (GRADE: A)

REI achieves exceptional values Alignment by living the co-op life—not just marketing it. The Cooperative Action Network engaged 1.1 million individuals in systemic change in 2023, with $3 million invested in strategic nonprofit partners that same year.[10] REI's gear repair programs, diversity in the outdoors initiatives, and OptOutside campaign reinforce values through policy and product rather than marketing alone. The co-op ownership structure proves their commitment to community over profits, earning them recognition on *Fast Company*'s Most Innovative Companies list for sustainability and social impact in 2024.[11] With 1.3 million new members added in 2023 and $200 million distributed through the Co-op Member Reward, REI demonstrates that authentic values integration drives both trust and business performance—outside and inside.[12]

MISSING THE MARK: WELLS FARGO (GRADE: D)

Wells Fargo represents a classic case of overdrawing trust and integrity messaging and underfunding the customer experience reality. In August 2023, the SEC found that Wells Fargo had steered thousands of investment advisory clients into higher-cost products inconsistent with their interests—resulting in a $26.6 million settlement including a $9 million civil penalty and approximately $17.6 million in reimbursements to affected clients.[13]

Meanwhile, Reuters reported throughout 2023 and 2024 that Wells Fargo remained under heightened regulatory supervision, continued asset cap restrictions, and ongoing remediation obligations tied to systemic failures in customer protection.[14] The bank's fake accounts scandal, whistleblower retaliation, and compounding regulatory record have created a significant gap between their stated commitment to customer focus and public perception. This is a textbook case of how legacy scandals can bankrupt values permanently—and no amount of smooth marketing copy can bail you out.

THE SUB-SUBJECTS: ADVOCACY

Advocacy is where brands put their money where their mouth is. It's the difference between posting a thoughtful Instagram story about social justice and actually funding programs that create change. Brand activism means actively addressing contentious social or political issues—systemic racism, reproductive rights, LGBTQ+ rights, gun control, immigration, sexual harassment, public health. You know, the stuff that makes Thanksgiving dinner awkward.

But here's where it gets tricky. When companies take a stance on social issues, they can antagonize large swaths of customers. Research shows the math is brutal: Customers who disagree with a brand's political stance are approximately twice as likely to defect as new aligned customers are to adopt—meaning the downside almost always outweighs the upside.[15] That's an even worse proposition than a holiday with your crazy uncle.

WHAT WE MEASURE

Primary Metric: Social Impact Investment

This is the percentage of revenue allocated to social causes and advocacy. This includes cash donations to nonprofits, donated products or services (valued at cost basis), employee service time with budget backing, legislative support and coalition building, crisis relief, and DEI advancement programs. We measure against revenue because it shows commitment regardless of profitability.

Secondary Indicators

- **Community partnership depth:** Number of long-term partners, geographic spread, and multiyear commitment percentages
- **Policy influence activity:** Amicus briefs, coalition memberships, public policy statements, and lobbying disclosure activity

- **Crisis response leadership:** Emergency aid response time and whether support is proactive vs. reactive

GRADING RUBRIC

For A-level Advocacy performance, benchmarks vary by industry based on margin structure and how much customers expect brands to show up beyond the product. Technology companies carry the highest expectations given their scale and cultural influence. As a result, the top performers invest 2 percent or more of revenue in social causes. Consumer goods and retail brands benchmark at 1.5 percent or above, where cause Alignment directly influences what customers put in their cart. B2B brands operate at a lower threshold—their customers care more about business outcomes than causes. Transparency and reporting standards, however, are equally high. But across all categories, the distinction between A- and B-level performance is less about the dollar amount spent on causes and more about depth—and authenticity—of impact. That means sustained partnerships, policy engagement, and proactive crisis response carry more weight than reactive or attention-grabbing social impact tactics.

Grading Rubric: Advocacy[16]

Grade	Description	Key Metric
A	Deep, sustained social impact with policy influence and proactive community leadership	Leading or above category benchmark revenue investment; multiyear partnerships
B	Active community partnerships with consistent investment	Above category median revenue investment; measurable community outcomes
C	Moderate, often reactive investment; selective cause support	At or just below category median revenue investment
D	Minimal investment; crisis-driven only; reactive positioning	Bottom quartile revenue investment; performative tactics over sustained impact
F	No meaningful Advocacy or actively harmful positions	Negligible or no investment; brand actions contradict stated values

MAKING THE GRADE: SALESFORCE (GRADE: A)

Salesforce is a force of good thanks to their comprehensive 1-1-1 model: 1 percent of product, 1 percent of equity, and 1 percent of employee time dedicated to philanthropy. In fiscal year 2024, Salesforce reported $86 million in annual grants and donations—part of nearly $800 million in lifetime giving—with more than 60,000 nonprofits and higher-education customers using Salesforce technology for free.[17] Employee volunteer hours reached 8.7 million cumulative by fiscal year 2024, including 900,000 annual hours that year.[18]

Beyond financial investment, Salesforce shows genuine policy engagement on climate legislation—supporting the Artificial Intelligence Environmental Impacts Act of 2024, backing the TAME Act, advocating for federal clean-energy transmission permitting reform, and engaging on California SB 253 implementation.[19]

During COVID-19, they founded the Work.com platform to help governments and organizations respond to the pandemic—an early signal of the proactive community leadership that has since become a Salesforce hallmark. Who says the Salesforce Tower is made of ivory?

MISSING THE MARK: COLUMBIA UNIVERSITY (GRADE: D)

Regardless of where one stands on the underlying issues, Columbia's protest response illustrates a classic Brand GPA failure: When your stated values and your actions diverge under pressure, stakeholders on all sides lose confidence.

Columbia University's 2024 campus debacle represents a textbook case of Advocacy leadership failure. Despite an institutional identity built around academic freedom, freedom of expression, and inclusion, the university's response to pro-Palestinian protests alienated people across the political spectrum. The administration's decision to call the NYPD onto campus, suspend students, and remove faculty was seen as both overly aggressive by protesters and too permissive by critics of anti-Semitism.[20]

The botched crisis response had severe repercussions. Robert Kraft paused donations to Columbia and Columbia Business School, expressing deep disappointment with the university's handling of protests.[21] The Russell Berrie Foundation—a long-standing institutional donor—also paused funding following the protest response.[22] Faculty dissent escalated sharply—Columbia's Faculty of Arts and Sciences passed a no-confidence vote in President Shafik in May 2024, with a clear majority of participating faculty in favor.[23]

Columbia's legacy of progressive activism and student engagement appears inconsistent with their police response and mixed messaging, proving that institutions face the same Advocacy challenges as corporations—and pay the same Ivy League price when they fail to lead authentically during a crisis.

THE SUB-SUBJECTS: CULTURAL RESONANCE

Cultural Resonance is about whether your brand feels like it belongs in the communities it serves. It's not just about being present; it's about being genuinely woven into the cultural fabric—otherwise, you're an interloper. Research confirms what most customers already know intuitively: Brands that connect to how people see themselves and their cultural identity earn loyalty, while those that don't can trigger an outsized negative response.[24]

According to Sprout Social research, 53 percent of people say they feel connected when a brand's values align with their own, and more than half (51 percent) say their relationship with a brand starts when they feel the brand understands them and their desires.[25] This goes beyond demographics to psychographics—understanding not just who your customers are but how they see themselves and their place in the world.

WHAT WE MEASURE

Primary Metric: Community Engagement Rate (CER)

This is the share of your audience that actively participates in cultural or community events, initiatives, or recognition programs. Unlike passive social media metrics, CER measures genuine participation—are people showing up, creating content, or collaborating with you in meaningful ways?

Secondary Indicators

- **Local partnership strength:** Number of active partnerships and years of collaboration with community organizations
- **Cultural trust score:** Brand reputation in community sentiment surveys (measured through net trust or favorability)
- **Trend leadership index:** Percentage of brand mentions tied to cultural events or viral themes

GRADING RUBRIC

For A-level Cultural Resonance performance, benchmarks vary significantly based on how locally rooted versus nationally scaled a brand is. Local and regional brands operate in tight communities where participation expectations are highest, so all eyes are on those brands. National brands carry lower but still meaningful thresholds, where Cultural Relevance is measured more broadly across communities and cultural moments—and also how they report out. Global brands, however, face the greatest challenge because they have to resonate authentically across diverse cultural contexts simultaneously. Across all categories, the distinction between A- and B-level performance comes down to one key question: Are you genuine? Customers can see cultural appropriation or camera-ready tactics from a mile away, so it's better to do nothing until you can do it the right way.

Grading Rubric: Cultural Resonance[26]

Grade	Description	Key Metric
A	Deep community integration; brand genuinely woven into cultural fabric	Top quartile CER for category; multiple sustained local partnerships
B	Active cultural participation; consistent community presence	Above category median CER; moderate partnership depth
C	Some community engagement; inconsistent cultural trust	At or just below category median CER
D	Minimal participation; weak or transactional partnerships	Bottom quartile CER; limited cultural presence
F	Little to no cultural presence; possible to likely negative sentiment	Category floor CER; culturally irrelevant or rejected

MAKING THE GRADE: LEGO (GRADE: A)

LEGO achieves exceptional Cultural Resonance by laying their bricks where it matters the most: in education, fan communities, and cultural institutions. The brand's Build the Change program and LEGO Education partnerships extend community engagement worldwide—a multigenerational community that keeps building over time across classrooms, living rooms, and cultural institutions globally.

The commercial scale tells the same story. Reuters reported that the Danish toy maker posted revenue of DKK 65.9 billion in 2023 and DKK 74.3 billion in 2024, with consumer sales up 12 percent in 2024—outperforming the broader toy industry while competitors struggled.[27] LEGO Ideas, their fan-driven product platform, continues to turn community passion directly into product. When it comes to Cultural Resonance, LEGO is a total stud.

MISSING THE MARK: TARGET (GRADE: D)

The typically culture-carrying retailer has gone quite off target when it comes to Cultural Resonance. The trouble started in Q2 2023, when Target's annual Pride collection triggered intense backlash from a portion of its customers, including violent confrontations with workers. On May 24, 2023, Target removed items from stores, citing "threats impacting our team members' sense of safety and well-being."[28] Damned if they do, indeed—comparable sales fell 5.4 percent that quarter, with Reuters and AP both reporting that the Pride backlash contributed to weakened traffic and sales.[29]

Rather than standing on principle, Target retreated further. In May 2024, the company scaled back Pride merchandise to select stores, citing "insights from last year's experience."[30] Meanwhile, Target had previously pledged more than $2 billion with Black-owned businesses under its Racial Equity Action and Change initiative—a commitment that sat awkwardly against a brand that blinked when cultural pressure arrived.[31]

Authentic Cultural Resonance requires sustained commitment. You don't get credit for showing up only when it's convenient, and you don't get to quietly exit when it gets hard. Target's customers noticed, and now Target's business results have gone from a bull's-eye to a black eye.

TOP AND BOTTOM OF THEIR CLASS: SOCIOLOGY

When it comes to Sociology, the difference between passing and failing often determines whether your brand is seen as a force for good or just another profit-maximizing entity. The brands that excel in this subject understand that being socially conscious isn't a marketing department add-on—it's a core business strategy that requires authentic commitment, consistent action, and genuine cultural understanding.

Brands earning the summa cum laude distinction in Sociology scored at or near the top of their class in Alignment, Advocacy, and Cultural Resonance. They demonstrate authentic values integration, meaningful social impact investment, and deep community connections that go beyond surface-level engagement. In contrast, Flunking Out brands often suffer from values misalignment, performative activism, or cultural tone deafness that alienates the communities they claim to serve.

To qualify as a "Best in Sociology" brand, we looked for the following:

- Values Alignment scores in the top quartile for category with demonstrated authenticity in messaging and actions
- Social impact investment above category benchmark with measurable community outcomes
- Top quartile community engagement with strong cultural relevance and local partnerships

Brands that flunked Sociology typically exhibited the following behaviors:

- Showed values Alignment in the bottom quartile for category with frequent messaging contradictions
- Invested below category median in Advocacy with minimal measurable impact
- Demonstrated weak Cultural Resonance with disconnected community presence

You'll notice Microsoft double-dipping—leading the Sociology honor roll at the corporate level while its Teams product struggled in Psychology. That's not a contradiction—that's the framework doing exactly what it's supposed to do. Microsoft earns its Sociology marks through sustained DEI commitments that span all products and services and AI for Good positioning that stood out among its peers. Meanwhile, Microsoft Teams—a product that has the scale to be its own stand-alone company—earned its Psychology struggles through governance failures and outages that stripped users of Control. In other words, a company can have its values in the right place and still ship a product that lets people down. The Brand GPA grades both—separately and honestly. You also might be surprised to see Grindr in the On-demand category. But when a roll in the hay is only a click away, it tracks.

Top and Bottom of Their Class: Sociology

Vertical	Summa Cum Laude	Why They Excel	Flunking Out	Why They Fail
Apparel and footwear	Patagonia[32]	B Impact Score of 166.0; #1 overall in the 2023 Axios Harris Poll 100, including #1 in Citizenship and Products & Services; Reuters reported Holdfast Collective planned to invest $4 million in a Chilean conservation initiative led by Puelo Patagonia	Shein[33]	Remake's *Fashion Accountability Report 2024* scored Shein 6 out of 150; Italian regulators said Shein's environmental claims could be generic, vague, confusing, and/or misleading per Reuters; 2024 peer-reviewed study found perceived betrayal correlated with reduced purchase intentions after environmental exposure
Consumer goods	Burt's Bees[34]	Ranked #13 overall in the 2024 Axios Harris Poll 100 among 16,310 Americans surveyed across trust, ethics, citizenship, and character—enduring natural-products positioning drives strong values Alignment with mainstream consumers	Bud Light[35]	Dylan Mulvaney partnership (April 1, 2023) triggered immediate backlash; Modelo Especial overtook Bud Light as #1 US beer by June 2023—the first time in decades; culture war fallout turned a mass-market brand into a case study in values misalignment and community fracture
Media and entertainment	PBS[36]	+25 net trust score in YouGov Trust in Media 2025—one of the most trusted news brands in America; public-service mission drives stronger Sociology evidence than any scale-focused competitor	X (Twitter)[37]	Kantar reported marketer trust in X ads fell from 22% to 12% between 2022 and 2024; only 4% of marketers consider it brand safe; Reuters cited CCDH findings that 209 misleading election posts drew 2.2 billion views without corrective notes

Fitness and wellness	Planet Fitness[38]	Maintained gender-identity locker room inclusion policy despite boycott pressure—standing by "Judgment Free Zone" ethos; *WSJ* cited policy as long-standing differentiator; BGCA partnership supported 475K youth through trauma-informed care programming	CrossFit[39]	Athlete death at 2024 CrossFit Games exposed major safety failures; CrossFit announced procedural changes November 20, 2024, following third-party investigation; safety governance failure undermined community trust at core
Health care	St. Jude[40]	#1 Most Trusted Nonprofit by Morning Consult 2024; recognized in *Fast Company*'s Brands That Matter 2023; mission-driven Advocacy and national donor trust set the category standard for values Alignment	OxyContin (Purdue Pharma)[41]	The Supreme Court's June 2024 rejection of Purdue's bankruptcy settlement pulled OxyContin back into the national spotlight; *Painkiller* and *Dopesick* kept the brand's role in the opioid crisis streaming into millions of homes; a $7.4B settlement in January 2025 was the final reminder that the brand's legacy is addiction, not healing
Consumer tech	Canva[42]	60M+ education users on free-access programs; design democratization mission embedded in product access policy; values Alignment demonstrated through scale of community impact across educators, students, and nonprofits globally	Tesla[43]	Fell from 8th to 63rd to 95th out of 100 in the Axios Harris Poll—a 32-point drop, the steepest of any brand in the survey; dead last in character; Axios attributed the collapse directly to Elon Musk's polarizing political activism
B2B tech	Microsoft[44]	#3 in 2025 Axios Harris Poll 100; reputation score rose 3.2 points YoY while maintaining DEI commitments during industry-wide rollback; AI for Good positioning reinforces values-led enterprise brand narrative	Palantir[45]	ICE awarded Palantir a $30M ImmigrationOS contract in April 2025 to build deportation-focused surveillance platform; privacy and civil liberties concerns remain central to brand perception; Advocacy gap compounds reputational drag

continued →

Education	Merit America[46]	Documented pathways into middle-class jobs for nondegree workers; average annual wage gain of nearly $21,000 for program completers; mission-driven Advocacy for underserved and low-wage populations	University of Phoenix[47]	DOE forgave nearly $37M in loans for 1,200+ students on FTC-backed findings; FTC's record $191M action documented systemic deceptive enrollment practices
Food service	Panera[48]	Day-End Dough-Nation donated unsold baked goods with a retail value of $83M in 2023; hunger-relief mission embedded in daily bakery operations across thousands of locations; 61% YouGov popularity among US consumers during the grading period	Starbucks[49]	52% of shareholders backed an independent labor-practices review in March 2023; 300+ stores on strike by late 2024; federal appeals court upheld NLRB ruling that Starbucks illegally fired unionizing baristas—a conflict that kept undermining the brand's social-purpose positioning
Travel	Marriott [50]	Serve 360 ESG program spanning 8,785 properties at year-end 2023; $51M+ contributed to communities and philanthropic causes in 2023; associates logged 3.1M volunteer hours in 2023 alone	Boeing[51]	January 5, 2024, Alaska Airlines door-plug blowout turned Boeing's safety culture into a consumer-facing crisis; CEO told Congress culture was far from perfect; Boeing agreed in July 2024 to plead guilty to criminal fraud conspiracy
On-demand	Instacart[52]	#5 in *Newsweek* and Statista's America's Best Online Platforms 2025 for Groceries & Delivery; 9.06 score across 29 criteria including impression, usage, and trust; consistent essential-service values Alignment	Grindr[53]	April 2024 UK lawsuit: HIV status and HIV test dates shared with third-party advertisers; privacy betrayal of a historically marginalized community; core trust promise broken for commercial gain

Financial services	Stripe[54]	Stripe Climate Orders launched November 2023, serving tens of thousands of businesses across 40+ countries; Frontier coalition committed $80M to carbon removal; ethical infrastructure positioning embedded directly in core product	Celsius Network[55]	FTC and SEC charged Celsius with fraud and consumer deception on July 13, 2023; $1.2B in uncollateralized loans concealed from customers; $4.7B judgment issued; ~600K customers left holding $4.4B in frozen accounts—crypto-trust collapse in real time

TOP SCHOLAR AND BOTTOM DWELLER

Sociology scholarship means talking the talk *and* walking the walk. Doing that double duty on the daily is Patagonia, a brand that proves social mission can be operationalized—not just advertised. On the other side of the social spectrum is fast-fashion icon Shein, a cautionary tale of what happens when a business model fundamentally contradicts the values of customers. When your entire operation runs counter to what your audience cares about, fast fashion can become a thing-of-the-past fashion in record time.

TOP SCHOLAR: PATAGONIA

Patagonia is down with its values. When founder Yvon Chouinard transferred Patagonia's voting stock to the Patagonia Purpose Trust and all nonvoting stock to the Holdfast Collective, a nonprofit dedicated to fighting the environmental crisis, he made Earth Patagonia's ultimate shareholder.

Hyperbolic as that sounds, the numbers back the conviction. Patagonia is a $1.5 billion revenue business—not just a hippy outdoors shop—and carries a B Corp Impact Score of 166.0.[56] B Corp certification, administered by the nonprofit B Lab, is one of the most rigorous third-party assessments of a company's social and environmental performance, accountability, and transparency. To earn it, a company must score at least 80 out of 200 points—and the median score for ordinary businesses completing the assessment is just 50.9.[57] Patagonia scores more than double the certification threshold and more than three times the median. In other words, Patagonia doesn't just clear the bar—it vaults it.

When it comes to external validation, Patagonia is a peak performer. The Axios Harris Poll 100 is an annual survey of more than 27,000 Americans that measures corporate reputation across six dimensions—Trust, Ethics, Growth, Products & Services, Citizenship, and Culture—producing a Reputation Quotient, or RQ, score out of 100. In the 2023 poll, Patagonia ranked #1 overall with an RQ score of 83.5—simultaneously taking the top spot in Ethics, Citizenship, and Products & Services.[58] And this isn't a one-time fluke—Patagonia has appeared in the top ten of the Axios Harris rankings multiple times since 2014.[59]

And when the DEI rollback period hit and brands across every category were quietly scrubbing sustainability language from their websites, Patagonia said hold my MiiR. The result: a jump from #8 in 2024 to #2 in 2025, with a +2.9 point reputation gain—one of the largest among companies that stayed the course.[60] KPMG's 2024 US Customer Experience Excellence ranking placed Patagonia at #3 as well, its first-ever top ten appearance, confirming that values-driven operations translate directly into how customers actually feel.[61]

The brand also puts their money where their mission is. The Holdfast Collective, the nonprofit vehicle of the brand, deploys Patagonia's profits directly into environmental causes after reinvestment, including a planned $4 million in a Chilean land conservation initiative.[62] They aren't just planting a few seeds—they're going full

Redwood. So Patagonia is the Sociology Top Scholar not just because it's at the top of the class—but because it keeps summiting.

Top Scholar Report Card: Patagonia

Sub-Subject	Grade	Metrics
Alignment	A	#1 Axios Harris Poll 100 overall in 2023; top spot in Ethics and Citizenship; B Corp certified since 2011
Advocacy	A	Holdfast Collective deploys profits to environmental causes; $4M to Chilean conservation initiative; held DEI commitments during industry-wide rollback
Cultural Resonance	A	Six top 10 Axios Harris appearances since 2014; #2 in 2025 with +2.9-point gain; #3 KPMG Customer Experience Excellence 2024

BOTTOM DWELLER: SHEIN

When it comes to Sociology, Shein is pretty dim. The fast-fashion giant has achieved massive scale while creating persistent trust deficits and cultural backlash—demonstrating how a business model built on values contradictions eventually collapses under its own weight.

The fundamental problem is misalignment at a structural level. Conscious consumers increasingly prioritize sustainability and ethical labor practices—the exact opposite of Shein's model. Despite attempts at extra-large "sustainability" messaging, the brand's underbelly is plenty exposed. Remake's *Fashion Accountability Report 2022*, published in January 2023, rated Shein at just 8 points out of 150 and described it as among the least transparent of the fast-fashion companies it evaluates.[63] By March 2024, Remake dropped Shein's score down to 6.[64] For a brand known for being a trendsetter, this isn't one to follow.

The cultural consequences are becoming impossible to ignore. CBS News reported in August 2023 that mounting ethical concerns were pushing some Gen Z consumers away, and by mid-2024, human rights groups had launched a legal campaign to block Shein's potential London IPO over labor practice concerns.[65] A peer-reviewed study published in the *Journal of Retailing and Consumer Services* in November 2024 examining 607 Shein consumers found that exposure to negative environmental information was positively correlated with negative attitudes toward Shein, perceived betrayal, and reduced purchase intentions.[66] In other words, when your own customers start turning against you, it's more than a fashion faux pas—it's a fait accompli.

Bottom Dweller Report Card: Shein

Sub-Subject	Grade	Metrics
Alignment	F	Remake's *Fashion Accountability Report 2022* scored Shein 8/150 in 2023, dropping to 6/150 in 2024; fundamental business model contradicts stated sustainability values; ranked least transparent among evaluated fast-fashion companies
Advocacy	F	Gen Z consumers questioning brand amid mounting ethical concerns; human rights groups launched legal campaign to block Shein IPO over labor practices; reactive communications versus proactive community investment
Cultural Resonance	F	Peer-reviewed study found perceived betrayal correlated with reduced purchase intentions after environmental exposure; organized activist opposition documented in named trade press

NEXT UP . . .

Sociology shows whether your brand is a good cultural citizen, but being socially conscious doesn't automatically translate to business success. That requires understanding the final piece of the Brand

GPA puzzle: Economics. It's time to talk money—both the value you create and the value customers perceive they're getting in return.

POP QUIZ: SOCIOLOGY

You can't overhaul your brand's societal impact overnight, but this short Sociology quiz can give you a directional sense of how your brand is doing in this subject. Answer each question with a checkmark (✓) for yes or leave blank for no. Then apply the weighting formula to calculate your back-of-the-envelope Sociology score.

ALIGNMENT (40 PERCENT)

- Do customer surveys show 70 percent+ agreement that your brand values align with their personal values?
- Can employees clearly articulate your brand's core values without looking them up?
- Are your marketing messages consistent with your actual business practices and policies?
- Have you avoided major values-related controversies or backlash in the past twelve months?

Industry benchmarks: consumer goods 75 percent+ Alignment, B2B 60 percent+ Alignment, fashion 80 percent+ Alignment

ADVOCACY (30 PERCENT)

- Do you invest at least 1 percent of revenue in social causes or community programs?
- Have you taken public stances on issues that matter to your customer base?
- Can you point to specific, measurable community impact from your Advocacy efforts?

- Do you have dedicated resources (staff, budget, partnerships) for social impact beyond marketing?

Industry benchmarks: tech 1.5 percent+ investment, consumer goods 1 percent+ investment, B2B 0.5 percent+ investment

CULTURAL RESONANCE (30 PERCENT)

- Are you regularly mentioned positively in community or industry conversations?
- Do you have meaningful partnerships with local organizations or cultural groups?
- Would your customers describe your brand as "understanding their community"?
- Do you actively participate in cultural moments and conversations relevant to your audience?

Industry benchmarks: local/regional brands 85 percent+ resonance, national brands 70 percent+ resonance, global brands 60 percent+ resonance

SCORING METHOD

Count your total "yes" answers in each section, then multiply your Alignment score by 0.40, your Personalization score by 0.30, and your Cultural Resonance score by 0.30. Add all three adjusted scores together to get your final Psychology score. See the next page for the scoring rubric (and sorry, there's no extra credit).

Pop Quiz Scoring Table: Sociology

Weighted Score Total	Sociology Grade	Interpretation
10–12	A	Top performance—your brand is a cultural leader with authentic values integration
8–9	B	Strong foundation, but room for deeper community impact in weaker areas
6–7	C	Mixed signals—focus on lowest-scoring sub-subject for improvement priorities
4–5	D	Trouble ahead—values Alignment and community connection need immediate attention
<4	F	Sociology crisis—urgent course correction required across all areas

Important note: Scoring should be interpreted within your industry context. Values Alignment and Advocacy benchmarks vary significantly by category—what qualifies as strong performance for a traditional manufacturing company would fall short of expectations for a lifestyle brand. Evaluate your results against your category peers, not the universal scale.

CHAPTER 6

ECONOMICS

THIS IS WHERE ALL THE OTHER SUBJECTS come home to roost. Unlike the rest of the Brand GPA framework where we redefine traditional academic concepts for a business context, Economics doesn't require a special interpretation. It's all about the numbers: Can customers afford what you're selling? Do they believe it's worth the price? Can you actually turn a profit?

Economics comes last on the report card for a reason. If there are serious issues with Chemistry, Communications, Psychology, or Sociology, a brand's Economics becomes increasingly vulnerable—and the math stops mathing.

WHY THIS MATTERS

No bones about it, brands have to make money to survive. Economics is where brand promise meets financial reality, and it's the ultimate stress test that separates sustainable businesses from venture-funded mirages. You can have the most beloved product, the clearest messaging, and the strongest emotional connection—but if your unit economics don't add up, a crash is en route. According to CB Insights' analysis of 101 start-up failures, 29 percent died because they ran out of cash.[1] That's a tale as old as time, but dig deeper and you'll find that cash problems are usually symptoms of fundamental issues across the business school classic "4 Ps"—product, price, place, and promotion.

Here's what separates the A students from the misfits: They don't just try to extract value from customers at every turn. Instead, they focus on creating value so that customers become more willing to pay a premium and, most importantly, come back for more. When Netflix spends jaw-dropping billions on content but that results in 90 percent+ retention rates, that's actually intelligent capital allocation that drives long-term value.

But Economics isn't about being cheap or expensive—it's about being profitable in a way that compounds over time. The brands that master Economics understand a fundamental truth: Sustainable growth comes from creating more value than you capture. But value is derived by mastering *all* the Brand GPA subjects. Get that consistently right and you have the makings of a moat of sustainability—and profitability.

WHAT WE MEASURE

Economics is evaluated across three key measurable sub-subjects. These were selected based on the most important—and measurable—criteria to determine if your business model actually works:

- **Value Perception:** Do customers believe you're worth what you charge?
- **Revenue Expansion:** Can you grow wallet share and lifetime value over time?
- **Economic Efficiency:** Are you achieving sustainable, profitable growth?

When a brand excels across these metrics, it demonstrates that it has built something customers willingly pay for, customers want more of, and can be delivered profitably—and at scale. With a subject weight of 20 percent of the overall Brand GPA, Economics serves as the crucial reality check on whether your brand fundamentals translate into business fundamentals.

The brands that score highest in Economics share a common trait: They've earned their pricing power through superior value delivery, not vaporware tactics. They understand that true economic strength comes from customers who *choose* to pay your prices because they believe in the value of your brand.

HOW WE GRADE

The three sub-subjects are weighted to determine a brand's overall Economics grade, which accounts for 20 percent of the overall Brand GPA. To calculate a brand's Economics grade, apply the internal sub-subject weightings (35 percent Value Perception, 35 percent Revenue Expansion, 30 percent Economic Efficiency) and then factor Economics as 20 percent of the overall GPA. The grading criteria for each sub-subject is explained further in their respective sections.

BRINGING IT ALL TOGETHER

Sub-Subject Weighting: Economics

Sub-Subject	Weighting	Primary Metric	A-Level Standard Description
Value Perception	35%	Price premium index	Premium pricing accepted by customers, strong willingness to pay
Revenue Expansion	35%	Net revenue retention (NRR)	Leading or above category benchmark NRR, expanding customer value over time
Economic Efficiency	30%	Customer lifetime value: customer acquisition cost (CLV:CAC) ratio	Above category benchmark CLV:CAC ratio, sustainable unit economics

Industry benchmark note: Economics benchmarks vary significantly by business model and market maturity. B2B software companies typically target different metrics than consumer goods brands. The key is ensuring your model generates sustainable returns within your industry context while building long-term competitive advantages.

THE SUB-SUBJECTS: VALUE PERCEPTION

Your customers are constantly making value calculations. They have endless choices and can compare prices instantly on their phones. In uncertain times, they're first asking, *Can I afford this?* but also, more importantly, *Is this worth it?* Value perception isn't about being the cheapest—it's about being worth the price.

Take Patagonia: They charge $279 for a down jacket you can get elsewhere for $80, yet customers shell out the bigger bucks because Patagonia products last forever—and it feels good to participate in a brand with such strong values (a Sociology A-student).

WHAT WE MEASURE

Primary Metric: Price Premium Index

(Your Average Price ÷ Category Average Price)

A score above 1.0 means customers are choosing you over cheaper alternatives—and that's the whole ball game. Below 1.0, price is doing the work your brand should be doing.

Secondary Indicators

- **Value-for-money NPS:** An NPS-style question reframed to assess price-value fit, isolating perceived value from overall brand sentiment
- **Willingness-to-pay delta:** The gap between what customers say they'd pay and what they're actually charged, indicating pricing headroom or churn risk
- **Price elasticity response:** How much demand shifts when price changes, with low elasticity signaling strong perceived value and high elasticity signaling a commoditized position

GRADING RUBRIC

For A-level Value Perception performance, benchmarks vary significantly by category and competitive set. High-end lifestyle and luxury brands command the highest price premiums—after all, customers are paying for identity as much as function—so a 1.25x or greater premium over category average is the threshold for top performance. Quality leaders in competitive consumer categories operate at a more moderate premium, where Value Perception is earned through product differentiation rather than brand cachet. Middle-market brands operating near price parity face the greatest pressure since any erosion of perceived value quickly shifts customers to cheaper alternatives.

Brands pricing below category average are typically signaling a real value proposition problem. They don't call it a fire sale for nothing!

Grading Rubric: Value Perception

Grade	Description	Key Metric
A	Strong premium justified by customer demand; identity and quality drive willingness to pay	Leading or above category benchmark price premium with stable or growing market share
B	Moderate premium accepted by market; quality differentiation sustains pricing	Above category median price premium
C	Parity pricing or small premium	At or just below category median pricing
D	Discount pricing or premium rejection	Bottom quartile pricing; declining share despite promotional pressure
F	Value proposition rejected by market; pricing indefensible	Category floor pricing or active customer flight regardless of price

Source: Simon-Kucher pricing studies, https://www.simon-kucher.com/

MAKING THE GRADE: IKEA (GRADE: A)

IKEA has cracked the code on Value Perception: They've convinced hundreds of millions of people to walk a literal mile through a blue-and-yellow labyrinth, buy furniture they have to assemble themselves, and feel great about it.[2] Talk about Stockholm Syndrome.

What makes IKEA an A-level performer is how they've turned cost consciousness into a cultural aesthetic. Customers aren't just buying tables and storage cubes—they're buying into a design philosophy that signals both affordability and taste. The flat-pack model isn't a bug—it's the feature. IKEA has conditioned entire generations to see DIY assembly as part of the value equation, not a compromise.

The economics reinforce this perception at every turn. IKEA's design-for-flat-pack model and cost discipline across sourcing and production keep prices low without sacrificing quality expectations.[3] Whether it's a lamp for about $12 or a $399 sofa, customers feel like they're beating the system—even when they're loading up on Swedish meatballs on the way out.

MISSING THE MARK: SUBWAY (GRADE: D)

In the battle of the QSRs, Subway snatched defeat from the jaws of victory when it messed around with its prized asset: the iconic $5 Footlong. For years, the brand built a reputation around affordable value—and incredibly memorable jingles. But Subway steadily destroyed their stronghold by raising prices without improving the experience—or the product quality.

The Subway Series came at a higher price point, and by August 2024, some twelve-inchers were hitting $14 in certain markets.[4] (That's a lot of dough!) YouGov data shows Consideration scores collapsed from 43.1 to 31.3, and Buzz cratered from 28.4 to 10.4 by 2023.[5] ACSI scores of 73 in 2024 and 76 in 2025 against a quick-service industry average of 79 confirm customers aren't feeling the love.[6] Franchisees pushed back on value promotions because they said they lost money—and the $6.99 Meal of the Day deal was pulled early when it didn't meet expectations.[7] It would be one thing if the brand was intent on becoming a premium deli, but instead of upping the taste, they abandoned their bread and butter: value.

THE SUB-SUBJECTS: REVENUE EXPANSION

Here's what most companies seem to forget: Acquiring new customers costs anywhere from 5x to 25x more than growing the existing base.[8] Yet most obsess over performance marketing and acquisition metrics while treating expansion like it's no big deal. That's completely backward!

The best brands don't just attract customers—they grow them. They also understand that the initial purchase is just the beginning of the economic (and overall) relationship. Revenue Expansion measures your brand's ability to deepen customer relationships and grow share of wallet over time. But that doesn't mean throwing a bunch of features on to a core offering that isn't sticky. Successful expansion means achieving great Chemistry with customers, then understanding what it takes for them to engage—and spend—more.

WHAT WE MEASURE

Primary Metric: (Annual) Net Revenue Retention Rate (NRR)

NRR measures revenue retained and grown from your existing base after upgrades, downgrades, and churn. Above 100 percent means your customers are spending more than last year—growth without acquisition. Below 100 percent means you have a leaky bucket.

Secondary Indicators

- **Customer lifetime value growth rate:** The year-over-year change in average lifetime value per customer, indicating whether the customer base is becoming more or less valuable over time
- **Expansion revenue percentage:** The share of total revenue from existing customers via upsells, cross-sells, or upgrades, reflecting a brand's ability to grow within its installed base
- **Cohort trends:** Retention and revenue patterns of customer groups acquired in the same period, tracked over time to assess whether newer cohorts are as loyal and valuable as earlier ones

GRADING RUBRIC

For A-level Revenue Expansion performance, benchmarks vary significantly by business model. B2B SaaS companies set the highest bar. Top performers target net revenue retention of 111 percent or above, meaning they rely on existing customers to punch above their weight and spend meaningfully more year over year without any new customer acquisition. Consumer subscription brands operate at a lower but still demanding threshold, where repeat purchase rates and order frequency signal whether the brand has genuinely earned a place in customers' lives. Traditional retail and consumer goods brands measure expansion differently—through basket size growth, category penetration, and repurchase frequency rather than NRR. Across all models, the distinction between A- and B-level performance comes down to one question: Are your existing customers spending more with you today than they were yesterday?

Grading Rubric: Revenue Expansion[9]

Grade	Description	Key Metric
A	Exceptional expansion engine; existing customers spending significantly more year over year	Leading or above category benchmark NRR; strong cohort growth
B	Solid growth from existing customers; consistent repeat purchase behavior	Above category median NRR; positive cohort trends
C	Maintaining customer value; flat expansion with minimal growth	At or just below category median NRR; stable but stagnant
D	Losing customer value over time; churn offsetting any expansion gains	Bottom quartile NRR; declining cohort performance
F	Customer value in freefall; expansion model has collapsed entirely	Category floor NRR; mass churn with no offsetting expansion

MAKING THE GRADE: NETFLIX (GRADE: A)

Netflix logged in to another sub-subject top spot, ironically, by cracking down on multiple logins. The password-sharing crackdown might have felt like being put into a time-out, but it was actually one of the most elegantly orchestrated revenue-expansion plays in streaming history. By forcing freeloaders to either pay up or log off, Netflix added 13.1 million subscribers in Q4 2023 alone—while simultaneously launching an ad-supported tier that now accounts for 55 percent of new sign-ups in available markets.[10]

The ad tier wasn't the historically commercial-free platform selling out—it was Netflix finding new ways to make bank and keep outpacing the competition. What started as a lower-cost entry point has scaled to ninety-four million users as of May 2025, up from seventy million just six months earlier.[11] Meanwhile, price increases in key markets including the US, UK, and France were absorbed without meaningful churn—a clear signal of elite pricing power thanks to delivering elite productions.[12]

MISSING THE MARK: STITCH FIX (GRADE: D)

Stitch Fix got boxed in when it came to Revenue Expansion. What began as a compelling value proposition—a subscription clothing model built on personalization—ultimately stalled when the company couldn't grow customer value over time. Between 2023 and 2025, Stitch Fix became a cautionary tale of a business that started out hot but couldn't translate early momentum into sustainable economic expansion.

Its active client base fell from its fiscal 2021 peak of more than 4.1 million to 2.5 million by fiscal 2024, while annual revenue declined from roughly $2.1 billion to $1.3 billion.[13] As order frequency dropped and clients spent less, stimulating repeat behavior became its Achilles' heel.

Freestyle—the big bet on direct shopping—required heightened spending on less efficient marketing and was ultimately restricted back to existing clients.[14] Challenges in acquiring and retaining clients compounded the damage, with net revenue per active client falling 9.3 percent year over year in fiscal 2023.[15]

Stitch Fix exposes a hard truth of subscription businesses: Revenue expansion is the engine that has to be running strong to offset acquisition costs and drive profitability—no matter how great the original idea is. Staying inside the "fix" took even this fashionable brand out of economic style quickly.

THE SUB-SUBJECTS: ECONOMIC EFFICIENCY

You can have A-level Value Perception and stellar Revenue Expansion, but if your unit economics don't pencil, it's like a house with a cracked foundation—eventually the brand will sink. That's why Economic Efficiency is the reality check that separates sustainable businesses from venture-funded mirages.

But it's more than a math equation; for your payback period to be as efficient as possible, the strength of your overall Brand GPA will reveal a lot. Are you finding customers in the right environments who are in the market? Is your value proposition clear? Is your path to purchase unobstructed? Are you adding value and earning more revenue per customer? Answer yes to all of these and your CFO will be your new BFF.

WHAT WE MEASURE

Primary Metric: CLV:CAC Ratio (Customer Lifetime Value ÷ Customer Acquisition Cost)

This ratio measures how much value a customer generates over their life as a customer relative to what it cost to acquire them initially. Above a 3:1 ratio is the baseline for healthy unit economics. Below that and it's just money out the door.

Secondary Indicators

- **CAC payback period:** The number of months required to recover customer acquisition cost from gross profit, with shorter payback indicating more efficient growth
- **Revenue per acquisition dollar:** Revenue generated for every dollar spent on customer acquisition, measuring the return on marketing and sales investment
- **Organic vs. paid channel mix:** The share of customers acquired through organic channels (SEO, word-of-mouth, referrals) vs. paid channels, with a higher organic share indicating stronger brand pull and lower long-term acquisition costs

GRADING RUBRIC

For A-level Economic Efficiency performance, benchmarks vary by business model and growth stage. With B2B SaaS companies and subscription businesses, a CLV:CAC ratio of 4:1 or above signals that the brand is generating substantial value from every dollar spent acquiring a customer. Consumer businesses operate at a similar threshold but measure payback differently, factoring in repeat purchase cycles and margins. Early-stage companies may sacrifice short-term efficiency for user or customer growth, but the leash should be short. Brands that master efficiency early build the most durable competitive advantages, while those that "pay to play"—meaning spending tons in paid acquisition that doesn't pay itself back—risk going sideways quickly. Across all models, the distinction between A- and B-level performance comes down to whether your unit economics improve as you scale—or whether you lose your shirt and become the brand with no clothes.

Grading Rubric: Economic Efficiency[16]

Grade	Description	Key Metrics
A	Exceptional unit economics; customer value compounds with scale	Above category benchmark CLV:CAC ratio; strong payback efficiency
B	Healthy unit economics; sustainable growth model with room to optimize	At or above category median CLV:CAC ratio
C	Marginal unit economics; efficiency improvements needed to sustain growth	At or just below category median CLV:CAC ratio
D	Poor unit economics; fundamental model issues requiring immediate attention	Bottom quartile CLV:CAC ratio; extended payback periods and no clear path to profitability
F	Unit economics have collapsed; survival requires external capital infusion	Category floor CLV:CAC ratio; cash burn accelerating toward existential crisis

MAKING THE GRADE: DUOLINGO (GRADE: A)

Duolingo has become fluent in how strong brand fundamentals translate into exceptional unit economics. The beloved language learning platform has built a business model that generates sustainable, profitable growth—powered by a freemium model that reduces acquisition friction and a learner community that has grown organically through word-of-mouth virality for nearly a decade, using paid acquisition only to complement and accelerate what the product already does naturally.[17]

Just like the multiple languages it offers, Duolingo benefits from multilayered value creation. The gamified learning experience creates natural viral loops—users share achievements, compete with friends, and generate community-driven marketing that feels authentic and creates FOMO in any language. When CMO Emmanuel Orssaud arrived, Duolingo's advertising had been built around big TV campaigns that "weren't driving much response."[18] What replaced it was a social-first strategy that generated 300 million YouTube Shorts impressions in Q1 2025 alone, with a single ten-episode Shorts run delivering 10.5 million views and 100,000 new followers.[19]

Their retention-focused product design means customers stay engaged longer, increasing lifetime value without driving up service costs. The result shows up directly in the financials: fiscal year 2024 adjusted EBITDA margin of 25.7 percent, Q4 2024 gross margin of 71.9 percent, and fiscal year 2024 free cash flow margin of 36.8 percent—proof that the brand's economics actually improve with its growing scale, creating sustainable competitive advantages that paid acquisition alone could never achieve.[20]

MISSING THE MARK: RENT THE RUNWAY (GRADE: D)

Rent the Runway was the dream solution for a fashionista on a budget. The premise resonated with so many: Why own when you can rent? But while the concept had a real runway, the unit economics fell off a cliff. Despite years of investment, fiscal year 2024 revenue was up just 2.3 percent year over year at $306.2 million while the company posted a $113.2 million net loss and negative-adjusted EBITDA of $20.5 million.[21] The devil can only rent so much Prada.

The business model's problems were hiding in plain sight. Every incremental customer required a lot of overhead: inventory, shipping, cleaning, and reverse logistics. Rent the Runway's April 2023 earnings release confirmed the company had struggled with profitability due to high operating costs tied to exactly those burdens.[22] When your cost structure prevents margin expansion even at scale, that's not a growth problem—that's a fashion emergency.

TOP AND BOTTOM OF THEIR CLASS: ECONOMICS

In Economics, the numbers don't lie. Customers either believe you're worth your price or they don't. You either build value that compounds or you constantly scramble for the next customer.

The Economics score in the Brand GPA framework reflects how well brands balance value creation with value capture across the entire customer life cycle. Brands earning the summa cum laude distinction have built economic models that work: Customers gladly pay their prices, stick around, and buy more over time, and the whole system operates efficiently enough to fund sustainable growth. In contrast, Flunking Out brands typically struggle with one or more fundamental economic challenges—pricing that customers reject, inability to expand customer relationships, or unit economics that require constant capital infusion.

To qualify as "Best in Economics," we looked for the following:

- Value Perception: Premium pricing accepted and defended by customer loyalty
- Revenue Expansion: Leading or above category benchmark net revenue retention or strong repeat purchase growth
- Economic Efficiency: Above category benchmark CLV:CAC ratio and reasonable payback periods

Brands that flunked Economics typically struggled in the following areas:

- Failed Value Perception: Pricing rejected by market or constant promotional pressure
- Poor Revenue Expansion: Declining customer value or high churn offsetting growth
- Inefficient economics: Unsustainable unit economics or excessive customer acquisition costs

Top and Bottom of Their Class: Economics

Vertical	Summa Cum Laude	Why They Excel	Flunking Out	Why They Fail
Apparel and footwear	Ralph Lauren[23]	Average selling price increased 10% in the quarter ending September 28, 2024; adjusted gross margin expanded 160 basis points to 67.0%; quarterly revenue rose 10.8% to $2.14B in fiscal Q3 2025; global DTC comparable store sales increased 6% in FY2024	Under Armour[24]	FY2025 North America revenue projected to decline 15%–17%; gross margin declined 310 basis points to 44.4% with a $150M operating loss; Reuters reported a $434M shareholder lawsuit settlement related to alleged misleading revenue disclosures
Consumer goods	YETI[25]	FY2024 net sales of $1.83B (+10% YoY); gross margin expanded 120bps to 58.1%; drinkware up 7% to $1.09B and coolers and equipment up 17% to $698.6M—premium pricing power anchored by product innovation and durable loyalty	Red Lobster[26]	Filed Chapter 11 on May 19, 2024, with $294M in debt; $76M net loss in 2023; $190.5M in annual rent including $64M on underperforming stores; "endless shrimp" promotion alone cost $11M—years of failing unit economics served on a platter
Media and entertainment	Tubi[27]	97M MAUs as of January 2025; ad revenue up 31% and then 35% in consecutive Fox-reported quarters—AVOD model scaling profitably while subscription platforms tighten their belts	X (Twitter)[28]	Fidelity markdowns implied a 71.5% valuation collapse from $44B to roughly $12.5B by November 2023; US ad revenue fell at least 55% YoY each month since the takeover with 2023 ad sales projected to drop to $2.5B—advertising exodus driven by brand safety collapse

Fitness and wellness	Equinox[29]	Revenues up 27% in 2023; memberships exceeding $300/month signal premium unit economics; $1.8B capital raise completed March 2024	Mirror[30]	Total after-tax charges of $442.7M disclosed in Lululemon's 2024 10-K; $98.2M additional pretax charges in 2023 including $44.2M asset impairments and $30.3M restructuring; ceased selling Mirror and new digital subscriptions December 2023
Health care	Ozempic (Novo Nordisk)[31]	~$16.8B in FY2024 brand sales (+26% YoY); became cultural shorthand for the entire weight loss drug category—the Xerox of GLP-1s	23andMe[32]	Revenue down 34% YoY; 40% workforce reduction with just $79.4M cash remaining; bankruptcy filed March 23, 2025—a business model built on genetic curiosity that never translated into sustainable economics
Consumer tech	Apple[33]	$96.2B in services revenue in FY2024 at 73.9% gross margin; ecosystem lock-in drives exceptional lifetime economics at a scale no consumer tech brand can match	Match Group[34]	Paying users declined nine straight quarters, falling to 14.6M in Q4 2024; Tinder payers down 5% YoY to 9.5M; total revenue down 1% to $860M; operating income fell 14% to $223M—a dating app that can't retain its own customers
B2B tech	Salesforce[35]	$37.9B FY2025 revenue; $63.4B in remaining performance obligations (+11% YoY) signals customers signing larger commitments; textbook land-and-expand economics at global scale	WeWork[36]	$13.3B long-term lease obligations vs. $2.4B committed revenue backlog on September 30, 2023, per SEC filing; Chapter 11 filed November 6, 2023; shares fell nearly 50% on November 1, 2023, as bankruptcy became inevitable

continued →

Education	Coursera[37]	168M registered learners; 1,612 paid enterprise customers, up 18% YoY; 94% enterprise NRR as of Q1 2024; $694.7M full-year 2024 revenue	University of Phoenix[38]	FTC $191M action; DOE $37M in federal loan forgiveness for 1,200+ harmed students; economic model built on deceptive enrollment, not durable student value
Food service	In-N-Out Burger[39]	$5.8M average unit volume across 415 locations in 2024—built on operational discipline, value pricing, and exceptional throughput efficiency	Boston Market[40]	Footprint collapsed from roughly 300 locations to just 27 by March 2024; New Jersey issued stop-work orders at 27 locations in August 2023 over $607,471 in unpaid wages owed to 314 workers; widespread creditor lawsuits and asset disputes throughout the grading period
Travel	Airbnb[41]	$11.1B revenue in 2024; 36% adjusted EBITDA margin; free cash flow grew from $3.8B in 2023 to $4.5B in 2024; $81.8B gross booking value up 12% YoY—all generated without owning a single property	Southwest Airlines[42]	Operating costs reached 99% of revenue; Q4 2024 CASM-X increased 11.1% YoY; Elliott Management disclosed a $1.9B stake in June 2024 demanding leadership change; Southwest announced end of open seating July 2024; DOT imposed $140M penalty with $600M+ in passenger refunds and reimbursements
On-demand	Uber[43]	$37.3B in 2023 revenue; $1.11B operating income marking first full year of operating profitability; sustained discipline across a high-cost, high-competition category	Bird[44]	$414M raised from shareholders via 2021 SPAC merger; Chapter 11 filed December 2023; $100M–$500M in liabilities; capital raised to survive became capital lost at scale for the electric scooter brand

Financial services	Progressive[45]	$74.4B in net written premiums in 2024 (+20.9% YoY); 34.95M policies in force (+18% YoY); 87.9 combined ratio demonstrates pricing power and underwriting efficiency at scale	Credit Suisse[46]	CHF 61.2B in net asset outflows in Q1 2023; emergency UBS rescue at CHF 3B (March 19, 2023); CHF 16B in AT1 bonds wiped out—catastrophic risk failures destroyed one of Europe's most storied financial institutions

THE TOP SCHOLAR AND BOTTOM DWELLER

Every class has its standout performer and its cautionary tale. For Economics, our Top Scholar is Apple—a brand that used hardware as a gateway to building a services juggernaut, compounding customer lifetime value at a scale no competitor can match. Our Bottom Dweller is WeWork, the ultimate example of how even cleaning up a toxic culture and generating positive PR couldn't save fundamentally broken unit economics.

TOP SCHOLAR: APPLE

An apple a day keeps the doctor away, but Apple today keeps the competition at bay. That's because their business is an economic flywheel that gets more valuable with every product launch and update. With $391 billion in total revenue and $93.7 billion in net income in fiscal year 2024, the consumer tech giant is giving NYC a run for the Big Apple title.[47] But the real Economics story isn't the hardware—it's what happens after you buy it.

The services engine is Apple's real economic genius. In fiscal year 2024, Apple generated $96.2 billion in services revenue at a 73.9 percent gross margin—compared to 37.2 percent on products.[48] That gap isn't a bug; it's a feature—and the result of a deliberate architecture: Sell the device once, monetize the customer forever. iCloud,

Apple Music, Apple TV+, AppleCare, the App Store—each one is a recurring revenue stream attached to a base of more than 2.35 billion active devices worldwide.[49]

The expansion economics are self-reinforcing. Every new device sale adds another node to the network. Every new subscriber adds margin without adding meaningful cost. Every year a customer stays inside the ecosystem makes leaving more expensive—not because Apple traps them but because the value compounds. Talk about Think Different.

Top Scholar Report Card: Apple

Sub-Subject	Grade	Metrics
Value Perception	A	$391B FY2024 revenue; $93.7B net income; premium pricing sustained at global scale across hardware and services
Revenue Expansion	A	$96.2B services revenue FY2024; 2.35B+ active devices; ecosystem architecture compounds lifetime value with every new product and subscriber
Economic Efficiency	A	73.9% services gross margin vs. 37.2% products; structural margin gap widens as services mix grows; self-reinforcing flywheel requires minimal incremental cost to scale

BOTTOM DWELLER: WEWORK

WeWork represents the ultimate Economics failure despite a noble effort to make the brand, well, work. Even after cleaning up leadership, culture, and messaging following the ouster of founder and former CEO Adam Neumann—after a master class in governance failure—the fundamental business model remained mathematically impossible. No amount of rebranding could save it.

But WeWork was never a tech company—it was a real estate company disguised in a tech bro hoodie that borrowed a tech company's valuation logic (land and expand, network effects, platform economics) and applied it to a business with the exact opposite cost structure (long-term fixed costs, short-term variable revenue). So even when the adults took over operations, there was no getting around the business challenges that made the dream of an Economics success story nothing more than a fairy tale.

The expansion model in particular made things worse for the beleaguered brand. Each new location meant more long-term lease commitments averaging fifteen years while customers signed only fifteen-month agreements. The result was $13.3 billion in long-term lease obligations against just $2.4 billion in committed revenue backlog as of September 30, 2023.[50]

The unit economics never worked. In Q2 2023 alone, WeWork posted a net loss of $397 million—not a temporary growing pain but a terminal illness.[51] The model required paying premium rents for long-term flexibility while charging customers for short-term convenience. The math couldn't math.

The November 2023 bankruptcy and shares that fell nearly 50 percent in a single day prove that when business fundamentals fail, no amount of kombucha fountains or community feels can make up for that over the long-term.[52] WeWork highlights that Economics might come last in the Brand GPA framework, but it's the subject that is the foundation and determines whether everything else has meaning.

Bottom Dweller Report Card: WeWork

Sub-Subject	Grade	Metrics
Value Perception	F	Mirage built on unsustainable economics; demand real but value proposition impossible; post-cleanup sentiment couldn't overcome math
Revenue Expansion	F	15-year leases vs. 15-month customer commitments; $47B lease obligations vs. $4B customer commitments; scaling amplified mismatch rather than improving unit economics
Economic Efficiency	F	$450 loss per member per month at full occupancy; $975 in costs before overhead; mathematical impossibility, not operational challenge

POP QUIZ: ECONOMICS

You can't run a comprehensive economic analysis overnight, but this short Economics quiz can give you a directional sense of how your brand is performing financially. Answer each question with a checkmark (✓) for yes or leave blank for no. Then apply the weighting formula to calculate your back-of-the-envelope Economics score.

VALUE PERCEPTION (35 PERCENT)

- Can you charge at least 10 percent more than your main competitors without significant customer loss?
- Do customers regularly choose your product/service even when cheaper alternatives are available?
- Are you seeing stable or growing market share despite premium pricing?
- Do customer surveys indicate satisfaction with price–value relationship (>70 percent positive)?

Industry benchmarks: Premium brands target 1.25x+ pricing with stable market share

REVENUE EXPANSION (35 PERCENT)

- Are existing customers buying more/upgrading over time (positive cohort trends)?
- Is your net revenue retention above 100 percent (or repeat purchase rates increasing)?
- Do at least 25 percent of your customers purchase additional products/services within twelve months?
- Are customer lifetime values growing year over year for comparable cohorts?

Industry benchmarks: SaaS targets 110 percent+ NRR; consumer brands seek 5 percent+ repeat rates

ECONOMIC EFFICIENCY (30 PERCENT)

- Is your CLV:CAC ratio above 3:1 across all major acquisition channels?
- Can you recover customer acquisition costs within eighteen months through gross margin?
- Are at least 30 percent of new customers coming through organic/referral channels?
- Are you profitable (or have clear path to profitability) without constant external funding?

Industry benchmarks: CLV:CAC above 3:1; payback periods under eighteen months for most models

SCORING METHOD

Count your total "yes" answers in each section, then multiply your Value Perception score by 0.35, your Revenue Expansion score by 0.35, and your Economic Efficiency score by 0.30. Add all three adjusted scores together to get your final Economics score. See the following scoring rubric (and sorry, there's no extra credit).

Pop Quiz Scoring Table: Economics

Weighted Score Total	Economics Grade	Interpretation
10–12	A	Economic excellence—your business model is working across all dimensions
8–9	B	Strong foundation—solid economics with room for optimization
6–7	C	Mixed signals—some economic strengths but need to address weak areas
4–5	D	Economic challenges—fundamental issues requiring strategic attention
<4	F	Economic crisis—urgent restructuring needed for sustainability

Important note: Scoring should be interpreted within your industry context. Unit Economics and Retention benchmarks vary significantly by category and business stage—what qualifies as strong performance for an early-stage company would fall short of expectations for a mature business. Evaluate your results against your category peers, not the universal scale.

PART TWO

THE REPORT CARD

IN PART 1, YOU LEARNED THE CURRICULUM—the five subjects, their respective sub-subjects, and the brands setting the bar, both high and low. Now it's time to see the sum of the parts.

Part 2 presents in-depth case studies of brands that have earned their stripes not just in one subject but across all five, consistently over time. These brands are the best in their respective classes, and they were selected because their GPAs tell a complete story: what happens when Chemistry, Communications, Psychology, Sociology, and Economics are all working in sync.

Now, if your brand is currently on the struggle bus, this might feel aspirational to the point of unattainable. That's why I've included inspiring turnaround stories—an in-depth look at brands that have put in the hard work and eventually gotten off academic probation. If you've ever had a rough semester but turned it around, you know changing GPAs is daunting—but doable.

You have the framework, and now you have the stories to help your brand go from passable to unsurpassable.

CHAPTER 7

THE VALEDICTORIANS

IT'S ONE THING TO ACE A SUBJECT OR TWO, but to consistently excel across all of the GPA subjects means a brand isn't just good—it's legitimately great. That also suggests that inside the organization, teams are already collaborating to solve real problems versus navel-gazing and grading their own homework.

But it's not just about the grade you achieve—it's about what you learned in the process. Recognize what works well, and repeat it relentlessly. That way, you won't be stuck pulling an all-nighter when a similar challenge arises. And delivering a high-quality customer experience means studying even when you don't need to. Customers are both predictable and, at times, unpredictable. Think of those moments that catch you off guard like that unexpected pop quiz. If you keep one eye on your Brand GPA, you'll be able to crush that quiz—and not skip a beat with even the most challenging customer.

HOW WE EVALUATED

Each brand's GPA reflects multiquarter performance across the five Brand GPA subjects:

- Chemistry—Activity, Affinity, Retention

- Communications—Clarity, Engagement, Responsiveness
- Psychology—Motivation, Personalization, Control
- Sociology—Alignment, Advocacy, Cultural Resonance
- Economics—Value Perception, Revenue Expansion, Economic Efficiency

To ensure this list reflects sustained excellence—not quarterly spikes or viral moments—each brand was evaluated over ten quarters, spanning Q1 2023 through Q2 2025, and only metrics with two or more independent data sources and established benchmark ranges were included. No brand earned Valedictorian status solely from a recent earnings boom, a breakout product launch, or a social media moment. These select brands are the "tortoises" of their respective categories, displaying enduring performance patterns that separate true category leadership from flash-in-the-pan success (looking at you, hares).

HOW WE GRADED

In an academic setting, an A is a perfect 4.0. But in the Brand GPA framework, an A is a 3.8—and that's intentional. That's because no brand is perfect, nor should it strive to be. When you're serving millions—sometimes billions—of customers, perfection is a fantasy. So, the 3.8 "cap" reflects the real-world truth that excellence is possible but perfection isn't. That's why you could see a top performer in a vertical with only a 3.4—maybe even lower.

Each subject grade is converted to its numeric equivalent and then weighted according to the earlier established rubric: Chemistry (30 percent), Communications (20 percent), Psychology (15 percent), Sociology (15 percent), and Economics (20 percent). These weighted scores are combined to produce a brand's final GPA. And because the scale tops out just below a 4.0, a GPA in the mid-to-high 3s is elite territory, namely because it signals consistent excellence across multiple dimensions over a longer period of time—not just a hot quarter or a standout moment. It's also important to note that despite some close scores, there is meaningful separation between brands. If one brand has an A (or a 3.8) in Chemistry while another has a B (or a 3.0), improving a score by 0.8 might seem simple, but mastering a subject isn't easy—and it can take some time. But slipping 0.8? That can happen in a flash.

Now it all comes together. Every brand in the following chapters was evaluated across all five subjects and all fifteen sub-subjects and against primary-source data from the grading period. And for those who loved AP Calculus, here's the formula:

$$=\text{Brand GPA} = \sum(s=1 \text{ to } 5)\ w_s \times \sum(i=1 \text{ to } 3)\ v_{s,i} \times g_{s,i}$$

Where:

w_s = subject weight (Chemistry 30%, Communications 20%, etc.)

$v_{s,i}$ = sub-subject weight within that subject (Activity 40%, Affinity 20%, etc.)

$g_{s,i}$ = numeric grade of each sub-subject (A=3.8, B=3.0, C=2.0, D=1.0, F=0.0)

$\sum_i v_{s,i} = 1$ for each subject (sub-subject weights sum to 100%)

HOW THEY GOT HERE

There are a few different pathways to the top of the class. Some Valedictorians earned their distinction by putting up dominant performances across multiple subjects—think of the brainiac in school who just crushes every exam en route to earning class MVP. But while flashy performances are impressive, sometimes, it's all sizzle and an underdone steak. As you read in Part 1, there were a couple of brands who led the way in one subject, only to be the class clown in another. Then there's the steady path toward greatness. Think of the student who was never the highest scorer in any single course but whose discipline across every subject produced the highest GPA in the class. They earn Valedictorian status sans sizzle—but the steak is perfectly cooked.

But no matter how they got there—sizzling all the way or sous viding their way to near-perfection—they earned it by making the grade consistently with their customers.

The following verticals feature the brand that earned their place at the top of the class—and one that didn't. Each Valedictorian got here by consistently making the grade with their customers, quarter after quarter, across all subjects—a master class in Brand GPA excellence.

APPAREL AND FOOTWEAR

VALEDICTORIAN: LULULEMON—WEIGHTED GPA: 3.62

Lululemon not only gets stellar grades but is like the kid at school who shows up early, stays late, and somehow looks effortlessly put together—and whom everyone wants to hang out with. Reuters reported in August 2023 that strong demand for Lululemon's core and newer products had enabled it to avoid heavy discounting and keep margins high—a feat that separates genuine brand love from manufactured loyalty in a category where promotions are practically a food group.[1] Baymard Institute ranked lululemon.com among the top 1 percent for overall e-commerce UX performance in 2024, placing it in unique company for digital clarity and customer experience in specialty apparel.[2]

Lululemon's top-tier Chemistry grade isn't powered by product alone, but the proprietary fabric group equivalent of the Spice Girls—Luon, Nulu, Luxtreme, Nulux, and Everlux—certainly helps the brand carry one of the strongest repeat engagement profiles in specialty retail. Global comparable sales rose 6 percent in the quarter that ended June 2024, with mainland China same-store sales up 26 percent—evidence that demand isn't just holding; it's compounding internationally.[3] The shopping experience is seamless in store and online, which is a major reason the brand consistently outperforms traditional apparel standards on retention and customer activity.

Psychologically, the brand occupies rare air. People don't buy Lululemon because they need leggings; they buy it because of what it says about them. The brand has been described as "high-end yoga wear for people who don't do yoga." That might be true, but Lululemon isn't posturing—among their core customer base, it's not a brand; it's a culture. Reuters reported in June 2024 that Chinese consumers, especially millennials and Gen Z, dubbed Lululemon the "Hermes of yoga" and were willing to pay a premium for niche, high-quality sportswear aligned with their lifestyles.[4] The stores, the language, and the product quality all reinforce the idea that purchasing from Lululemon is an investment in a better, more intentional version of oneself.

Then there's the Economics grade, one of the clearest indicators of Lululemon's Valedictorian status. Lululemon sells high-quality products at a premium, but that doesn't chase away customers, even in wobbly economic times. Reuters reported improved inventory and strong full-price sales helped lift gross margin to 57.7 percent in June 2024—and gross margin climbed further to 58.3 percent in Q1 fiscal 2025, up sixty basis points year over year.[5] Direct-to-consumer revenue continued to expand across the grading period, with company-operated store net revenue up 14 percent and e-commerce net revenue up 6 percent in fiscal 2024.[6] Building a consistently great brand isn't child's play, but with its distinctive identity, elite customer retention, and category-leading economics, Lululemon makes it look as effortless as a child's pose.

Report Card: Lululemon

CHEMISTRY	COMMUNICATIONS	PSYCHOLOGY	SOCIOLOGY	ECONOMICS
A	B	A	B	A
Activity: A Affinity: A Retention: A	Clarity: A Engagement: B Responsiveness: B	Motivation: A Personalization: A Control: A	Alignment: A Advocacy: B Cultural Resonance: B	Value Perception: A Revenue Expansion: A Economic Efficiency: A

STRUGGLING STUDENT: UNDER ARMOUR—WEIGHTED GPA: 1.80

Oh, how the mighty have fallen. Under Armour, the brand once known as the "Nike Slayer," ended up cutting off their own identity and losing their way. Years of heightened promotional activity trained customers to wait for discounts rather than pay full price, cultural relevance faded as lifestyle competitors moved in, and inconsistent messaging left the brand mid-reset with no clear voice. North America revenue was projected to decline 15–17 percent, and gross margin fell 310 basis points to 44.4 percent.[7] When your Chemistry and Economics grades are consistently in the tank, you've earned your place at the bottom of the brand bin.

Report Card: Under Armour

CHEMISTRY	COMMUNICATIONS	PSYCHOLOGY	SOCIOLOGY	ECONOMICS
C	C	C	C	D
Activity: C Affinity: C Retention: C	Clarity: C Engagement: C Responsiveness: C	Motivation: C Personalization: C Control: C	Alignment: C Advocacy: C Cultural Resonance: C	Value Perception: D Revenue Expansion: D Economic Efficiency: D
North America demand eroding with repeat purchase behavior weakening as discounts replace loyalty	Years of promotional dependency left messaging fragmented and brand direction unclear	Lost the next generation of athletes to lifestyle competitors with a sharper point of view	Cultural relevance faded as the brand chased volume over identity	Gross margin fell 310 basis points to 44.4%, North America revenue down 15–17%, and a $434M lawsuit erased the premium story

CONSUMER GOODS

VALEDICTORIAN: TRADER JOE'S—WEIGHTED GPA: 3.65

Sure, Trader Joe's is a retail grocer, but with approximately 80 percent of its products private label, the brand is less a grocery store and more a CPG wonderland.[8] That's where its off-the-charts Chemistry score comes from: limited SKUs, constant product rotation, and creative seasonal drops that generate Cabbage Patch Kids–like fever.

But it's not just about their unique (and highly addictive) snacks and wide variety of frozen meals. The quirky, friendly atmosphere shows up in their Communications, from the *Fearless Flyer* free publication to the folksy handwritten signs to the Morse code–style bell ringing to the checkout experience that feels like catching up with an old pal. And there's a real sense of cultural belonging—just say, "Trader Joe's" at a dinner party, and the cool kids will flock right to you.

So it's no surprise that ol' Joe is an Economics phenom. With 608 compact stores generating an estimated $16.5B in revenue in 2023 and $18B in 2024—roughly $27–30M per location—TJs ranks among the most productive grocers in America.[9] Placer.ai reported in November 2024 that Trader Joe's drew a median fifty-six visits per square foot versus just twenty-three for H-E-B, the second-strongest grocery performer, and visits per location rose another 3.2% in 2024.[10] The private-label strategy and compact footprints allow the brand to stay laser focused on high-quality products at consistently competitive prices, and that means consistently happy customers—despite their notoriously horrendous parking lots.

Report Card: Trader Joe's

CHEMISTRY	COMMUNICATIONS	PSYCHOLOGY	SOCIOLOGY	ECONOMICS
A	B	A	A	A
Activity: A Affinity: A Retention: A	Clarity: B Engagement: A Responsiveness: B	Motivation: A Personalization: B Control: A	Alignment: A Advocacy: A Cultural Resonance: A	Value Perception: A Revenue Expansion: A Economic Efficiency: A

STRUGGLING STUDENT: KIND—WEIGHTED GPA: 1.70

Once upon a time, KIND was the snack bar in everyone's shopping basket. But across the ten-quarter evaluation window, KIND faced real category headwinds—snack bars fell 5 percent in dollars and 7 percent in units per SPINS—while KIND's own core segment sales dropped 10.7 percent to $268.7M as Quest surged 22.8 percent in the same period.[11] The consumer had moved on to protein, and KIND's belated Protein MAX launch confirmed what the data already showed: They were following, not leading. To paraphrase the classic pop song, these days it's cruel to be KIND.

Report Card: KIND

CHEMISTRY	COMMUNICATIONS	PSYCHOLOGY	SOCIOLOGY	ECONOMICS
D	C	C	C	D
Activity: D Affinity: C Retention: D	Clarity: C Engagement: C Responsiveness: C	Motivation: C Personalization: C Control: C	Alignment: B Advocacy: C Cultural Resonance: C	Value Perception: C Revenue Expansion: D Economic Efficiency: D
Lost ground while the category gained; repeat purchase and brand pull both in retreat	Protein MAX signals adaptation, not leadership; messaging trailing the shift	"Better for you" no longer commands the emotional premium it once did	"Do the KIND thing" intact—brand's best subject—but cultural momentum has moved on	Down 10.7% in core segment; squeezed between private label below and protein brands above

MEDIA AND ENTERTAINMENT

VALEDICTORIAN: TUBI—WEIGHTED GPA: 3.67

Tubi rewrote the streaming playbook by proving that free doesn't have to suck. While the subscription wars carried on between the usual suspects, Tubi exploded from roughly 64 million monthly active users in early 2023 to 78 million by March 2024 and surpassed 97 million by January 2025—outpacing every major SVOD competitor in year-over-year growth.[12]

It found its way to outstanding Chemistry by curating a library of classic TV shows and movies that are a Gen Xer's must-see TV dream. (And for the Gen Zers curious about life in the 1900s, it's a playground of pre-internet nostalgia.) From '90s rom-coms to '80s sitcoms to original programming, Tubi truly has something for anyone. And it shows—total viewing time surged 59 percent year over year in 2023, surpassing 8.5 billion streaming hours.[13] But it's not just about comfort viewing. In 2025, Tubi featured Super Bowl LIX, which drew a 13.6 million average-minute audience and peaked at 15.5 million concurrent streams—making it the most-streamed Super Bowl in history.[14]

One would think that commercials would impede that kind of growth, but Tubi offers a lighter ad load than traditional broadcast television and many other free ad-supported streaming services—a key part of its strategy to delight customers with killer content and docile interruptions. That's because, from a Psychology perspective, Tubi understands what we are all feeling: subscription fatigue. Cutting the cord was meant to be freeing, but annual fee hikes, restrictions on password sharing, and questions of quality have made consumers long for something cheaper—and easier.

Tubi delivers real entertainment value without forcing consumers into yet another billing cycle. And it's paid off—literally. Ad revenue growth came in at 31 percent, then 19 percent, then 35 percent across multiple reported periods—while subscription-led platforms tighten their belts and desperately roll out ad-supported models of their own.[15] Diff'rent strokes, indeed.

Report Card: Tubi

CHEMISTRY	COMMUNICATIONS	PSYCHOLOGY	SOCIOLOGY	ECONOMICS
A	A	A	A	B
Activity: A Affinity: A Retention: A	Clarity: A Engagement: A Responsiveness: A	Motivation: A Personalization: B Control: A	Alignment: A Advocacy: A Cultural Resonance: A	Value Perception: A Revenue Expansion: B Economic Efficiency: B

STRUGGLING STUDENT: *THE WASHINGTON POST* —WEIGHTED GPA: 1.79

WaPo is having a bit of an identity crisis. While much of its journalism remains world class, this is a story of a Psychology fumble that cascaded into Economics collapse. Across the ten-quarter evaluation window, digital subscriptions fell from roughly 3 million to 2.5 million—then lost another 250,000 after owner Jeff Bezos backed the decision not to endorse a presidential candidate.[16] The turmoil was hard to miss: Executive editor Sally Buzbee stepped down in June 2024, Pulitzer-winning cartoonist Ann Telnaes resigned after the paper killed her cartoon critical of Bezos, and longtime columnist Ruth Marcus walked out after management blocked her column criticizing Bezos's editorial policy.[17] Two rounds of cuts—240 buyouts in 2023 and nearly 100 layoffs in 2025—shrank the newsroom to roughly 940 journalists.[18] *The Post*'s Brand GPA slump shows that even legacy giants need more than just Pulitzers to make the grade with readers.

Report Card: ***The Washington Post***

CHEMISTRY	COMMUNICATIONS	PSYCHOLOGY	SOCIOLOGY	ECONOMICS
D	C	C	C	D
Activity: C Affinity: C Retention: D	Clarity: B Engagement: C Responsiveness: C	Motivation: C Personalization: C Control: D	Alignment: C Advocacy: C Cultural Resonance: C	Value Perception: C Revenue Expansion: D Economic Efficiency: D
Digital subscriptions in retreat; declining repeat engagement signals readers are disengaging faster than new audiences can be cultivated	Journalism quality remains strong, but identity confusion in messaging undermines clarity and trust at the brand level	Owner controversy and journalist departures eroded the trust that made *The Post* a destination—motivation to subscribe weakened significantly	A reputation built on fair, impartial journalism now competes with headlines about its own internal turmoil	Subscription revenue declining, losses mounting—the business model under pressure from both sides of the ledger

FITNESS AND WELLNESS

VALEDICTORIAN: EQUINOX—WEIGHTED GPA: 3.50

When it comes to maintaining a consistently high Brand GPA, Equinox is a flex. The health and wellness vertical is a crowded space, but no other brand delivers a premium, high-touch customer experience with this level of consistency. Across the grading period, Equinox maintained some of the strongest (literally!) Retention in the category, the clearest sense of brand identity, and the most durable economics—all while expanding its footprint and maintaining luxury-tier member satisfaction (which ain't easy!).[19]

Equinox has made the act of going to the gym a status symbol of sorts. From the greeters to the expertly designed main floor and studios to the luxurious bathrooms with steam rooms and complimentary bougie hair and skin products, the brand has turned high-end fitness into a lifestyle aspiration—and a case study in endorphin-fueled Chemistry. Members visited clubs at a rate 12 percent above the prior year in January 2024, even as traffic across major gym chains remained flat.[20]

The brand walks the walk, but they can certainly talk the talk. Their Communications are A-level thanks to their disciplined brand voice, intuitive digital UX, and famously bold brand campaigns. Psychologically, the environment is engineered for Motivation. Everything from the diverse offering of group fitness classes to the high-end equipment to the evolving personalization of the Equinox app makes it clear that phoning it in isn't an option—members are expected to push themselves hard.

Where Equinox is all muscle, however, is Economics. During the grading period, Equinox was fueled by 27 percent revenue growth, while raising prices annually without sending members running for the hills and opening new clubs in some of the trendiest—and most expensive—locations.[21] Premium pricing plus a premium experience has led them to a premium brand GPA—and that only happens when your unit economics are as chiseled as your personal trainers.

Report Card: Equinox

CHEMISTRY	COMMUNICATIONS	PSYCHOLOGY	SOCIOLOGY	ECONOMICS
A	A	B	B	A
Activity: A Affinity: A Retention: A	Clarity: A Engagement: A Responsiveness: B	Motivation: B Personalization: B Control: B	Alignment: B Advocacy: B Cultural Resonance: B	Value Perception: A Revenue Expansion: A Economic Efficiency: A

STRUGGLING STUDENT:
WW INTERNATIONAL—WEIGHTED GPA: 1.46

WW (formerly Weight Watchers) has some dead weight dragging their Brand GPA down to perilous levels. Between Q1 2024 and Q1 2025, subscribers fell from 4.0 million to 3.4 million as GLP-1 medications like Ozempic and Zepbound reshaped consumer expectations around weight loss. Subscription revenue dropped 7.2 percent in Q4 2024, and the company filed for Chapter 11 bankruptcy by May 2025 carrying approximately $1.6 billion in debt.[22] By May 2025, WW had filed for Chapter 11 bankruptcy protection carrying approximately $1.6 billion in debt—the kind of loss that the brand doesn't like to celebrate.[23]

Report Card: WW International

CHEMISTRY	COMMUNICATIONS	PSYCHOLOGY	SOCIOLOGY	ECONOMICS
C	C	C	C	F
Activity: C Affinity: D Retention: C	Clarity: C Engagement: D Responsiveness: C	Motivation: D Personalization: C Control: C	Alignment: C Advocacy: C Cultural Resonance: D	Value Perception: D Revenue Expansion: F Economic Efficiency: F
Subscriber erosion and weakening Affinity signal a brand losing its grip on core customers	Engagement collapsed alongside the subscriber base; Clarity and Responsiveness offered no offsetting strength	GLP-1 alternatives dismantled the motivational foundation the legacy behavioral program was built on	Cultural relevance faded as the weight loss category shifted beneath the brand's feet	Bankruptcy, $1.6B in debt, and collapsing subscription revenue define a total economic failure

HEALTH CARE

VALEDICTORIAN: CLEVELAND CLINIC—WEIGHTED GPA: 3.64

Most people want to send the entire US health-care system to permanent detention, but Cleveland Clinic proves you can perform at the highest clinical levels while delivering an experience patients actually trust. Across the ten-quarter evaluation window, Cleveland Clinic ranked among the leading US health systems in patient satisfaction, care coordination, and long-term patient trust—a rare medical triple lutz when most providers just tumble on the ice.

Its Chemistry strength comes from vast scale—82,608 caregivers, 23 hospitals, and 280 outpatient facilities—and a care model that keeps patients coming back.[24] Outpatient encounters grew from 12.8 million in 2022 to 14.1 million in 2024, with patients moving through the system without friction thanks to shared records, tight specialist integration, and predictable handoffs.[25]

Communications is a standout—counter to the typical fragmented, confusing experience found with most modern health-care providers. Cleveland Clinic benchmarks against Press Ganey and HCAHPS national standards and reports above-national-average outpatient performance across the grading period.[26] Patient-facing materials avoid jargon without dumbing things down, and MyChart remains one of the clearest digital experiences in the category.

The Psychology advantage follows naturally. Dealing with your health is emotional and often frightening—but consistent above-benchmark patient experience scores across primary care, cardiology, neurology, oncology, and surgical services prove Cleveland Clinic understands that. And while the health-care industry writ large struggled with inflation and staffing shortages, this nonprofit delivered $275.7 million in operating income at a 1.7 percent margin in 2024—all the while earning *Newsweek*'s #2 global hospital ranking in 2024.[27] Those are some serious rock star results from the rock and roll capital of the world.

Report Card: Cleveland Clinic

CHEMISTRY	COMMUNICATIONS	PSYCHOLOGY	SOCIOLOGY	ECONOMICS
A	A	A	A	B
Activity: A Affinity: A Retention: A	Clarity: A Engagement: A Responsiveness: A	Motivation: A Personalization: A Control: A	Alignment: A Advocacy: A Cultural Resonance: A	Value Perception: B Revenue Expansion: B Economic Efficiency: B

STRUGGLING STUDENT: 23ANDME—WEIGHTED GPA: 0.50

23andMe was a truly revolutionary idea. To put the boilerplate "democratizing access to personal genetic data" into plain English, they helped people get in control of their health destiny and connected long-lost family members, one DNA strand at a time. But things went from twenty-three to zero pretty quickly after a 2023 data breach exposed nearly 6.9 million customers' most intimate data—and the company's response was slow and opaque.[28] Revenue fell 34 percent year over year, then a 40 percent workforce cut left just $79.4 million in cash.[29] On March 23, 2025, the company filed for bankruptcy—and twenty-seven states filed suit to make sure no one could buy what was left of its customers' genetic data without consent.[30] 23andMe started with good intentions—but all that was left in the end was some bad genes.

Report Card: 23andMe

CHEMISTRY	COMMUNICATIONS	PSYCHOLOGY	SOCIOLOGY	ECONOMICS
D	D	F	F	F
Activity: D Affinity: D Retention: D	Clarity: D Engagement: D Responsiveness: D	Motivation: F Personalization: F Control: F	Alignment: F Advocacy: F Cultural Resonance: F	Value Perception: F Revenue Expansion: F Economic Efficiency: F
A breach affecting 6.9M customers accelerated user erosion, and Retention collapsed as trust evaporated across the entire platform	A slow and opaque breach response demonstrated crisis communications failure at every level when it mattered most	The psychological contract was permanently severed when twenty-seven states filed suit to block the sale of customers' genetic data without consent	A brand built on personal empowerment became synonymous with genetic data exploitation—values Alignment destroyed beyond repair	Revenue fell 34% YoY while a 40% workforce cut left just $79.4M in cash before bankruptcy filing in March 2025

CONSUMER TECH

VALEDICTORIAN: CANVA—WEIGHTED GPA: 3.70

Canva has done what Google, Apple, and many others have been unable to do: make anyone a designer. And they've struck a perfectly pixelated nerve: Monthly active users grew from 135 million to more than 220 million across the grading period.[31] Talk about up-and-to-the-right.

What drives Canva's elite Chemistry grade is its ability to make nondesigners not only create something remarkable but feel remarkable in the process, meaning they are also crushing it in Psychology (function + feeling FTW!). Teachers, students, SMB owners, tech professionals, and first-time creators all have the same experience: They get a high-quality result in minutes, not hours. Getting started can often be the hardest part, but Canva has thought of every touchpoint.

The interface guides users intuitively to their first meaningful action, and enhanced features are introduced with the same "you got this!" spirit as the more basic tools. And while tech companies often overuse (and never deliver) the term *democratize* in their mission statements, Canva puts their Magic Studio where their mouth is by enabling more than sixty million educators and students around the world to access the platform for free.[32]

So it's no surprise that Canva's mastery across Chemistry, Communications, Psychology, and Sociology has enabled them to be a standout in Economics. By offering powerful tools for free and indispensable tools for paid tiers, the company built one of the most sustainable product-led growth engines in tech, and the immediate value delivery makes becoming a paid customer a no-brainer. Canva generated approximately $1.7B in annualized recurring revenue in late 2023, surging to more than $2.5B by early 2025—and the numbers keep climbing.[33]

But the most remarkable thing about Canva isn't the 220 million users or the $2.5 billion in ARR—it's what enabled that kind of scale to happen. Canva has cured nearly a quarter of a billion people of their presentation anxiety. In other words, the subscription is the new prescription.

Report Card: Canva

CHEMISTRY	COMMUNICATIONS	PSYCHOLOGY	SOCIOLOGY	ECONOMICS
A	A	A	A	A
Activity: A Affinity: A Retention: B	Clarity: A Engagement: A Responsiveness: A	Motivation: A Personalization: A Control: A	Alignment: A Advocacy: A Cultural resonance: A	Value perception: A Revenue Expansion: A Efficiency: A

STRUGGLING STUDENT: SONOS—WEIGHTED GPA: 1.27

Sonos's recent tagline is "Feel More," but they probably didn't mean more frustration. A disastrous 2024 app overhaul sent the platform's rating crashing from 4.6 to 1.3 stars on Google Play in just three months—hitting Chemistry, Communications, and Psychology hard across the grading window.[34] The botched redesign cost the company $20–30M to fix, shares fell over 30 percent from the day before launch, and CEO Patrick Spence resigned in January 2025.[35] Once the darling of home audio, Sonos proves that even a songbird can fall out of tune.

Report Card: Sonos

CHEMISTRY	COMMUNICATIONS	PSYCHOLOGY	SOCIOLOGY	ECONOMICS
D	D	D	C	D
Activity: D Affinity: C Retention: D	Clarity: D Engagement: C Responsiveness: D	Motivation: D Personalization: C Control: D	Alignment: C Advocacy: D Cultural Resonance: C	Value Perception: D Revenue Expansion: D Economic Efficiency: D
App collapse killed engagement and drove user exodus; seamless audio promise broken publicly	Redesign created immediate friction; crisis response slow, leaving customers without answers	Trust evaporated overnight; CEO departure compounded the free fall	Community backlash across platforms signaled broad disconnection from the brand's core audience	Revenue decline, $20–30M remediation cost, and 30%+ share drop tell the full story

B2B TECH

VALEDICTORIAN: SALESFORCE—WEIGHTED GPA: 3.76

Salesforce is the BMOC: brand mastering our curriculum. But more than scoring the highest marks across the board, Salesforce has earned its big mover (and shaker) on campus status by creating the SaaS playbook that nearly every tech company now follows. What makes Salesforce exceptional is that even at colossal scale, it continues to behave like a hungry, customer-obsessed growth company rather than a complacent legacy incumbent (looking at you, Cisco).

Across the full ten-quarter grading period, Salesforce delivered elite Retention, expansion, and platform engagement—the holy trinity of enterprise Chemistry. Those who adopt one cloud product almost always expand to two, three, or more, and multicloud customers retain at some of the highest rates in B2B tech. In fact, eight of the top ten deals in fiscal 2024 included six or more clouds.[36]

Communications is where Salesforce still sets the industry curve. Trailhead and Dreamforce—which drew 45,000+ Trailblazers from 140+ countries in 2024—are not only huge engagement drivers but also successful brands within the brand.[37] Dual Gartner Magic Quadrant leadership in Customer Data Platforms and Multichannel Marketing Hubs seals it.[38]

And while a B2B brand might not seem to have a soul, Salesforce masters Sociology thanks to the 1-1-1 model, $86 million in annual grants, and 60,000+ nonprofits using Salesforce technology for free—a community that genuinely behaves like a movement.[39]

While the Brand GPA doesn't use pluses or minuses, an honorary A+ goes to Salesforce's Economics. Fiscal year 2025 total revenue hit $37.9 billion, with $63.4 billion in remaining performance obligations, up 11 percent year over year.[40] The brand wrote the textbook on land-and-expand economics and executes at global scale—making Salesforce a true enterprise tour de (Sales) force.

Report Card: Salesforce

CHEMISTRY	COMMUNICATIONS	PSYCHOLOGY	SOCIOLOGY	ECONOMICS
A	A	B	A	A
Activity: A Affinity: A Retention: A	Clarity: A Engagement: A Responsiveness: A	Motivation: A Personalization: A Control: B	Alignment: A Advocacy: A Cultural Resonance: A	Value Perception: A Revenue Expansion: A Economic Efficiency: A

STRUGGLING STUDENT: ZOOM—WEIGHTED GPA: 2.00

Once upon a time Zoom had the verb—and the verve—as COVID reduced everything to video conferencing and ushered in remote work as the new normal. But across the ten-quarter evaluation window, Zoom lost its pandemic-era zip. Revenue flatlined from $1.105 billion to $1.184 billion—barely moving despite a growing enterprise software market.[41] Enterprise customers fell from 220,400 to 192,600—a 12.6 percent decline—as hybrid work stabilized and Microsoft bundled Teams "for free" with Microsoft 365, eroding Zoom's psychological stronghold.[42] Net dollar expansion fell from 115 percent to 98 percent, meaning existing customers were spending less, not more.[43] While AI Companion showed product ambition, the return to in-office culture and a very well-resourced competitor meant that analog killed the video conferencing star.

Report Card: Zoom

CHEMISTRY	COMMUNICATIONS	PSYCHOLOGY	SOCIOLOGY	ECONOMICS
C	C	C	C	C
Activity: C Affinity: C Retention: C	Clarity: C Engagement: C Responsiveness: C	Motivation: C Personalization: C Control: C	Alignment: C Advocacy: C Cultural Resonance: C	Value Perception: C Revenue Expansion: C Economic Efficiency: C
Revenue flatlined from $1.105B to $1.184B as enterprise customers fell 12.6% YoY—pandemic tailwind became structural headwind	Clear product, undifferentiated messaging—no evidence of category-leading Engagement or Responsiveness within window	AI Companion showed ambition, but Microsoft bundling eroded Zoom's psychological stronghold faster than new features could replace it	ESG present but not externally validated; cultural relevance peaked with the pandemic and hasn't been rebuilt	Revenue grew just 3.1% YoY to $4.665B while enterprise NDE fell from 115% to 98%—profitable but structurally stagnant

EDUCATION

VALEDICTORIAN: DUOLINGO—WEIGHTED GPA: 3.76

The international language is love, but the international language learning platform customers love is our education Valedictorian, Duolingo. What makes the brand so distinct is that it takes something complex like learning a new language and makes it fun, which is a big reason why during the ten-quarter grading period, the platform grew from roughly 60 million to nearly 100 million monthly active users—with daily active users reaching 37.2 million by Q3 2024—while maintaining a day-thirty retention rate of roughly 38 percent—a number that is a foreign concept (hey-o!) to other education apps, which often average below 10 percent retention.[44] And because users keep coming back, subscription revenue surged throughout the period, highlighted by Duolingo Max, the premium AI-powered tier offering interactive conversational practice.[45]

Duolingo's growth seems effortless, and that's because of how effortlessly people fall into the habit of learning. Thanks to dopamine hits via quick wins, streak tracking, and adaptive difficulty—plus personality-filled nudges from Duo, the mascot-cum-guilt-inducing owl—the brand creates both instant gratification and long-term motivation. People don't open Duolingo because they have to—they open it because it scratches the same itch as Wordle (except in French, Spanish, or for the Trekkies reading this book, Klingon).

As you read earlier, Duolingo was the Communications Top Scholar, and rightfully so—the brand's comms are light-years ahead of typical edtech. Seamless onboarding, cheerful "you got this!" reinforcements, and a booming TikTok presence (now over 17 million followers) have helped transcend Duolingo into a cultural phenomenon.[46] And what has made it such a cult-of-personality brand is its instant access—and in turn, soaring Sociology score—thanks to its free core offering and meaningfully powerful features without cumbersome paywalls. Duolingo democratized language learning for millions globally, building a classroom where people share streaks, milestones, jokes, and memes across forty languages.

Given their commitment to a feature-rich freemium model, one might think their Economics score might need tutoring, but the opposite proved true. Subscription revenue climbed more than 45 percent, paid subscribers grew from roughly 4.8 million to over 7 million, net revenue retention stayed above 100 percent, and gross margins held in the mid-70 percent range.[47] The product-led engine scales without massive sales teams, and Duolingo Max pushed ARPU steadily upward. It's a master class in product-led growth—delivering value instantly, making Personalization a cornerstone, and using creativity and humor to build a sticky experience and strong global community. What's not to love/aimer/amar/bangwI' SoH?

Report Card: Duolingo

CHEMISTRY	COMMUNICATIONS	PSYCHOLOGY	SOCIOLOGY	ECONOMICS
A	A	A	A	A
Activity: A Affinity: A Retention: A	Clarity: A Engagement: A Responsiveness: A	Motivation: A Personalization: A Control: B	Alignment: A Advocacy: A Cultural Resonance: A	Value Perception: A Revenue Expansion: A Economic Efficiency: A

STRUGGLING STUDENT: CHEGG—WEIGHTED GPA: 0.44

Chegg is barely chugging along. Across the grading period, subscribers fell 31 percent to just 3.2 million, and revenue dropped 30 percent to $121 million in Q1 2025—numbers that reflect not an economic stumble but a structural collapse.[48] The tutoring company publicly admitted that ChatGPT was materially cannibalizing demand for its core homework-help model, one of the earliest brands to wave the white flag at AI.[49]

Chegg, whose name combines "chicken" and "egg" in reference to the classic chicken vs. egg dilemma, created their own Communications dilemma by delivering confused messaging about AI partnerships and product pivots that blurred the value proposition at precisely the moment customers needed clarity.[50]

Meanwhile, Psychology cratered as students no longer felt they needed Chegg when large language models at the tips of their fingers answered questions instantly—and for free. With guidance repeatedly revised downward and revenue declining 30 percent to $121 million in Q1 2025, Chegg, sadly, is the new chump.[51]

Report Card: Chegg

CHEMISTRY	COMMUNICATIONS	PSYCHOLOGY	SOCIOLOGY	ECONOMICS
F	D	F	D	F
Activity: F Affinity: D Retention: F	Clarity: D Engagement: F Responsiveness: D	Motivation: F Personalization: D Control: D	Alignment: D Advocacy: D Cultural Resonance: D	Value Perception: F Revenue Expansion: F Economic Efficiency: F
Nonsubscriber traffic down 49% YoY; subscribers fell 31% to 3.2M—dual-axis collapse with no recovery signal	Muddled AI pivot messaging destroyed clarity at precisely the moment students needed a reason to stay	Students defected to free LLMs instantly; no feature retained them; motivational pull evaporated overnight	Academic integrity fault line; mass student defection; Trustpilot 2.0/5 from 6,692 reviews	Revenue down 30% to $121M; gross margin compressed to 56%; $17.5M net loss; 22% workforce cut

FOOD SERVICE

VALEDICTORIAN: IN-N-OUT BURGER—WEIGHTED GPA: 3.73

Bruce Lee famously said, "I fear not the man who has practiced 10,000 kicks once, but I fear the man who has practiced one kick 10,000 times." It's a good thing he never had to face In-N-Out. The iconic fast-food chain is the big cheese of the food service category with an incredibly simple menu offering of just burgers, fries, and shakes. But their constant practice gives the brand a real Chemistry kick (well, three of them), and across the ten-quarter grading period, no competitor matched their consistency.

Every In-N-Out delivers the same experience: fresh ingredients (they don't have freezers), made-to-order preparation (no heat lamps fossilizing your food), and enthusiastic service (the Pleasantville of fast food). That tight operating model produces customer confidence rare in QSR—to the tune of $5.8 million per-store average unit volumes across 415 locations in 2024.[52]

But more than tasty food, it's the In-N-Out lore that turns customers into superfans—a Psychological win. The not-so-secret menu and special lingo make it feel more like a speakeasy than a burger joint. IYKYK. Amirite? Its Sociology score also spikes thanks to family ownership, community ethos, and an exceptionally strong employee culture. In-N-Out publicly displays its commitment to paying well above industry wages, and its LEARN program and promote-from-within track record create a more motivated workforce than the QSR norm, which in turn makes for a better customer experience.[53]

The brand's Communications strategy embraces simplicity over complexity because they've never strayed from their core customer: the hungry traveler. The famously minimal menu focuses attention on quality, not choice overload, and you can consume every menu item with one hand (although protein style really does require two). But don't expect to come across a big billboard or hear a catchy jingle. In-N-Out spends minimally on national media.[54] Instead, word of mouth keeps the business as searing hot as its grills.

But it's the value that keeps people coming back—and the Economics grade soaring. As consumer prices skyrocketed across the QSR space during the ten-quarter period, In-N-Out's stick-to-your-guns strategy around simplicity delivered a double-double in its own right: an impressively high-quality experience at a modest price and tremendous volume efficiency.

Report Card: In-N-Out Burger

CHEMISTRY	COMMUNICATIONS	PSYCHOLOGY	SOCIOLOGY	ECONOMICS
A	A	A	B	A
Activity: A Affinity: A Retention: A	Clarity: A Engagement: A Responsiveness: A	Motivation: A Personalization: A Control: A	Alignment: A Advocacy: B Cultural Resonance: B	Value Perception: A Revenue Expansion: A Economic Efficiency: A

STRUGGLING STUDENT: BOSTON MARKET—WEIGHTED GPA: 0.34

Boston Market has almost no more clucks to give. Between Q1 2023 and Q1 2024, the chain practically evaporated, shrinking from roughly three hundred locations to just twenty-seven, making it one of the fastest brand implosions in QSR history.[55] In August 2023, the New Jersey Department of Labor issued stop-work orders across twenty-seven locations over $607,471 in unpaid wages owed to 314 workers.[56] By February 2024, a federal judge had granted US Foods an $11.9 million default judgment against the company.[57] Clearly the legal system isn't playing chicken, and with so few locations left, neither is the brand.

Report Card: Boston Market

CHEMISTRY	COMMUNICATIONS	PSYCHOLOGY	SOCIOLOGY	ECONOMICS
F	F	D	D	F
Activity: F Affinity: D Retention: F	Clarity: D Engagement: F Responsiveness: F	Motivation: D Personaliza-tion: F Control: D	Alignment: D Advocacy: F Cultural Reso-nance: D	Value Percep-tion: F Revenue Expansion: F Economic Efficiency: F
300 locations to 27 in under 12 months; customers didn't churn—they ran out of places to go	A 2.7/5 app rating, unanswered emails, and stop-work orders—the brand stopped talking long before it stopped operating	86% brand awareness with nowhere to eat—the memory of the brand outlasted the brand itself	$607,471 in unpaid wages to 314 workers—hard to claim com-munity values when you're stiffing the community	An $11.9 million federal judgment and 27 locations left; the unit economics didn't just fail—they filed for contempt

TRAVEL

VALEDICTORIAN: AIRBNB—WEIGHTED GPA: 3.58

Airbnb didn't just disrupt travel—it changed a paradigm and built a marketplace that scales profitably while the asset owners absorb the overhead. For the grading period, Airbnb books itself a spot atop the travel class, with Nights and Experiences bookings growing from 448 million in 2023 to 491.5 million in 2024 and Q1 2025 adding another 143.1 million—up 8 percent year over year. That's a full board of industry-leading achievements that demonstrates demand isn't plateauing.[58] Active listings crossed 7.7 million by end of 2023 and surpassed 8 million by end of 2024, meaning supply kept pace with demand—five-star marketplace dynamics.[59] That balance is the engine behind Airbnb's A in Chemistry: The platform grows as it attracts new customers and as repeat guests increase their activity—creating a self-reinforcing loop that has no signs of slowing down any time soon.[60]

No brand is flawless, and Airbnb's B grades in Communications and Sociology are rock solid—but far from perfect. The framework's weighting matters here: Communications carries 20 percent and Sociology 15 percent, so neither is a GPA killer—but neither should be glossed over. On the Communications side, Airbnb's transparency investments—total price display, Guest Favorites surfacing, and a booking flow benchmarked among travel's best—earn genuine Clarity credit.[61] Where it loses ground is Engagement and Responsiveness: Host–guest disputes, inconsistent service standards across eight million listings, and a support experience that still frustrates at scale keep the A ever so elusive. Sociology tells a similar story: Airbnb's community framing is genuine, but regulatory battles from New York to Barcelona—and an ongoing tension between platform growth and neighborhood impact—reflect a brand still working through its relationship with the communities its hosts operate in.

What seals the Valedictorian designation is the solid A in Economics—and specifically what those Economics reveal about the model itself. Airbnb's revenue reached $11.1 billion in 2024 with a 36 percent adjusted EBITDA margin, while free cash flow hit $4.5 billion, up from $3.8 billion in 2023.[62] Those numbers, generated without owning a single property, represent a capital efficiency that has the brand walking on air—and running circles around the competition.

Report Card: Airbnb

CHEMISTRY	COMMUNICATIONS	PSYCHOLOGY	SOCIOLOGY	ECONOMICS
A	B	A	B	A
Activity: A Affinity: A Retention: A	Clarity: A Engagement: B Responsiveness: B	Motivation: A Personalization: A Control: A	Alignment: B Advocacy: B Cultural Resonance: B	Value Perception: A Revenue Expansion: A Efficiency: A

STRUGGLING STUDENT:
CARNIVAL CRUISE LINE—WEIGHTED GPA: 1.50

Carnival is on the verge of becoming a clown show of a brand, despite having full boats during the grading period. Demand for cruising came back after the COVID dry dock, and Carnival rode that wave back to profitability. But $27 billion in remaining debt; D grades in Psychology, Sociology, and Economics; and a brand identity that begins and ends at "affordable cruise" are true signs of a sinking ship.[63] Last-minute deals, deposit sales, early-booking discounts—the promotional tidal wave never relents, and Carnival is exceptionally good at generating the next booking. What it doesn't generate, however, is loyalty, trust, or a reason to choose Carnival—especially when a competitor offers a better deal. In other words, the Carnival brand is just performance marketing in a captain's hat.

Report Card: Carnival Cruise Line

CHEMISTRY	COMMUNICATIONS	PSYCHOLOGY	SOCIOLOGY	ECONOMICS
C	C	D	D	D
Activity: C Affinity: C Retention: C	Clarity: C Engagement: C Responsiveness: C	Motivation: D Personalization: D Control: D	Alignment: D Advocacy: D Cultural Resonance: D	Value Perception: D Revenue Expansion: D Economic Efficiency: D
Demand came back post-pandemic, but loyalty didn't follow—full ships reflect a category with limited alternatives, not a brand customers actively choose	Promotional noise fills the silence where a brand voice should be; last-minute deals and deposit sales talk loudly but say very little	Customers book Carnival because it's affordable, not because they feel something—transactional by design, forgettable by default	Environmental scrutiny, regulatory pressure, and a brand identity that begins and ends at "cheap cruise" leave little room for values Alignment	$27 billion in debt and a promotional dependency that never relents—a business model built on volume, not value

ON-DEMAND

VALEDICTORIAN: DOORDASH—WEIGHTED GPA: 3.43

DoorDash is the valedashtorian (hey-o!) of the on-demand vertical because it consistently delivers what people actually want from this kind of brand: reliability, clarity, and a friction-free experience. Recent industry data places DoorDash at approximately 65 percent of US restaurant delivery sales, thanks to high order frequency and strong subscription retention through DashPass, which gives subscribers an elevated experience with no delivery fees and a percentage back on pickup orders in the form of credits.[64]

Success in this space isn't easy. Many companies struggle to stay sticky after seasonal surges or big marketing pushes, but DoorDash has earned household status with millions of dedicated customers. The user experience is intuitive and consistent, helping to elevate the brand's Chemistry. When it comes to Communications, frequent updates via push notifications and real-time tracking of the order sets clear expectations and puts the customer in the driver's seat (well, technically, the passenger's seat). From a Psychology perspective, DoorDash also delivers emotional assurance—something that didn't exist with delivery services of yesteryear.

Where DoorDash firmly slams the, ahem, door on the competition is with its Economics grade. While no delivery company is immune to fee frustration, DoorDash has made material improvements in price transparency and restaurant-level clarity, helping reduce ambiguity across the experience, which in turn strengthens their Psychology position. DoorDash clocked $1.19 billion in full-year 2023 adjusted EBITDA—positive across all four quarters—proving they can live large long after the COVID bubble that pushed the demand for on-demand off the charts.[65] With stable ARR through DashPass, which counted twenty-two million combined DashPass and Wolt+ subscribers as of Q1 2025, DoorDash shows that customer-centric operations and financial discipline can't be treated like side dishes if you want to build a great on-demand brand.[66]

Report Card: DoorDash

CHEMISTRY	COMMUNICATIONS	PSYCHOLOGY	SOCIOLOGY	ECONOMICS
A	A	B	C	A
Activity: A Affinity: A Retention: A	Clarity: A Engagement: A Responsiveness: A	Motivation: B Personaliza-tion: B Control: B	Alignment: C Advocacy: C Cultural Reso-nance: A	Value Percep-tion: B Revenue Expansion: A Economic Efficiency: A

STRUGGLING STUDENT: ANGI (FORMERLY ANGIE'S LIST)—WEIGHTED GPA: 1.41

Oh, Angi. The brand is covered in clouds thanks to low trust, confusing lead-selling practices, inconsistent contractor quality, and poor communication, which leave it at the bottom of the on-demand class. An FTC action against Angi's HomeAdvisor subsidiary—resulting in up to $7.2 million in contractor refunds—confirmed persistent frustration around Angi's paid lead-generation model, including allegations of low-quality leads, repeated charges, and poor contractor vetting, a brutal indication of collapsing Chemistry and Communications.[67] When the little *e* was dropped in the brand's name, it was a foreshadowing of a collapse of its big *E*: Economics.

Report Card: Angi

CHEMISTRY	COMMUNICATIONS	PSYCHOLOGY	SOCIOLOGY	ECONOMICS
D	D	D	D	D
Activity: D Affinity: B Retention: D	Clarity: D Engagement: B Responsiveness: C	Motivation: D Personalization: C Control: D	Alignment: D Advocacy: F Cultural Resonance: C	Value Perception: D Revenue Expansion: F Economic Efficiency: B
Service requests down 26% and a shrinking professional network tell the same story—customers aren't coming back, and the pros they need aren't staying either	Users can't exit a project once started and contractors flood their phones the moment they do; clarity isn't missing—it's been replaced by friction	The FTC found HomeAdvisor, an Angi affiliate, used deceptive tactics to sell leads—when the government has to define your trust problem, you've already lost the customer	A $7.2M FTC redress for defrauded service providers isn't a footnote—it's a verdict on how Angi treats the contractors its entire model depends on	Ads and leads revenue down 14%, services down 21%—the one bright spot is improved EBITDA, but you can't cost-cut your way to a brand customers believe in

FINANCIAL SERVICES

VALEDICTORIAN: VANGUARD—WEIGHTED GPA: 3.70

If the name of your brand is a superlative, you've set customer expectations pretty darn high. But for Vanguard, their brand name isn't a haughty flex—it's a commitment. Known for their low-key vibe and laser focus on driving results—and delight—for their customers, the brand is trusted to the tune of trillions. Across the ten-quarter evaluation window, Vanguard's advised assets grew from approximately $7.2 trillion at year-end 2023 to $8.6 trillion at year-end 2024.[68] Morningstar reported $222 billion in 2024 US long-term fund inflows—second only to BlackRock—while the *Financial Times* reported Vanguard led all US ETF flows with $308.2 billion.[69] Its Chemistry score remains unmatched, driven by a pure, unflashy passive investing ethos: low-cost index funds that consistently beat high-fee alternatives over the long term.

While competitors flood social channels with sizzle and celebrities, Vanguard communicates in plain English, backed by research, clarity, and transparency, giving them strong marks for Communications. It's not the flashiest or most creative, but their digital planning tools and client education center are to the point and see some of the highest repeat engagement in the industry, and their customer support consistently ranks at or near the top among major investment firms.

The Psychology and Sociology advantages are intertwined by the value of transparency: The company is client owned, not shareholder owned, a powerful differentiator that reinforces integrity and aligned incentives. That stability is especially potent during periods of volatility, and during the ten-quarter grading period, Vanguard maintained exceptional long-term investor loyalty even as markets swung up and down. True to their name, Vanguard is at the forefront of low-cost, long-term investing, from Boomer retirees to Gen Zers opening a 401(k) for the first time, cementing its status as the de facto brand for building financial stability across generations.

Economically, Vanguard remains a juggernaut. Its asset-weighted average expense ratio held at roughly 0.07–0.08 percent—among the lowest in the industry—and Vanguard funds outperformed peer-group averages in 84 percent of cited comparisons.[70] Meanwhile, Schwab disclosed multibillion-dollar quarterly outflows across multiple quarters in 2024, underscoring Vanguard's relative stability.[71] With retirement contributions growing steadily and long-term investor loyalty remaining exceptional, the brand's Economics score stayed top-notch despite competitive pressure. The financial crisis of 2009 taught us that no financial institution is too big to fail, but with a Brand GPA like Vanguard's, it's safe to say it will continue putting the *V* in Valedictorian.

Report Card: Vanguard

CHEMISTRY	COMMUNICATIONS	PSYCHOLOGY	SOCIOLOGY	ECONOMICS
A	B	A	A	A
Activity: A Affinity: A Retention: A	Clarity: B Engagement: B Responsiveness: A	Motivation: A Personalization: A Control: A	Alignment: A Advocacy: A Cultural Resonance: A	Value Perception: A Revenue Expansion: A Economic Efficiency: A

STRUGGLING STUDENT: LEMONADE—WEIGHTED GPA: 1.92

Lemonade hoped to sweeten a generally sour insurance category with a tech disruptor attitude wrapped in a whimsical brand—but the Brand GPA tells a different story. An 85 percent gross loss ratio in fiscal year 2023 and $119.1 million in operating cash burn revealed the gap between growth ambition and profitable scale.[72] A Texas Department of Insurance consent order in August 2024 documented a rating system failure affecting more than 16,000 policyholders, and an April 2025 SEC disclosure revealed approximately 190,000 individuals had driver's license numbers exposed through a flaw in Lemonade's own quote flow.[73] In a category built entirely on trust, that's not a speed bump—that's a sinkhole. Lemonade intended to make insurance easy and delightful. But in the end, the brand turned out to be a real, well, lemon.

Report Card: Lemonade

CHEMISTRY	COMMUNICATIONS	PSYCHOLOGY	SOCIOLOGY	ECONOMICS
D	D	C	B	C
Activity: C Affinity: C Retention: D	Clarity: C Engagement: C Responsiveness: D	Motivation: C Personalization: B Control: D	Alignment: B Advocacy: B Cultural Resonance: C	Value Perception: C Revenue Expansion: B Economic Efficiency: D
Growth in customer count masked an 85% loss ratio—when your economics undermine your promise, retention suffers	Whimsical brand promise undermined by category sprawl; core message clarity lost as product pivots outpaced positioning	A Texas consent order and a 190,000-person data breach; in insurance, trust isn't a nice-to-have—it's the whole product	Their Giveback donated $2.1M—genuine but hard to lean on when regulators are documenting your pricing failures	$119.1M in cash burn and an 85% loss ratio in 2023—improvement came, but confidence left first

THE RUNNERS-UP

Avis, the car rental company, proudly staked their claim as the #2 brand (behind Hertz) with their iconic 1962 slogan, "We Try Harder." It's unlikely any of the brands on this list would be content being the silver medalist of their respective industry, so we decided to give them a few hints around why they are a tad behind—and what it would take to overcome the incumbent. In some verticals, the margins are incredibly slim, and in others there's a little more breathing room for the #1s. But in the event the current Valedictorians can't fulfill their duties in the eyes of their customers, there's a competitive batch of first runners-up ready to pounce.

VERTICAL	SALUTATORIAN	GPA	DELTA vs. VALEDICTORIAN	WHERE THEY SHINE	WHAT IT WOULD TAKE
Apparel and footwear	On[74]	2.94	0.68	Chemistry and Economics—46.6% revenue growth and 59% gross margin signal a premium performance brand hitting its stride; consumer enthusiasm and athlete partnerships drive category-leading demand	One of the wider gaps on this list; focus on closing the gap in Communications, Psychology, and Sociology—a younger brand still building the third-party CX, ESG, and engagement proof that comes with scale
Consumer goods	YETI[75]	3.60	0.05	Chemistry, Sociology, and Economics—DTC sales growing to 55%+ of revenue, 58.1% gross margin, and NPS of 74 signal a premium outdoor brand with elite customer loyalty and pricing power	The gap to Valedictorian is razor thin at 0.05—close it by building stronger independent CSAT and engagement data to match the brand's already elite Chemistry and Economics
Media and entertainment	Reddit[76]	3.62	0.05	Chemistry and Economics—DAU grew from 82.7M to 108.1M in five quarters; ad revenue up 50% to $1.2B in 2024; $203M in data licensing deals; IPO priced at $6.4B valuation in March 2024	To gain the mere inches needed for a Valedictorian takeover, strengthen Responsiveness and Advocacy—where community-first platforms must prove they can scale without losing the trust of the communities that made them

Fitness and wellness	Oura[77]	3.38	0.12	Psychology and Economics—category-leading personalization through sleep, HRV, and readiness scoring; more than $500M in revenue in 2024 (more than double the prior year); ~80% global smart ring market share per IDC (2023); 4.9/5 App Store rating across 193K reviews	Close the gap in Communications and Sociology—without disclosed CSAT benchmarks or third-party Responsiveness data, and with limited Advocacy evidence, the framework can't award the grades the product experience probably deserves
Health care	Hims & Hers[78]	3.50	0.14	Economics and Chemistry—$1.4765B FY2024 revenue (+69% YoY), 79% gross margin, 97% recurring online revenue, and 2.2M+ subscribers signal a DTC health-care model firing on all cylinders	Close the gap in Communications and Sociology—the prescription for success is stronger third-party CX validation and a more mission-driven cultural narrative, otherwise the framework can't give credit where it's probably due
Consumer tech	Sony[79]	3.40	0.30	Chemistry and Economics—118M PlayStation MAUs signals sustained platform engagement and cross-category revenue discipline across gaming, imaging, and audio simultaneously	Close the gap in Sociology and Communications—Canva is a big star, so a quietly dominant legacy brand that under-punches its cultural weight and lacks the digital-native engagement paper trail will remain second fiddle

continued →

B2B tech	ServiceNow[80]	3.48	0.28	Chemistry and Economics—98% renewal rates, subscription revenue growing from $2.024B to $2.866B, and cRPO of $10.27B (+19% YoY) signal elite retention and expansion economics at enterprise scale	Close the gap in Communications and Sociology—challenging Salesforce is no small feat; stronger third-party CX Validation and Cultural Resonance are needed to earn higher grades and compete
Education	MIT[81]	3.58	0.19	Chemistry, Sociology, and Economics—#1 globally in QS rankings, 99% first-year retention, 30,000+ alumni companies employing 4.6 million people, $1.1B+ in annual research expenditures, and a $126K median early-career salary that redefines the value equation for higher education	A duo-able takeover if Communications and Psychology have disclosed CSAT benchmarks, student satisfaction scores, or third-party Responsiveness data; otherwise, the framework can't award the A the brainiac brand has likely earned
Food service	Texas Roadhouse[82]	3.57	0.16	Chemistry and Economics—same-store sales rose 7.7–9.3% every quarter in 2024; AUV exceeded $8M for the first time in brand history; net income grew 42.2% to $433.6M, and total revenue increased 16.0% to $5.37B in 2024	Close the gap in Communications—without disclosed CSAT benchmarks, third-party Responsiveness data, or scaled digital engagement metrics comparable to category leaders, the framework can only grant "well done" instead of the top prize

Travel	Emirates[83]	3.28	0.30	Psychology and Economics—a product so differentiated it generates loyalty through experience alone; record $4.7B profit on $33B revenue in FY2023–2024 proves premium positioning at scale	Close the Chemistry and Communications gaps—without disclosed repeat-traveler retention metrics comparable to Airbnb's marketplace data, the framework can't give Emirates the platinum status it's soaring toward
On-demand	Waymo[84]	3.17	0.26	Psychology and Sociology—safety data showing 73% fewer injury crashes and documented accessibility Advocacy for disabled communities reflects a brand building genuine trust at every touchpoint	Close the Chemistry and Economics gaps—without geographic scale beyond four cities and no stand-alone revenue or profitability disclosure, the framework can't navigate the brand's full potential
Financial services	Wealthfront[85]	3.48	0.22	Chemistry and Economics—competitive 0.25% fee, best-in-class cash management recognition, and platform trust drive strong Retention and Value Perception among cost-conscious investors	Close the gap in Sociology and Communications—the lack of more robust third-party CX data and cultural visibility keeps the brand a few basis points behind the top spot

GREAT GRADES, GREAT BUSINESS

The performance gap between category leaders and those that regularly ride the struggle bus isn't just about pride—it's about profit. Across the Brand GPA dataset, Valedictorians average a 3.62 GPA, while the Struggling Students average just a 1.30, a 64 percent performance differential. But more than just a stark contrast in grades, when you look under the hood, Valedictorians consistently show retention rates 2–3x higher, NPS scores 20–40 points stronger, and unit economics that get more efficient with scale.

Trader Joe's, In-N-Out, and Airbnb demonstrate how operational excellence fuels customer obsession. Canva, Salesforce, and Duolingo prove that clarity and ease of use translate not just into brand momentum but market dominance. Equinox, Vanguard, and Lululemon show how premium value delivery justifies premium pricing. Tubi, Cleveland Clinic, and DoorDash reveal how trust and everyday reliability can turn customer satisfaction into real scale—and category leadership.

An important reminder: None of these top brass brands carries a cumulative 4.0 (or on the Brand GPA scale, a flawless 3.80). While a perfect GPA works as an aspirational North Star in an academic context, in business nothing is ever perfect, and even the best brands stumble occasionally. But what separates these Valedictorians from the rest is their relentless pursuit of A-level work across all subjects.

In fact, these GPA outcomes mirror broader industry research: Companies delivering superior customer experience dramatically outperform laggards—in one long-running analysis, CX leaders generated more than five times the shareholder return of CX laggards, while separate loyalty research finds that improving retention by just 5 percent can increase profits by 25–95 percent.[86] Valedictorians don't just earn better grades—they earn a competitive advantage that feels totally out of reach for struggling brands. But if your brand is having a tough time making the grade, there's a lot to learn from the Valedictorians. In other words, you *don't* have to keep your eyes on your own paper.

CHAPTER 8

THE COMEBACK KIDS

THERE'S NOTHING LIKE A GREAT COMEBACK STORY. From Rocky to Rudy to Ricky Martin, people love to get behind the underdog or will the person down on their luck over the hump. The same is true with brands. When a business starts to tank, odds are customers aren't cheering on its demise (though I doubt there's a Bring Back Enron group on Facebook). Frankly, it's a bummer when a product or service you once loved—or even depended on—no longer shows up in the way you need it. Even though people are quite comfortable airing their brand grievances online, customers can be forgiving if—and only if—a business looks itself in the mirror and takes steps (drastic as they might need to be) to course correct. Or in the Brand GPA context, corrects the courses—or subjects—where they have faltered the most.

So on the heels of the Valedictorian chapter, where the brightest and shiniest industry stars were given their well-deserved A-grade flowers, it's time to focus on another set of apt pupils. The Comeback Kids are meant to give hope to the hopeless, as it's easy to see nothing but downside when your brand is firmly belted into the struggle bus. But as these twelve brands will show you, a turnaround is possible—however, it takes time, patience, and perseverance. Not every company can rebound to their peak success, but they *can* operate in a new and more sustainable way that keeps their customers top of mind—and their report cards top of the class.

HOW WE EVALUATED

Unlike the Valedictorians, who earned their spots based on an analysis of ten consecutive quarters of consistent, top-tier performance, the Comeback Kids had to show material improvement over a longer horizon. In order to highlight the most recent and relevant examples, we looked at data over a five-year window from 2020 to 2025 to determine if a brand displayed the following:

- **A clear decline:** Not a bad month or a soft quarter but a real, documented downturn—operational, financial, cultural, or all three.
- **A meaningful rebuild:** Leadership changes, product reinvention, cultural reset, economic discipline, or customer experience improvements that can be traced to credible sources. Survival alone didn't count. Surface-level rebrands didn't count. Spin definitely didn't count.
- **A sustained recovery:** Evidence that the brand didn't just bounce off the bottom but actually charted a healthier, more durable course—reflected in customer sentiment, product-market fit, financial stability, or renewed relevance.

Some brands experienced the sting of COVID and had to work their way out of a pandemic hole. Others actually benefited greatly during the shutdown but got thrust into detention once life got back to normal. And others were struggling for years, even decades, until the 2020s brought on new prosperity.

Each Comeback Kid was evaluated against the same five Brand GPA subjects used throughout this book—Chemistry,

Communications, Psychology, Sociology, and Economics—using the exact same grading structure. (Remember, there's no such thing as perfect!) Some companies had bigger holes to dig out of, and no one rebounded with straight As. But that's okay! Instead, they improved well enough to earn something much harder to achieve when your brand is in the gutter: a second chance.

APPAREL AND FOOTWEAR: ABERCROMBIE & FITCH

BRAND GPA TRANSFORMATION: 1.1 → 3.3

THE POSTMORTEM

By 2020, Abercrombie was a hot mess. Outdated aesthetics, changing cultural norms, and years of negative press—including discrimination claims resolved in 2004 through a $50 million consent decree with the EEOC and the 2022 Netflix documentary *White Hot: The Rise & Fall of Abercrombie & Fitch* revisiting the brand's exclusionary past—pushed younger shoppers away in droves.[1] The decline was years in the making: Comparable sales stagnated across the late 2010s, significant store rationalization followed including 137 closures in fiscal 2020, and the brand's cultural icon status had eroded to near irrelevance.[2] Under CEO Fran Horowitz, appointed on February 1, 2017, the brand did serious soul searching and focused on modernizing product offerings, cleaning up its reputation, and rebuilding trust with churned consumers.[3] By the end of the grading period, Abercrombie tidied up their point of view and got a new attitude: The outdated mall relic had become a modern, inclusive, fashion-forward retailer with renewed momentum.

THE FIVE DRIVERS OF THE COMEBACK

1. Chemistry: From Midriff Mall Rats to Haute Heroes

Abercrombie rebuilt its product engine around elevated casual wear, focusing on expertly cut basics, year-round staples, and denim that gave premium labels a run for their money. Denim became one of the brand's most significant category growth drivers, average unit retail climbed through double-digit increases as the brand reduced markdown dependency, and the better assortment discipline—neutral palettes, quality fabrics, improved fits, expanded dress and activewear—brought lapsed customers back, particularly millennial women. If you build great fashion-forward products, they will come, and customers found a fashion field of dreams with these new looks.

2. Communications: Sex No Longer Sells

Once upon a time, only the beautiful people "qualified" to shop at Abercrombie. The catalog and in-store imagery were hypersexualized and oh so white, but a comms overhaul shifted messaging from elitism to inclusivity, embracing diverse body types and real-life contexts—grounding the brand in a more thoughtful tone. The "A&F's New Look" campaign repositioned the brand through creator partnerships including curve model and influencer Remi Bader, whose denim try-on content helped drive massive organic reach on TikTok. Brand sentiment shifted from negative to positive according to YouGov BrandIndex, and customers rediscovered the brand through creators, not controversies.[4]

3. Psychology: Far from the Maddening Crowd

Instead of delivering an inferiority complex, every customer touchpoint evolved to focus on inspiring style, individual expression, and inclusivity—meeting shoppers where they are with great fashion and healthier emotional bonds. Store traffic rebounded significantly post-COVID alongside double-digit e-commerce growth, and customer confidence returned as repeat purchase behavior strengthened meaningfully during the grading period.

4. Sociology: All Sizes Fit All

Waify chic was the norm during Abercrombie's initial ascent, but the reformed brand significantly expanded its extended size offerings between 2020 and 2022 and embedded inclusion into all company practices through ESG commitments, confronting its cultural missteps head-on and earning back trust. Campaign representation shifted to reflect real diversity—racial, body, and LGBTQ+ representation—instead of nostalgic exclusivity.

5. Economics: Margins Without Markdowns

By mending their missteps, the business opportunity became clearer, leading to better demand forecasting, lower markdown dependency, and improved omnichannel fulfillment. The payoff was real: Net sales grew 16 percent in fiscal 2024 to $4.95 billion, operating margin expanded 370 basis points to 15 percent, and comparable sales climbed double digits across all four quarters of fiscal 2024—Q1 +21 percent, Q2 +18 percent, Q3 +16 percent, Q4 +14 percent.[5] Abercrombie became a profit powerhouse instead of a past-tense punchline.

LESSONS LEARNED

Abercrombie's transformation shows that a fashion faux pas of this magnitude might seem devastating, but introspection, accountability, and renewed focus on the customer clears the runway for a big comeback. Unlike some brands benefiting from '90s and early aughts nostalgia, the Abercrombie turnaround wasn't about being retro for profit. It's a case study in doing the hard work and staying the course—and fashionably making the grade.

Abercrombie & Fitch: A Monumental Makeover

Subject	2020 Grade	2025 Grade
Chemistry	D	A
Communications	C	A
Psychology	D	B
Sociology	F	B
Economics	D	B
Overall GPA	1.1	3.3

CONSUMER TECH: POLAROID

BRAND GPA TRANSFORMATION: 1.7 → 3.2

THE POSTMORTEM

The start of the millennium was a bit of a photobomb for Polaroid. After its 2001 bankruptcy, the 2008 end of instant film production, and a line of fairly crappy electronics that stripped the brand name of meaning, Polaroid was overexposed and underwater. But March 2020 marked a real reset: Polaroid dropped the Originals sub-brand and consolidated under a single Polaroid name.[6] Bolstered by the launch of the Polaroid Now—featuring an autofocus lens system, self-timer, and double-exposure capability—and a Gen Z–driven analog resurgence, instant photography entered a legitimate comeback. As of 2023, the global instant-print market stood at $1.62 illion, growing at a 5.6 percent annual clip, and a fresh crop of GPA graders.[7]

THE FIVE DRIVERS OF THE COMEBACK

1. Chemistry: Point-Click Fit

Polaroid stopped chasing cheap electronics and rebuilt around instant analog photography. The Polaroid Now combined vintage appeal with modern enhancements—autofocus lens system, improved light-sensing and flash adjustment, self-timer, and double exposure. The brand expanded its product line with the Now+, the pocket-sized Go, and the premium I-2 with LiDAR autofocus, giving customers multiple entry points. While Fujifilm's Instax line clearly dominates the instant-camera category—with cumulative sales exceeding 100 million units—Polaroid focused on differentiating through design, build quality, and higher-end features.[8] The broader instant-print camera category itself has expanded, with the global market estimated at $1.62 billion and projected to grow at roughly a 5.6 percent annual rate.[9] Turns out legacy product-market fit can come back into focus.

2. Communications: The Bigger Picture

Polaroid had fragmented its identity across sub-brands and licensing deals, but the March 2020 reset unified everything under one brand, one website, one company.[10] The "Forever Now" relaunch campaign leaned into creativity and real-world moments rather than nostalgia gimmicks. Social engagement grew meaningfully—Instagram reached 763,000 followers—and high-profile collaborations with the Jean-Michel Basquiat Foundation in 2024 and MoMA in 2025 strengthened brand recall as artistic influencers adopted Polaroid as their visual tool kit.[11] The brand was widely available at Urban Outfitters, Target, and Best Buy, signaling mainstream retail confidence.

3. Psychology: Back to the Future

As social media feeds became increasingly algorithmic and curated, interest in analog media began rising among younger consumers.

Film photography, vinyl records, and other tactile formats all experienced renewed attention in the 2020s, particularly among Gen Z seeking alternatives to fully digital experiences. Instant photography benefited from this shift toward physical artifacts and imperfect images, positioning Polaroid's cameras as tools for spontaneous, real-world moments rather than digitally optimized content.

4. Sociology: Offline Is the New Online

The brand arrived at a moment when analog tools—from vinyl records to film cameras—were gaining renewed attention among younger creators seeking alternatives to algorithm-driven digital culture. Polaroid's Basquiat Edition campaign and MoMA collaboration placed the brand squarely within fashion, street culture, and creator communities, with Hypebeast and PetaPixel both covering the Basquiat launch as a cultural moment.[12] Younger creators used instant cameras to stand out in an increasingly homogenized and inauthentic digital world.

5. Economics: Focus on Sustainable Growth

Polaroid's strategy centered on a simpler business model: cameras paired with proprietary instant film. As of 2023, the global instant-print market was estimated at $1.62 billion and growing at roughly 5.6 percent annually, providing a stable backdrop for the category.[13] Fujifilm's Instax line alone has surpassed 100 million cumulative unit sales, illustrating the scale of demand for instant photography products.[14] Within that expanding category, Polaroid focused on a tiered product ladder—from the pocket-sized Go to the premium I-2—supported by repeat purchases of film packs.

LESSONS LEARNED

Polaroid's revival shows that sometimes a selfie is what a brand needs to look inward and see where it needs to make the right changes.

By simplifying the product line and proudly reembracing its analog photography roots, Polaroid developed a new generation of instant photography lovers—and bolstered its Brand GPA in the process.

Polaroid: A Transformation Worth a 1,000 Words

Subject	2020 Grade	2025 Grade
Chemistry	C	A
Communications	C	B
Psychology	C	B
Sociology	D	B
Economics	D	B
Overall GPA	1.7	3.2

CONSUMER GOODS: NERDS

BRAND GPA TRANSFORMATION: 1.9 → 3.4

THE POSTMORTEM

For most of the 2000s and 2010s, Nerds were far from the cool kids' table. The tiny, misshapen sugar bombs couldn't break past chocolate confections, the dominant Mean Girls of the candy category. (So fetch!) When Ferrara took over Nerds, the brand had roughly $40 million in sales; by 2019, *The Wall Street Journal* put the figure at about $50 million.[15] But the 2020s saw a nerdy metamorphosis: Ferrara reimagined Nerds through product innovation with the launch of Nerds Gummy Clusters in 2020.[16] The chewy transformation paid off spectacularly: By late October 2024, Gummy Clusters alone had already crossed $500 million in 2024 sales—before Halloween.[17] By June 2025, *Food Dive* reported Nerds was on track to exceed $900 million in sales, up more than

1,700 percent from its roughly $50 million base.[18] The original Nerds Gummy Clusters won Best in Show at the 2021 NCA Most Innovative New Product Awards.[19]

THE FIVE DRIVERS OF THE COMEBACK

1. Chemistry: Biting Off All They Can Chew

Tinkering with the original formula paid off, as Gummy Clusters became a cult product that drove massive trial. The mash-up of Nerds flavors with a chewy texture tapped into industry trends favoring multi-sensorial, multi-flavorful, and multi-texture experiences. In the fifty-two weeks ending May 15, 2022, Nerds led the non-chocolate novelty category with $251.9 million in sales, up 145.7 percent year over year.[20] Ferrara expanded the line with Very Berry Gummy Clusters in 2022, which won the Most Innovative New Product Award in the non-chocolate category at the Sweets & Snacks Expo.[21] The innovation vaulted Nerds into the top tier of non-chocolate novelty brands and opened the door for future product line extensions including seasonal Spooky and Frosty Gummy Clusters.

2. Communications: From Clusters to Loops

Nerds' social momentum did the heavy lifting. Gummy Clusters became a fixture of snack content on TikTok, with Ferrara leaning into the platform's candy-salad trend—creators mixing candies including Nerds Frosty Gummy Clusters into viral food content. Nerds kept its messaging playful and simple, allowing the organic social proof to drive awareness the old-fashioned way: through word of mouth (specifically, the taste buds).[22]

3. Psychology: Nostalgia Meets Novelty

The emotional magic came from bridging the familiar with the unexpected. Millennials recognized a brand from childhood, while Gen

Z—a demographic where over 57 percent enjoy gummy candies according to category research—adopted Nerds as an expressive, hyper-textural snack that felt different from traditional gummies.[23] This combination created an emotional relevance the original tiny-piece format never achieved, generating genuine stickiness (quite literally) courtesy of a little silliness.

4. Sociology: I Want Candy

Nerds became a must-have snackcessory wherever snacking was the norm, from movie nights to road trips to dorm room hang-outs. Ferrara leaned into TikTok Shop's candy-salad phenomenon, positioning Nerds Gummy Clusters as a social ingredient rather than just a snack. Trade coverage documented the brand's cultural resurgence throughout the grading period, helping Nerds slay the candy category.[24]

5. Economics: Sugar on Top

From 2020 to 2025, non-chocolate candy benefited from shifting consumer preferences toward gummy and chewy textures—non-chocolate chewy candy sales reached $6 billion in 2024, up 5.7 percent year over year.[25] Nerds became a top contributor to that surge, with Gummy Clusters growing at a 40 percent clip as of 2024.[26] As *Food Dive* reported, without Gummy Clusters, the brand would be closer to $100 million annually—instead, it's on track to exceed $900 million.[27] Not bad for a bunch of Nerds.

LESSONS LEARNED

Nerds proves that successful turnarounds can come from simple reinvention borne out of modern customer needs and wants. By integrating the best of a legacy brand into a high-demand new format, Ferrara created a "new original" for Gen Z—and sugary fuel for the TikTok fire.

Nerds: Sweet Revenge

Subject	2020 Grade	2025 Grade
Chemistry	C	A
Communications	C	B
Psychology	C	B
Sociology	D	B
Economics	C	A
Overall GPA	1.9	3.4

MEDIA AND ENTERTAINMENT: SNAP

BRAND GPA TRANSFORMATION: 1.8 → 3.0

THE POSTMORTEM

By 2020, Snap was in a quandary: culturally relevant but commercially stalled. TikTok was on fire—reaching 100 million US monthly active users by 2020—while Instagram had cloned Snapchat's signature feature with Stories in August 2016.[28] Wall Street still questioned whether Snap could grow beyond an ephemeral messaging app for teens. Daily active users climbed modestly from 218 million in Q4 2019 to 265 million by year-end 2020.[29] Everyone wondered if Snap would pull a disappearing act of its own. But between 2020 and 2025, the company snapped out of its funk by doubling down on what made it successful: messages and lenses. Daily active users climbed to 443 million by Q3 2024, and augmented reality engagement grew to over 300 thousand AR creators and more than 3 million lenses by Q4 2022, making Snap a fire starter of its own.[30]

THE FIVE DRIVERS OF THE COMEBACK

1. Chemistry: Don't Go Chasing Waterfalls

Snap went back to the rivers and lakes that differentiated it from the start: being the fastest, lowest-pressure way to communicate directly with friends. Snap also rebuilt its Android app, and company engineering documentation said the effort reduced slow cold starts and crash rates by 60 percent, cut frozen frames by 45 percent, and trimmed the APK size by 25MB.[31] Daily active users grew from 265 million in Q4 2020 to 319 million in 2021, 375 million in 2022, and 443 million by Q3 2024, with strong gains in international markets including Europe and Rest of World.[32] With 432 million DAUs against more than 850 million disclosed MAUs as of Q2 2024, Snap's DAU/MAU ratio of roughly 50 percent reflects strong habitual daily engagement.[33] The renewed focus on tight-knit communication—streaks, private stories, camera-first messaging—ensured product-market fit wouldn't expire ten seconds later.

2. Communications: Unfiltered and Unapologetic

By leaning into creativity, connection, and AR innovation rather than chasing TikTok and Instagram, Snap's voice grew stronger. That strategic clarity helped the business scale revenue from $2.51 billion in 2020 to $4.12 billion in 2021 and $4.60 billion in 2022—numbers that tell a better story than any estimate could.[34]

3. Psychology: Less Exposed, More Composed

As social media continued to make teens feel worse about themselves, Snap emphasized its ability to foster more authentic, less performative conversations. Independent research from the University of Amsterdam, published in 2025, found that time spent on TikTok, Instagram, and YouTube had consistent negative effects across measured mental health dimensions, while time spent on Snapchat positively affected friendship closeness and well-being with no significant impact on self-esteem.[35] Pew Research found 59 percent of US teens used Snapchat in 2022, while a 2024 Pew update put that figure at 55 percent.[36] Snap also reinforced trust with privacy-conscious users and their parents through persistent safety features—friend-only messaging defaults for teens, ephemeral content by default, and an experience centered more on direct communication than on a public algorithmic feed.

4. Sociology: I'll Be There for You

While TikTok and Instagram pushed users toward global broadcast, Snap focused on something different: friends. Snap reached more than 850 million monthly active users in Q2 2024, and Spotlight—launched in November 2020—exceeded 300 million monthly active users by Q3 2022.[37] While Spotlight gave Snap a TikTok-style surface, the platform's bigger win was investing in streaks, private stories, and group chats: features borne from the natural rituals of a younger generation.

5. Economics: Augmented Revenue

Snap's AR ad formats became a serious revenue stream, with over 300 thousand AR creators and 3 million lenses fueling a creator-to-advertiser ecosystem at scale.[38] Snapchat+—launched in June 2022 at $3.99 per month—surpassed 7 million subscribers by Q4 2023, growing further to 12 million by Q3 2024 and 14 million by Q4 2024.[39] Combined with a 20 percent workforce reduction in August 2022, Snap's adjusted EBITDA grew from $45 million in 2020 to $162 million in 2023, with the business delivering $617 million in adjusted EBITDA at its 2021 peak.[40] Oh, snap!

LESSONS LEARNED

Snap emerged as a formidable opponent to TikTok and Instagram by being true to itself. By leaning into intimacy, safety, and a camera-first thesis, the company rebuilt relevance with a generation that relied on it to shield them from performative pressures. In a world of algorithmic interference, Snap proved small circles and gated communication aren't ephemeral—they're essential.

Snap: A Snappy Comeback

Subject	2020 Grade	2025 Grade
Chemistry	C	A
Communications	C	B
Psychology	C	B
Sociology	C	B
Economics	D	B
Overall GPA	1.8	3.0

FITNESS AND WELLNESS: LIFE TIME

BRAND GPA TRANSFORMATION: 2.2 → 3.3

THE POSTMORTEM

By 2020, Life Time was totally out of shape. The pandemic forced 149 centers to close for some period during the quarter ended June 30, 2020, and the damage was swift and severe: Revenue fell from $1.90 billion in 2019 to $948 million in 2020, while adjusted EBITDA dropped from $437.9 million to negative $63.0 million.[41] Center memberships declined from approximately 854,000 to 501,000.[42] The company's long-term debt reached $2.399 billion by September 30, 2021.[43] But between 2020 and 2025, Life Time rebuilt its operating model. By fiscal year 2024, revenue rose to $2.62 billion, adjusted EBITDA reached $676.8 million with 25.8 percent margins, and center memberships climbed to

812,062.[44] The company completed an IPO in October 2021 and expanded to 179 centers by year-end 2024.[45] Talk about a flex.

THE FIVE DRIVERS OF THE COMEBACK

1. Chemistry: Product-Market Fitness

Life Time doubled down on its competitive advantage: a premium, multispace fitness environment that members continued to use frequently once conditions normalized. Center memberships rebounded from 500,948 in 2020 to 649,373 in 2021; 725,206 in 2022; 763,216 in 2023; and 812,062 in 2024.[46] Average visits per membership rose from 124 in 2022 to 135 in 2023 and 143 in 2024, while total visits climbed from 86 million in 2022 to over 114 million in 2024.[47] In other words, the brand was back in fit form.

2. Communications: A Clean Bill of Health

Life Time returned to its core "Healthy Way of Life" positioning and continued to build in affluent suburban and urban markets. Average revenue per center membership climbed from $1,317 in 2020 to $2,528 in 2022; $2,810 in 2023; and $3,160 in 2024, reinforcing the brand's ability to command premium pricing and proving that A-level messaging coupled with execution enhances performance the natural way.[48]

3. Psychology: Membership Has Its Privileges

Life Time's psychological edge came from making the membership feel worth returning to. The company's filings emphasize community, experience, and engagement, and the numbers show those qualities translating into behavior: Average revenue per center membership rose from $1,317 in 2020 to $3,160 in 2024,[49] so members were not only coming back—they were using the clubs more often and paying more for the experience. Life Time got extra reps in what matters most: customer experience.

4. Sociology: Not Just a Regular Gym but a Cool Gym

As wellness became more central to consumer identity, Life Time positioned itself as more than a stand-alone gym. The company continued expanding its "Healthy Way of Life" ecosystem in affluent suburban and urban locations, while also building adjacent offerings such as Life Time Work and Life Time Living.[50] That broadened the brand from a fitness destination into a more comprehensive wellness platform.

5. Economics: Returning to Growth and Discipline

Life Time executed a remarkable financial turnaround: Revenue rebounded from $948 million in 2020 to $2.22 billion in 2023 and $2.62 billion in 2024.[51] Adjusted EBITDA swung from negative $63.0 million in 2020 to $536.8 million in 2023 and $676.8 million in 2024, with margins expanding from negative 6.6 percent to 25.8 percent—above the company's 23 percent pre-pandemic margin in 2019.[52] Long-term debt fell to $1.556 billion at year-end 2024 from $2.399 billion on September 30, 2021.[53] The brand didn't just regain the strength it lost—it hit a slew of new PRs.

LESSONS LEARNED

Unlike other brands, Life Time's challenges weren't self-inflicted. While some businesses got a boost during the pandemic, Life Time—like many physical-first brands—saw its Brand GPA wasting away. Rather than waiting it out, the brand went into beast mode and used the downtime to get into even better shape by reinforcing premium value, elevating member experience, and operating with more financial discipline.

Life Time: From Pain to Gain

Subject	2020 Grade	2025 Grade
Chemistry	C	B
Communications	C	B
Psychology	C	B
Sociology	C	A
Economics	D	B
Overall GPA	2.2	3.1

HEALTH CARE: OSCAR HEALTH

BRAND GPA TRANSFORMATION: 1.6 → 3.0

THE POSTMORTEM

By 2021, Oscar Health was losing oxygen. Annual losses swelled from $406.8 million in 2020 to $572.7 million in 2021, medical loss ratios reached 88.9 percent, and the $39 IPO stock fell below $3 by late 2022.[54] Membership stood at 598,169 at year-end 2021.[55] Oscar exited Medicare Advantage for the 2024 plan year and pulled out of Arkansas and Colorado for 2023.[56] But there was still a pulse. Between 2021 and 2025, Oscar rebuilt its business with tighter underwriting and market discipline. By 2024, it posted its first profitable year with net income of $25.4 million, MLRs improved to 81.7 percent, membership surged to 1,698,000, and revenue hit $9.18 billion—more than quadrupling from $2.04 billion in 2020.[57] The stock staged a 957 percent rebound from its November 2022 low of $2.25 to a peak of $23.79 in February 2024.[58] The Brand GPA looked DOA, but the recovery was as miraculous as modern medicine.

THE FIVE DRIVERS OF THE COMEBACK

1. Chemistry: Vitals Stabilized

Oscar's Chemistry recovery is best measured through the metric regulators and insurers use to assess pricing discipline: medical loss ratio. An MLR of 88.9 percent in 2021 meant the plan was paying out nearly $0.89 of every premium dollar in claims—leaving almost nothing for operations, improvement, or stability. By 2024, Oscar had brought that figure down to 81.7 percent, a 720 basis-point improvement reflecting materially better underwriting discipline and claims management.[59] Membership grew from 598,169 in 2021 to 1,006,000 in 2022; 1,367,000 in 2023; and 1,698,000 in 2024—a 184 percent increase—demonstrating that when vital product fundamentals work, the relationship with customers stays healthy.[60]

2. Communications: Cured of Jargon

For years, Oscar talked the talk of a tech start-up, selling cleverness instead of clarity. But when it comes to health care, patients want just the facts. The brand's strategic pivot—exiting Medicare Advantage, pulling back from unprofitable markets, and refocusing on ACA individual plans—sent a clear signal to brokers, regulators, and members alike that Oscar was prioritizing sustainability over scale. Revenue grew from $3.79 billion in 2021 to $6.72 billion in 2022, $8.39 billion in 2023, and $9.18 billion in 2024, reflecting rapid membership expansion and stronger positioning in ACA marketplace plans.[61]

3. Psychology: No More Headaches

Navigating your health is daunting, so when the logistics are easier, it's less overwhelming. Oscar rebuilt confidence by tackling the emotional friction points that once made members more fearful of the brand than of their own health challenges. CMS Marketplace

Quality Rating System star ratings—which incorporate member experience measures derived from CAHPS surveys—showed Oscar individual marketplace plans receiving 3 to 3.5 stars across several state marketplace plans in the 2023 QRS release.[62] With more stable pricing and product offerings, Oscar moved closer to the performance range of top ACA plans.

4. Sociology: A Better Bedside Manner

Oscar's ACA-focused membership skews younger and more digitally engaged compared to traditional health insurance populations, according to the company's own SEC filings.[63] Its geographic concentration in highly populated metropolitan markets allowed Oscar to scale efficiently in communities where tech-savvy, ACA-eligible consumers were most concentrated.[64] As Oscar toned down the start-up swagger and became more vocal about protecting marketplace access and simplifying coverage—issues frequently cited by regulators and marketplace stakeholders—the brand's personality evolved from VC to MD, earning back trust from the customers who mattered most.

5. Economics: From Code Blue to Code Green

After a brutal $572.7 million loss in 2021, Oscar came off life support and achieved its first profitable year in 2024, posting net income of $25.4 million.[65] Revenue hit $9.18 billion as membership expanded from 598,169 in 2021 to 1,698,000 by 2024.[66] Medical loss ratios improved from 88.9 percent in 2021 to 81.7 percent in 2024, a 720 basis-point swing reflecting materially improved underwriting discipline.[67] And the stock told the whole story: from a low of $2.25 on November 3, 2022, to a peak of $23.79 on February 6, 2024—a 957 percent rebound.[68] Just what the doctor—well, the CFO—ordered.

LESSONS LEARNED

Oscar's rebound proves that *disruption* is really just a buzzword that gets in the way of the term that matters most: *discipline*. Once the brand turned its focus on customers and fixed the fundamentals, the company earned back trust by delivering a customer experience and cost structure that worked *for* members, not against them. And while this turnaround isn't a medical marvel, it certainly brought Oscar's Brand GPA back to life.

Oscar Health: A *Better* Pill to Swallow

Subject	2020 Grade	2025 Grade
Chemistry	D	B
Communications	D	B
Psychology	D	B
Sociology	C	B
Economics	D	B
Overall GPA	1.2	3.0

B2B TECH: ATLASSIAN

BRAND GPA TRANSFORMATION: 2.3 → 3.4

The Postmortem

By 2020 and into 2023, Atlassian had lost its way despite having a massive footprint across corporate IT. Growth slowed, paid seat expansion was challenged, particularly in SMB, and the forced server-to-cloud shift frustrated IT leaders who were once brand champions. Cloud deadlines confused customers, migrations felt rushed, and enterprise buyers started wondering what surprises might come next. The stock took a hit, and brand confidence needed a Jira ticket of its own. Between 2023 and 2025, the company clarified its cloud road map and gave admins predictable migration paths. Revenue and enterprise cloud customer expansion accelerated, the equivalent of putting "fixed" in the brand's resolution field.

THE FIVE DRIVERS OF THE COMEBACK

1. Chemistry: Cloud Illusions

The early cloud transition was, in a word, a disaster. System crashes were common, migration tools were confusing, and IT admins dreaded the process. By 2024–2025, Atlassian fixed the basics and the black cloud parted: Reliability improved, and migration tools could handle massive corporate moves without breaking everything. Cloud revenue grew 31 percent year over year in Q4 fiscal 2024 and 25 percent year over year in Q3 fiscal 2025, and customers with more than $10,000 in Cloud ARR reached 45,842 in fiscal 2024, up 18 percent year over year.[69] In enterprise software, 110 percent NRR is the benchmark for strong retention—18 percent enterprise customer expansion on top of that is taking names. How's that for a silver lining?

2. Communications: Less Surprise, More Delight

Atlassian's biggest problem wasn't what they said—it was when. The company announced in 2020 that server support would end, but the timeline felt abrupt to IT teams that need years to plan.[70] By 2023, Atlassian had built a more empathetic communications infrastructure: a cloud migration guide and migration resource hub, a public road map with quarterly email updates, and dedicated migration support.[71] They reinforced the February 15, 2024, deadline with countdown content, including hundred-day and day-by-day blogs.[72] See, sometimes in tech it is okay to take it offline, think outside the box, and circle back.

3. Psychology: Reassuring Through Reliability

Enterprise teams live inside Jira all day, so reliability and market confidence are priority one. In 2022, Atlassian was named a Leader in the Gartner Magic Quadrant for IT Service Management Platforms—up from Visionary in 2021—reflecting a meaningful shift in how enterprise buyers perceived the platform's maturity and trustworthiness.[73] Atlassian backed that positioning with Premium cloud products carrying a 99.9 percent uptime SLA and Enterprise products carrying 99.95 percent.[74] Jira Service Management earned a 4.5/5 rating on Gartner Peer Insights across more than 1,000 verified enterprise reviews, confirming that the confidence rebuild wasn't just analyst speak—it was showing up in real customer experience.[75] Now, if only engineers actually slept.

4. Sociology: Hybrid Is the New Black

The hybrid boom brought on by COVID reengineered how teams collaborate. Atlassian invested in ensuring Jira and Confluence became more dependable hubs for cross-functional work—and by fiscal 2025, approximately 50 percent of users of its core apps were business users, not just engineers.[76] Its Marketplace ecosystem grew from over 5,300 apps in 2022 to over 5,700 by April 2023, giving companies customization for specialized workflows.[77] Hy-Vee modernized ITSM with Jira Service Management Cloud and reported 100+ downtime hours saved annually.[78] That's the land-and-expand opportunity most enterprise brands only dream of.

5. Economics: Back to Basics

When Atlassian pushed the server-to-cloud shift, the math wasn't exactly mathing. Server revenue dried up, cloud migration costs piled up, and investors were about to give up. Once the transition got cleaned up, the economic skies cleared: Cloud revenue grew

31 percent year over year in Q4 fiscal 2024 and 25 percent year over year in Q3 fiscal 2025, and customers with more than $10,000 in Cloud ARR reached 45,842, up 18 percent year over year in fiscal 2024 as Premium and Enterprise tiers expanded.[79] Free cash flow strengthened to $555 million in Q3 fiscal 2024, up 59 percent year over year.[80] Atlassian shares rebounded sharply from their 2022 lows and jumped approximately 20 percent after strong Q2 fiscal 2025 results.[81] Revenue didn't just rebound—the brand did.

LESSONS LEARNED

Atlassian's comeback shows that even the most beloved enterprise tools can lose the room if they move faster than their customers can follow. The recovery wasn't about a new product—it was about earning back trust through transparency, predictability, and reliability. In enterprise software, confidence is the real killer app.

Atlassian: A Confluence of Comebacks

Subject	2020 Grade	2025 Grade
Chemistry	B	A
Communications	C	B
Psychology	C	B
Sociology	C	B
Economics	C	A
Overall GPA	2.3	3.4

EDUCATION: BLOOMTECH

BRAND GPA TRANSFORMATION: 1.6 → 3.0

The Postmortem

By 2020, BloomTech—then Lambda School—was failing fast. Independent reporting found that Lambda publicly claimed 86 percent of students landed tech jobs, while internal documents showed placement rates closer to 50 percent.[82] The CFPB later confirmed those findings, adding that for 2020 graduates, the placement rate in the first half of 2021 was only around 30 percent.[83] California regulators ordered Lambda to cease recruiting and enrolling students after finding it was operating without state approval.[84] Former students sued over alleged misrepresentation of placement rates and the ISA financing model, and the CFPB found BloomTech had issued more than 11,000 ISA loans between 2017 and 2023—falsely telling students the agreements were not loans, did not create debt, and were risk-free.[85] BloomTech cut roughly half its staff in December 2022, and the CFPB ultimately permanently barred BloomTech from consumer lending and banned founder Austen Allred from student-lending activities for ten years.[86] The rebrand to Bloom Institute of Technology was announced in November 2021, with the legal name change to BloomTech Inc. following in 2022.[87] After enrolling in the school of hard knocks, BloomTech is starting to blossom again.

THE FIVE DRIVERS OF THE COMEBACK

1. Chemistry: Moving the Goal Post

When the brand was Lambda, the core issue wasn't getting people into courses—it was getting them out. California's BPPE performance data showed Full Stack Web Development on-time completion rates of just 27 percent in 2021 and 0 percent in 2022, with placement rates of 44 percent in 2021 and 40 percent in 2022.[88] BloomTech's California-approved program structure set a maximum completion window of eighteen consecutive calendar months.[89] BloomTech's programs typically ran six to nine months, per the CFPB consent order, giving students a clearer path to completion.[90] Sometimes less really is more.

2. Communications: Radical Transparency

When Lambda was at its worst, students couldn't get a straight answer about outcomes or financing—a communications F-bomb that tanked trust. As part of the rebrand, BloomTech published company-authored outcomes reports and, according to BloomTech, rewrote financing terms to offer up-front and deferred tuition options alongside the Tuition Refund Guarantee as a credibility anchor.[91] The shift wasn't just cosmetic—it was a direct response to being caught grading their own homework with inflated numbers.

3. Psychology: School Ties

Lambda's old model left students feeling lost, with sprawling timelines and uneven instruction—and the tales they told out of school were damaging. The shift to BloomTech addressed the emotional friction points directly: Programs typically running six to nine months meant students could see the finish line, and according to BloomTech, the Tuition Refund Guarantee replaced anxiety about outcomes with a contractual commitment.[92] When expectations became more predictable and financing terms became more transparent, the brand had at least earned the right to be trusted again.

4. Sociology: New School of Thought

By the early 2020s, the coding bootcamp boom had cooled because employers weren't buying it—literally. Many programs promised six-figure dream jobs after twelve weeks, but hype rarely translated into career advancement. BloomTech shied away from the fantastical and focused on workforce reality. Programs became more structured, focusing on entry-level paths across Backend Development, Full Stack Web Development, and Data Science.[93] The brand's pivot away from ISA-funded growth toward outcome-anchored programming repositioned it as a more credible player in a category desperately in need of one.

5. Economics: From Burn to Earn

The financial model under the Lambda name was a cash sinkhole. The CFPB found BloomTech issued more than 11,000 ISA loans between 2017 and 2023—a model that ultimately collapsed under regulatory and legal pressure.[94] The CFPB permanently barred BloomTech from consumer lending and banned its founder from the student-lending business for ten years.[95] The BloomTech rebrand ushered in a structural overhaul: Shorter programs reduced time to completion, and according to BloomTech, fixed-cost tuition and deferred payment options reduced dependence on ISA financing.[96] With the regulatory overhang addressed and the program model simplified, BloomTech had the clean code of growth it needed: a more predictable economic model.

LESSONS LEARNED

BloomTech's comeback proves you can't just rebrand your way out of a credibility crisis—you have to earn your way out. Once the company stopped promising miracle jobs and aligned to how people actually get hired, things rebounded. Shorter programs, clearer financing, and a guarantee backed by real eligibility requirements didn't just fix the academic experience—they made the business model smarter. Lambda got schooled by hype and hope, but BloomTech made the grade with simplicity and substance.

BloomTech: Coming into Bloom

Subject	2020 Grade	2025 Grade
Chemistry	C	B
Communications	D	B
Psychology	C	B
Sociology	C	B
Economics	C	B
Overall GPA	1.6	3.0

FOOD SERVICE: CHIPOTLE

BRAND GPA TRANSFORMATION: 2.0 → 3.4

The Postmortem

By the early 2020s, Chipotle was no longer all that and a bag of tortilla chips. Portion-size frustration spread across TikTok (when it comes to food, less is never more), delivery fees ate into Value Perception, and same-store sales growth cooled from its post-pandemic surge of 19.3 percent in 2021 to 8.0 percent in 2022 and 7.9 percent in 2023.[97] Digital sales, once hotter than a habanero at 45.6 percent of sales in 2021, eased to 37.4 percent in 2023 and 35.1 percent in 2024.[98] Between 2023 and 2025, the company tightened operations, invested in faster service, and leaned into menu innovation. Revenue climbed to record highs and the brand got its mojo back.

THE FIVE DRIVERS OF THE COMEBACK

1. Chemistry: Bowled Over

After getting roasted online for stingy portions, Chipotle acknowledged that roughly 10 percent of the system needed retraining and moved to reemphasize consistent, generous portions across all locations.[99] It sped up service and doubled down on throughput improvements. Chicken al Pastor returned to the menu in 2024, giving customers a fresh reason to come back in.[100] The company opened 271 new restaurants in 2024, the majority with Chipotlanes—now in over 80 percent of planned new locations—keeping wait times down for digital orders.[101] Online ordering once again became their bread and butter (well, tortilla and salsa).

2. Communications: Substance, with a Side of Style

For a while, the exact same menu item had different prices depending on how you ordered. The brand rewrote in-app pricing explanations so customers understood what was menu price vs. delivery markup, and used short-form video to demonstrate what a full serving looked like. The Chipotle app held a 4.6 rating on Apple's App Store.[102] Chipotle Rewards surpassed thirty-six million members, with Freepotle as a named 2023 promotion within the program.[103] Ingredient spotlight videos routinely racked up massive view counts, helping Chipotle steer the conversation instead of playing defense with the TikTok haters.

3. Psychology: Confidence on the Line

Chipotle rebuilt customer confidence by ensuring customers didn't leave hangry. The app featured a redesigned build flow so people could see calorie counts, ingredient swaps, and portion options before checking out. The brand gave control back with predictable ready times, better order tracking, and distinct Chipotlanes that improved access and convenience. Restaurant-level operating margin improved to 27.5 percent in 2024, reflecting an operation that was running cleaner, faster, and more reliably than it had in years.[104] But more importantly, it left customers satiated—and appreciated.

4. Sociology: Catching Some Zs

Chipotle isn't just a brand—it's part of culture. So when the vibe dipped online, Chipotle faced the harsh music, fixed the issues, then built content to earn cheers from younger audiences. Its content strategy focused on real ingredients—zero artificial colors, flavors, or preservatives, as confirmed in the company's 2024 10-K—support for local growers, and investment in workforce education.[105] It paired those moves with creator partnerships through the Chipotle Creator Class, launched in 2021, and worker POV videos that racked up massive view counts across platforms.[106] The brand didn't chase Gen Z—it earned them.

5. Economics: A Little Reset Goes a Long Way

When inflation spiked in 2022, some pain was self-inflicted—portion inconsistencies and clunky digital pricing made value feel like it was slipping. But comparable restaurant transactions turned positive in 2023 and 2024, climbing 5.0 percent and 5.3 percent respectively.[107] Average unit volumes reached $3.2 million per restaurant in 2024, full-year revenue hit $11.3 billion—a record—and operating income exceeded $2.1 billion.[108] The stock surged above $3,000 before a June 2024 50-for-1 stock split.[109] Chipotle didn't just stop being stingy with portions—it stopped being stingy with results.

LESSONS LEARNED

Chipotle's rebound proves you don't need to hit rock bottom to stage a comeback. Sometimes, it's getting back to basics that gets your Brand GPA back in strong standing. Portions that felt fair, waits that felt reasonable, and digital ordering that felt honest—none of these was a headline-grabbing strategy MBA students will study for decades. But all of them moved the needle, proving that when Value Perception heats up and logistical challenges simmer down, the money—and brand love—will flow. Chipotle didn't reinvent the wheel (or in their case, the bowl)—they listened to customers and took care of business. And that's a wrap.

Chipotle: A Tasty Turnaround

Subject	2020 Grade	2025 Grade
Chemistry	C	A
Communications	C	B
Psychology	C	B
Sociology	C	B
Economics	C	A
Overall GPA	2.0	3.4

TRAVEL: NORWEGIAN CRUISE LINE

BRAND GPA TRANSFORMATION: 1.5 → 3.0

The Postmortem

To the cruise industry, the onset of COVID was like hitting an iceberg. Norwegian ships sat idle, monthly cash burn averaged about $345 million in Q4 2021 and was projected to reach roughly $390 million entering Q1 2022, and the brand loaded up on expensive debt just to stay afloat—reaching $13.9 billion by September 30, 2022.[110] Customer trust was also low. Long hold times and refund delays left travelers frustrated, booking volumes lagged competitors' early rebound, and the stock hit multiyear lows in 2022. But by 2023–2025, the brand showed real signs of comeback: Norwegian *Prima* (2022), Norwegian *Viva* (2023), and Norwegian *Aqua* (2025) launched to strong demand, advance ticket sales reached $3.1 billion in Q3 2023—59 percent above Q3 2019 levels—and the Q4 2023 booked position hit record levels at higher pricing.[111] Finally, the wind was at the brand's back.

THE FIVE DRIVERS OF THE COMEBACK

1. Chemistry: Putting the Love Back into the Boat

Norwegian's product is its ships, so to win customers back, the brand focused on the onboard experience. The *Prima*-class ships expanded the premium onboard product, and Norwegian reported robust onboard revenue generation across all revenue streams during the recovery period.[112] The newer vessels consistently generated strong onboard revenue, forward bookings, and higher onboard spending—creating a self-reinforcing loop that had customers falling back in love with the open sea.

2. Communications: Steering Toward Clarity

Nothing eroded Norwegian's brand faster between 2020 and 2022 than confusing messaging. Refund timelines dragged on for months, COVID rules changed faster than passengers could rebook, and itinerary updates were buried in legalese. By 2023–2025, the company's most visible customer-facing move was replacing Free at Sea with the more straightforward More at Sea package beginning January 1, 2025.[113] The rest of the communications cleanup is harder to prove with primary sources, but we give Norwegian credit for the policy simplification, letting the booking numbers do the real talking.

3. Psychology: Smooth Sailing Ahead

Between 2020 and 2022, Norwegian guests were anxious, but the brand did little to ease concerns. Cruises were routinely overbooked, last-minute policy changes felt constant, and communications were a mess. By 2023–2025, the return of forward bookings at higher pricing told the real story: Travelers were once again willing to commit earlier and pay more—an important proxy for restored confidence.[114] In March 2024, S&P upgraded NCL Corporation's issuer credit rating to B+, citing the company's forward-booked position, occupancy recovery, and higher pricing—outside validation that the comeback had become structurally credible, not just cosmetically better.[115] Finally, some cruise control.

4. Sociology: Back in the Social Current

Air travel is a means to an end, but cruising is culture. For a while, Norwegian struggled as travelers gravitated toward brands with simpler bundles. But from 2023 to 2025, as younger travelers showed rising interest in cruising industry-wide, Norwegian's newer *Prima*-class product gave the brand a more contemporary platform to compete for that demand.[116] CLIA's 2024 *State of the Cruise Industry Report* confirmed that millennial and Gen Z interest in cruising was climbing, and Norwegian certainly put in the work to benefit from the generational shift.[117]

5. Economics: Staying Afloat

Norwegian's business faced serious challenges between 2020 and 2022. Debt climbed to $13.9 billion by September 30, 2022, monthly cash burn was severe, and advanced-ticket booking collapsed.[118] But over the next three years, revenue jumped from $4.844 billion in 2022 to $9.480 billion in 2024, powered by occupancy reaching 104.9 percent and strong onboard spending.[119] Net yield increased 8.7 percent year over year in Q3 2024, and adjusted EBITDA reached approximately $2.45 billion in 2024.[120] The stock staged a significant recovery as demand normalized. The financial anchors were, at last, aweigh.

LESSONS LEARNED

Norwegian's comeback shows that running a tight ship on the basics is the fastest path toward recovery. The brand earned back trust not through reinvention but through discipline—simplifying policies, improving reliability, and upgrading the onboard experience. The takeaway is straightforward: When a company's actions become predictable, transparent, and customer centric, rising tides can lift the Brand GPA back to great heights.

Norwegian: Running a Tight(er) Ship

Subject	2020 Grade	2025 Grade
Chemistry	D	B
Communications	D	B
Psychology	D	B
Sociology	C	B
Economics	D	B
Overall GPA	1.5	3.0

ON-DEMAND: INSTACART

BRAND GPA TRANSFORMATION: 2.3 → 3.1

The Postmortem

Unlike Norwegian Cruise Line, the pandemic was a business boom for Instacart. But like most pandemic beneficiaries, the high highs were a false positive. As in-person grocery shopping normalized, GTV growth moderated—reaching $28.823 billion in 2022, then growing to $30.322 billion in 2023 and $33.461 billion in 2024.[121] Delivery fees felt unnecessary, app issues were routine, and the delayed IPO launched in September 2023 at a $9.9 billion valuation—fueling speculation that the model wasn't sustainable.[122] But between 2023 and 2025, Instacart cleaned up all of its messy aisles, clarified pricing, and tightened operations, turning a pandemic fling into a sustainable business.

THE FIVE DRIVERS OF THE COMEBACK

1. Chemistry: Putting the Wheels Back on the Cart

Instacart improved what mattered most: accuracy, speed, and reliability. Batch assignment improvements meant more predictable delivery windows, and as customers blended orders across multiple stores, repeat usage strengthened. The retailer network expanded from more than 1,400 banners at IPO to more than 1,800 banners in North America by 2024, giving customers access to more of what they actually wanted.[123] Full-year 2024 orders reached 294 million, up 9 percent year over year, making the brand a weekly essential instead of a crisis one-off.[124]

2. Communications: SKUing Toward Clarity

For a brand that's supposed to take the hassle out of grocery shopping, Instacart's communication tactics often did the opposite—customers didn't always understand pricing and didn't always get timely updates. Instacart rewired its communications: Service, delivery, and item-level price differences were separated into clear explanations in-app, and real-time stock signals surfaced earlier in the shopping flow. Full-year 2024 total revenue reached $3.378 billion, up 11 percent year over year, reflecting a platform customers were increasingly willing to pay for.[125] Shoppers more gleefully filled their carts.

3. Psychology: Gutting the Grocery Guesswork

It felt like you needed a fortune teller when using Instacart. Would orders be on time? Would you get what you actually selected? Instacart tightened the predelivery journey. Real-time tracking became more accurate, shopper chat became faster, and clearer ETA windows reduced the "where is my order?" anxiety. As reliability improved, customers responded: Orders grew 14 percent year over year in Q3 2025.[126]

4. Sociology: Aligning with Retail Rather Than Competing with It

As life normalized post-COVID, grocery delivery risked slipping back into "nice to have" territory. The brand leaned into how people actually shop: mixing delivery with curbside pickup, blending multiple stores in a single order, and honoring local preferences through retailer partnerships. By 2024, Instacart had partnered with more than 1,800 retail banners, reaching 98 percent of households in North America.[127] By mirroring how people shop, Instacart became less of a calamity commodity and more of a cultural constant.

5. Economics: Retail Media Becomes the Engine

Instacart had a pandemic boom, but the stronger story came later. The brand leaned into retail media ads, the one-time side hustle that ballooned into a major profit driver. Advertising and other revenue reached $958 million in 2024, up 10 percent year over year, and by Q3 2025, the advertising business was generating $269 million quarterly—powered by more than 7,500 brands that advertise on Instacart.[128] Full-year 2024 adjusted EBITDA reached $885 million, up 38 percent year over year, and by Q4 2024, Instacart posted $148 million in net income and $252 million in adjusted EBITDA.[129] With ads helping subsidize fulfillment, Instacart made its whole business basket better and smarter.

LESSONS LEARNED

Instacart has had quite a journey: from novelty to necessity to not sure back to necessity—but in a different context. During the pandemic, it was critical, but when the coast cleared, the value wasn't strong enough to stay essential. Today, it's a preference—and more shoppers are opting in. The brand's rebound shows that you don't need a breakthrough idea to win customers; you just need to understand them and their needs—preferably before their wheels get squeaky.

Instacart: From Buggy to Baddie

Subject	2020 Grade	2025 Grade
Chemistry	B	B
Communications	C	B
Psychology	C	B
Sociology	C	A
Economics	C	B
Overall GPA	2.3	3.1

FINANCIAL SERVICES: ALLY

BRAND GPA TRANSFORMATION: 2.3 → 3.2

The Postmortem

Ally entered 2020 loaded with fanfare, and it banked on that buzz to grow in the new decade. But then near-zero interest rates wiped out much of the company's earning power—net interest margin fell to 2.40 percent in Q2 2020, down twenty-six basis points from the prior year.[130] Auto-loan delinquencies edged higher through 2024, call-center wait times spiked, and customers questioned whether an online-only bank could keep pace with traditional institutions.[131] Hold times were long, dispute resolution felt sluggish, and the brand went from digital darling to something closer to a dot-com dud. Fortunately, that didn't break the bank, and from 2023 to 2025,

Ally regained momentum. Rates normalized, deposits held steady, service stabilized, and financial performance strengthened, helping rebuild customer trust—and a Brand GPA in default.

THE FIVE DRIVERS OF THE COMEBACK

1. Chemistry: A Bank to Count On

When interest rates fell to near zero in 2020, the bank's appeal took a major hit. A digital bank without yield is, well, unremarkable. The brand expanded features like early direct deposit and other digital banking tools as part of its strategy to deepen primary customer relationships and engagement.[132] Total deposits at Ally Bank were $152.3 billion at year-end 2022, $154.7 billion at year-end 2023, and $154.8 billion by year-end 2024—making Ally one of the largest digital-only banks in the US, with approximately three million retail customers.[133] When APYs climbed back up—reaching 4.20 percent in September 2024, according to Ally Bank—that was just gravy.[134] Customers now valued the broader suite, and Ally had the beginnings of a meaningful recovery.

2. Communications: Doing It Right

Managing money can be daunting, so customers depend on banks to be available when they need them and to communicate clearly—and simply. Unfortunately, during the pandemic, Ally's communication playbook lost the plot. Customers faced long hold times, statement disclosures were confusing, and basic updates—from rate changes to dispute timelines—weren't clear. But between 2023 and 2025, Ally got back to its "Do It Right" roots and did just that. It overhauled its support routing so response times returned to pre-COVID norms, rewrote product pages and rate explanations to cut out the jargon, and expanded its educational content so people actually understood how to use its tools—and customers started feeling like more than just a number.

3. Psychology: Becoming a True Ally

Sadly, money doesn't grow on trees, but most people still rely on branches—unless you're Ally. The strictly online bank made customers feel in line between 2020 and 2022, with seemingly endless wait times on the phone preventing swift solutions for opaque account summaries and many other issues. By 2023–2025, Ally saw the light and rebuilt customer trust with accurate account data, faster dispute resolution, and financial literacy content delivered in plain language, not banker-speak. By giving customers better support and a sense of control over their money, the brand started living up to its own name.

4. Sociology: A Mission of Mobility

Big banks poured billions into becoming more digital, making consumer fintech vulnerable. But Ally showed that standing behind the causes your customers care about builds sustainable brand credibility. The brand expanded financial literacy programs, funded women- and minority-owned businesses through Moguls in the Making—a program run with the Thurgood Marshall College Fund that has supported nearly four hundred students with nearly $1.5 million in scholarships and prizes—committed over $150 million to workforce development initiatives, and provided nearly $3 million in grants to 113 nonprofit partners.[135] A bank with a soul—who knew?

5. Economics: A Diversified Portfolio

Rate recovery helped, but Ally had already done the hard work. Total deposits held firm at $152.3 billion in 2022, $154.7 billion in 2023, and $154.8 billion in 2024, while GAAP net financing revenue came in at $6.201 billion in 2023 and $6.014 billion in 2024.[136] Net interest margin recovered to 3.33 percent in Q4 2024 and 3.47 percent for full-year 2025, demonstrating post-rate-cycle recovery.[137] Auto credit performance stabilized under tighter underwriting even as delinquencies edged higher through 2024.[138] New businesses like credit cards and SMB banking reduced reliance on auto lending, and Ally remained fee free with no overdraft fees or monthly maintenance charges.[139] That's the ultimate win for customers trying to build wealth—and a business trying to build a moat.

LESSONS LEARNED

When rates collapsed and service faltered, customers questioned whether a bank without branches could weather the storm. But Ally proved that bricks and mortar is just an illusion of trust. By tightening operations, clarifying communications, and ensuring "Do It Right" was literal, not figurative, Ally got back on a path of Brand GPA greatness. When you bank on what customers actually value, you don't just survive rate cycles—you compound trust.

Ally: Unbreaking the Bank

Subject	2020 Grade	2025 Grade
Chemistry	B	B
Communications	C	B
Psychology	C	B
Sociology	C	B
Economics	C	A
Overall GPA	2.3	3.2

GETTING AHEAD OF THE CURVE

Turnarounds rarely happen quickly. Progress happens quarter by quarter, not overnight. The Comeback Kids featured here prove something essential: A low Brand GPA doesn't have to be a death sentence. Every brand in this chapter started in a slump, but over five years, each rebuilt its way to better and more consistent performance across the five subjects of the Brand GPA.

Brands that pull themselves out of decline do so by recommitting to product relevance, clarifying their message, rebuilding emotional trust, aligning with cultural expectations, and operating with sharper financial discipline. Abercrombie modernized its identity. Chipotle rebuilt its kitchen. Atlassian stabilized its road map. Oscar fixed its fundamentals. Their specifics differ, but their major Brand GPA improvements unify them.

And just like in academia, a rough semester doesn't get you expelled. Falling behind over a quarter (or in many cases, several quarters) doesn't mean your brand is finished. But you have to study the subjects where you're struggling, seek out extra help, cut out the distractions, and put in the work so you can score points toward prosperity with your customers.

That's the real lesson of the Comeback Kids: Even when your brand is behind the curve, all hope is not lost. The data might be grim, but with self-reflection, patience, and cross-functional alignment, *any* organization can raise its GPA—and become customers' pet once again.

CHAPTER 9

CLASS SUMMARY

WELL, YOU DID IT. YOU MADE IT TO THE END. And just like Colonel Steve Austin, aka the Six Million Dollar Man, you're now better, stronger, and faster than you were before. The Brand GPA will allow you to add the right bionics to your brand so that you can consistently earn straight As from the people who matter most: your customers. You've studied the framework, marveled at the Valedictorians, and cheered on the Comeback Kids, so now you know what it takes to be top of the class.

Now what?

Before you do anything else, here are three things you can do this week to start improving your Brand GPA:

1. **Take the pop quizzes (again):** If you haven't yet, you're ready to ace this. Already took them? Gold star! But it's a great idea to revisit the subjects where your scores were lowest—Chemistry if product engagement is shaky, Communications if complaints are piling up, Psychology if churn is increasing, Sociology if you're getting blown up on social media, or Economics if revenue is flatlining. There's a good chance your score will look different now that you've read the whole playbook.

2. **Focus on the metrics that matter:** You don't need a complete syllabus on day one. Just grab five key numbers that are critical to the customer experience, such as your retention rate (Chemistry), your CSAT score (Communications), your self-service resolution rate (Psychology), your values Alignment survey result (Sociology), and your price-to-value satisfaction score (Economics). Put them in a spreadsheet. Congratulations—you just created your back-of-the-envelope Brand GPA report card!
3. **Use the buddy system:** Don't keep this framework to yourself—or solely in your department. Whether it's your CEO, your product lead, your head of customer success, or your finance point person, start a conversation about the five subjects and your initial assessment. Then build consensus and run a full diagnostic so you can improve not only your Brand GPA but also how your organization works together.

CHANGE (AI)GENT

Implementation will no doubt be the hardest part, namely because change is hard, but also because there are distractions everywhere. You're not only trying to make the grade with your customers, but your board, shareholders, and employees all have their red pens out as well. And then there's the artificial elephant in the room: AI.

I know most leaders are getting bogged down with how to implement AI ASAP, while also living in fear that they've already flunked out. But here's the deal: It comes down to noise vs. signal. AI is the big, noisy bot on campus, and every day on LinkedIn, there are a slew of hot takes and heated "taste great/less filling" arguments about whether SEO is dead, if AEO or GEO is the future, if AI rank trackers are legitimate tools or complete BS, and oh, here are the fifty-two prompts you must use every day to get ahead. Calgon, take me away!

This can leave you confused about what to do and paranoid that you aren't doing enough. Yet in all the AI noise, there's one signal that cuts through clearly: your customer's assessment of your brand. And that signal has been remarkably consistent across every technological shift we've seen, from web 1.0 to smartphones to social media to now. So I go back to basics—sort of like the three Rs of academia—and ask the question, "How might AI help me improve my Brand GPA?" If an AI solution can help you accelerate a better experience for your customers, bring it on. If it will only augment the problem, run fast.

As my former colleague at both Google and Northwestern, Jim Lecinski, a professor and leading voice on AI and marketing, notes, most businesses are stuck asking AI to do the same things "faster, cheaper, easier."[1] But the companies actually winning are using AI to do things that were never possible for their customers before. In other words, they're using AI to enhance the customer experience, not replace it.

YES, *AND* . . .

When MTV launched in 1981, their very first video was the Buggles' "Video Killed the Radio Star," an ominous choice of a generally underground song meant to subtly warn of the changes to come. But in reality, video enhanced the radio star, by giving consumers the ability to see their favorite artists and appreciate their music in a whole new light.

The same things have happened in business, particularly over the last thirty years. First the dot-com boom in the late '90s meant every brand had to be online or else. But the internet bubble burst in the early 2000s—not because the technology was overhyped but because businesses whose only real brand value was being online got exposed quickly by always-discerning consumers. They failed not because they didn't use the internet correctly but because they were all sizzle and no steak (or in academic terms, all electives).

In the words of actor Anne Hathaway to a gaggle of her most impassioned Italian fans: *Calma!* It's easy (and expected) to feel anxious, especially given that AI is moving at breakneck speed.

But to borrow the golden rule of improv, we need to adopt a "yes, and . . ." approach when it comes to AI (and anything else that is bound to appear down the road). For those not familiar, that simple little phrase is a powerful rule that teaches performers to build on and accept their scene partner's ideas rather than shutting them down. So yes, we need to ensure that we are making the grade with our customers, and we need to be open to AI (and other technologies) that can help us earn a better GPA more swiftly. And vice versa.

According to Salesforce's 2024 *State of the Connected Customer* report, 61 percent of customers say advances in AI make it more important that companies are trustworthy—meaning AI is raising the trust bar, not lowering it.[2] Meanwhile, PwC found that 82 percent of consumers still want more human interaction in customer service experiences as technology increases, and Zendesk's 2024 CX Trends report shows that 53 percent say it's important that companies provide a human option when AI is involved.[3] That doesn't mean customers are anti-AI—just like they weren't anti-dot-com, anti-mobile, or anti-social. New technologies always enter the chat, and inevitably, brands scramble to adopt them at breakneck speed.

But consumers are often on a different timeline, so be careful not to over-index on what's hot technologically within a business but lukewarm outside of it. Leverage AI to deliver a great experience more often than you could without it and your brand will thrive. Use it to water down what makes your brand special, and you'll hear about it—loudly.

Am I saying that AI doesn't have the chops to be bigger and more transformative than any technology we've seen before? Absolutely not. It's a massive redwood that seems to get taller every day. But don't lose the customer forest for the AI trees. If history repeats itself (and I am betting big—in the form of a book!—that it will), both brands and customers will eventually find common ground with AI.

But even then customers will continue to be tough graders. No matter what technological tidal wave is beating down on your business, customers still want brands to deliver real value, communicate clearly, create emotional connections, and align with their values if they expect them to keep coming back. The Valedictorians and Comeback Kids we studied didn't get there by chasing the latest technology—they got there by mastering the fundamentals and letting technology serve the customer, not replace them.

BRAND GPA—OR BUST

Think of the Brand GPA as insurance against uncertainty. You can't predict which AI tool will win, which optimization tactic will work, or what the next big disruption will be. But you can predict that customers will continue to reward brands that understand them, serve them well, and earn their loyalty day after day.

The question isn't if you're being graded or not—you are, constantly. Customers are evaluating your Chemistry through their usage and retention. They're scoring your Communications through every interaction and touchpoint. They're measuring your Psychology through how you make them feel. They're judging your Sociology through your values and actions. They're calculating your Economics through the value you deliver relative to what you charge. The question is whether you're going to take those grades seriously, measure them systematically, and use them to guide your decisions.

As you audit your own brand, you might find that it earns high marks in one subject but is a total slacker in another. That's a feature of the Brand GPA, not a bug. Why? Because it happens more often than you think. For instance, a brand can be a Communications misfit, but in Sociology it performs like a completely different pupil. Same brand, same time period, two wildly diverging grades. And for those of you reading who were great at math but not so hot in history, this might sound familiar.

That's why the Brand GPA is so important. It surfaces where you're winning and where you're losing across every part of the customer experience. Just like when you were in school, your report card revealed how you were really doing despite what you might have told your parents. It's the same thing with the Brand GPA: It won't let your brand take a premature victory lap unless all cylinders are firing.

HAPPILY EVER AFTER

Imagine presenting at your next quarterly company all-hands or walking into your next board meeting with a simple but transparent Brand GPA dashboard: Your Chemistry grade is trending up due to improved retention, your Communications grade dropped after support-response-time issues, your Psychology grade is steady quarter over quarter, Sociology is going strong despite some temporary political pressures, and Economics is where you want it, but pricing pressure in a few key markets means some tough tests are ahead. Suddenly, resource allocation decisions become clear. Team priorities align around improving specific grades rather than chasing whatever tactic dominated last week's LinkedIn debates. Eureka!

The Brand GPA is more than a measurement tool—it's a Swiss Army knife methodology that delivers a brand health diagnostic, a strategic planning framework, and a common language for measuring what your customers actually care about—rolled into one score that's easy to track, defend, and act on over time.

It's also a vehicle that allows you to integrate the latest and greatest AI—or any other hot new technology that comes along—while keeping your focus locked on the one thing AI will never replace: your customer.

Class dismissed.

ACKNOWLEDGMENTS

WRITING A BOOK IS NOT FOR THE FAINT OF HEART, and it takes a mighty cast of people to help get you over the finish line. So here comes some gratitude.

First, I want to thank the teams at Fast Company Press and Greenleaf for their guidance and support—especially Justin, Jen, Divine, Brittany, Rachel, and Gwen. Thanks a million times over to my editors, Elizabeth Brown, Hayden Seder, and Tess Newton, for keeping me honest and making me better, and to Brian Phillips for the brilliant cover art. I also want to thank Tania Rahman for the introduction that changed everything.

Next, I want to thank my muse Jennifer Aaker for telling me never to write a book, but when I did, giving me nothing but tremendous advice and support. I also want to thank my other muses Kim Scott, Andy Cunningham, Leslie Blodgett, and Sarah Robb O'Hagan, whose journeys into authorship and unique points of view motivated me to share mine more than they will know.

I have to give special credit to my past teams and colleagues who helped me fight the good fight when it came to trying to give brand a permanent seat at the table. I also thank those who were the antagonists—I wouldn't have the perspective I have without those sparring matches! And to my OG sensei Dick Costolo, thanks for teaching me that a little humor helps sell the point.

I also need to acknowledge First Republic Bank (RIP) for being such an exceptional brand and Chase for acquiring them and absorbing none of their goodness. That's what got me thinking about what makes a brand really tick and what motivated me to flesh out the framework, so I guess in a strange way, I'm expressing my gratitude for corporate M&A.

And then there's the behind-the-scenes crew who deserve their moment in the spotlight. I want to thank my friends and family who cheered from the sidelines and gave me feedback along the way. Sadia Harper—your gumption to tell your story gave me the spark to tell this one, so thanks for giving me the writing bug. Elsa Broeker—thanks for those sharp legal eyes. Nick Cromydas, Kate Garmey, AJ Hassan, Dan Hickle, Julie Homan, Anne Mercogliano, Grant Muenter, Andrea Perez, Mandana Varahrami, Stuart Winchester, and my forever veep Katie Stanton—thank you all for being my tribal council, for your honest feedback, and for convincing me there is an audience for this.

To my parents, Kathi and Bruce, and sisters, Jess and Mel—thanks for pretending to understand what the book is about and for being so proud (especially Mom). To my godmother Darryln and stepmother Karen—thanks for cheering me on as always. Sonya Grimaldi—thanks for kicking my ass in seventh grade and teaching me how to write. Ashley, Jon, Claire, Julie, the Rxs and the Modern Family near and far—I couldn't have done it without you checking in and telling me I could. Thank you for being the best group of friends/hype squad ever. And last but not least, Michael—thank you for enduring my manic writing fits and making me take breaks when I started seeing spots. You helped me do this.

NOTES

INTRODUCTION: TO BRAND OR NOT TO BRAND . . .

1. Gartner, "Gartner Predicts Over 40% of CMOs Who Push for Larger Brand Budgets Will Lose Influence with the C-Suite," press release, February 12, 2026, gartner.com/en/newsroom/press-releases/2026-2-12-gartner-predicts-over-40-percent-of-cmos-who-push-for-larger-brand-budgets-will-lose-influence-with-the-c-suite.

2. Barry Diller, interview by Kara Swisher, *On with Kara Swisher*, "Barry Diller Unfiltered: on Family, Fortune, Elon, Trump & AI," Vox Media Podcast Network, May 19, 2025, https://podcasts.apple.com/us/podcast/barry-diller-unfiltered-on-family-fortune-elon-trump-ai/id1643307527?i=1000708970882.

3. Gartner, "Gartner Predicts over 40%."

4. Elena Verna, "Brand . . . a Product Job Now?" *Elena's Growth Scoop*, Nov 24, 2025, https://www.elenaverna.com/p/brand-a-product-job-now.

CHAPTER 1: THE BRAND GPA

1. "Retaining Customers Is the Real Challenge," Bain & Company, January 2006, https://www.bain.com/insights/retaining-customers-is-the-real-challenge/.

2. Nidhi Arora et al., "The Value of Getting Personalization Right—or Wrong—Is Multiplying," McKinsey & Company, November 12, 2021, https://www.mckinsey.com/capabilities/growth-marketing-and-sales/our-insights/the-value-of-getting-personalization-right-or-wrong-is-multiplying.

3. *Experience Is Everything: Here's How to Get It Right* (PwC, 2018), https://www.pwc.de/de/consulting/pwc-consumer-intelligence-series-customer-experience.pdf.

4. *2024 Edelman Trust Barometer* (Edelman, 2024), edelman.com/trust/2024/trust-barometer.

CHAPTER 2: CHEMISTRY

1. *The State of Personalization 2022* (Twilio Segment, April 2022), https://www.scribd.com/document/587861199/State-of-Personalization-Report-Twilio-Segment-2022.

2. Pew Research Center, "About Half of U.S. Adults Have Stopped Doing Business with a Company Because of Poor Customer Service," February 1, 2024, https://www.pewresearch.org/short-reads/2024/02/01/about-half-of-us-adults-have-stopped-doing-business-with-a-company-because-of-poor-customer-service/.

3. Brian Balfour, "Product Market Fit Collapse: Why Your Company Could Be Next," *Reforge*, January 22, 2025, https://www.reforge.com/blog/product-market-fit-collapse.

4. "Retaining Customers Is the Real Challenge," Bain & Company, January 2006, https://www.bain.com/insights/retaining-customers-is-the-real-challenge/.

5. Netflix, "Q4 2024 Shareholder Letter," January 21, 2025, https://cdn.arstechnica.net/wp-content/uploads/2025/01/FINAL-Q4-24-Shareholder-Letter.pdf; Netflix, "Form 10-K for the Fiscal Year Ended December 31, 2023," US Securities and Exchange Commission, filed January 26, 2024, ht tps://www.sec.gov/Archives/edgar/data/1065280/000106528024000030/nflx-20231231.htm.

6. Reuters, "Netflix Adds 5.1 Million Subscribers, Beats Forecasts as Ads, Crackdown Pay Off," October 17, 2024, https://www.reuters.com/technology/netflix-adds-subscribers-beats-forecasts-ads-crackdown-pay-off-2024-10-17/; Jay Peters, "Netflix Adds Millions of Subscribers as Its Password-Sharing Crackdown Continues to Pay Off," *The Verge*, October 17, 2024, https://www.theverge.com/2024/10/17/23920969/netflix-q3-2024-earnings-subscribers-password-sharing.

7. Jonathan Carson and Brendan Brady, *State of Subscriptions* (Antenna, 2024), https://cdn.prod.website-files.com/6756b521db09e280168a4cf3/67bdc1527f0c1577a2ff0fd6_Antenna%20x%20State%20of%20Subscriptions%20-%20Premium%20SVOD.pdf.

8. Carson and Brady, *State of Subscriptions*.

9. Peloton Interactive, Inc., "Peloton Interactive, Inc. Reports Third Quarter Fiscal 2023 Financial Results," news release, May 10, 2023, https://investor.onepeloton.com/news-releases/news-release-details/peloton-interactive-inc-reports-third-quarter-fiscal-2023; Peloton Interactive, Inc., "Q2 FY2025 Shareholder Letter," February 6, 2025, https://investor.onepeloton.com/static-files/9404c038-4c2e-4652-8069-c6b5cd393b46.

10. Synthesized from Kantar BrandZ, Sprout Social Benchmark Reports, and CustomerGauge NPS data.

11. YETI Holdings Inc., "YETI Reports Fourth Quarter and Fiscal Year 2023 Results," news release, February 15, 2024, https://investors.yeti.com/news/news-details/2024/YETI-Reports-Fourth-Quarter-and-Fiscal-Year-2023-Results/.

12. *2023 Social Media Industry Benchmark Report* (RivalIQ, 2023), https://get.rivaliq.com/hubfs/eBooks/2023-social-media-benchmark-report.pdf.

13. Allbirds Inc., "Allbirds Reports First Quarter 2025 Financial Results," news release, May 8, 2025, https://ir.allbirds.com/news-releases/news-release-details/allbirds-reports-first-quarter-2025-financial-results.

14. Allbirds Inc., "Form 10-K for Fiscal Year Ending December 31, 2023," US Securities and Exchange Commission, filed March 13, 2024, https://www.sec.gov/Archives/edgar/data/1653909/000165390924000015/bird-20231231.htm; Allbirds Inc., "Form 10-Q for Quarterly Period Ended June 30, 2025," US Securities and Exchange Commission, filed August 8, 2025, https://www.sec.gov/Archives/edgar/data/1653909/000165390925000051/bird-20250630.htm; Aidin Vaziri, "Allbirds Is Closing Its Last San Francisco Store," *San Francisco Chronicle*, January 28, 2026, https://www.sfchronicle.com/sf/article/allbirds-closes-last-store-21320307.php.

15. "Retaining Customers Is the Real Challenge," Bain & Company; "What Is Customer Churn?" Recurly, 2024, https://recurly.com/research/churn-rate-benchmarks/.

16. "Quarterly Results," monday.com, accessed April 27, 2026, https://ir.monday.com/financials-and-filings/sec-filings/default.aspx.

17. "SEC Filings," monday.com, https://ir.monday.com/financials-and-filings/sec-filings/default.aspx.

18. monday.com, "monday.com Announces Second Q0uarter 2024 Results," news release, August 12, 2024, https://ir.monday.com/news-and-events/news-releases/news-details/2024/monday.com-Announces-Second-Quarter-2024-Results/default.aspx; monday.com, "monday.com Announces Third Quarter 2024 Results," news release, November 11, 2024, https://ir.monday.com/news-and-events/news-releases/news-details/2024/monday.com-Announces-Third-Quarter-2024-Results/default.aspx.

19. "Press Releases," HelloFresh, accessed April 27, 2026, https://hellofreshgroup.com/en/newsroom/press-releases/.

20. HelloFresh SE, "HelloFresh SE Met Outlook for the Fiscal Year 2023, Provides Outlook for the Fiscal Year 2024 and Removes Its Midterm Targets," news release, March 7, 2024, https://assets.ctfassets.net/irplh84t0tdt/6UgWf8TFNFNI0epkwgNcHV/e94eec70d9f8452ac5c9d0f14bee16a6/2024-03-07_Ad_hoc_Announcement_Guidance_2024_EN.pdf.

21. HelloFresh, "HelloFresh SE Reports Quarterly Revenue of Approx. €2.07 Bn," press release, April 25, 2024, https://assets.ctfassets.net/irplh84t0tdt/3yUD7O1vfEjRCr6UEcYDCg/0f477219c195fca577590146d78e2871/HelloFresh_Group_Press_Release_Q1_2024.pdf.

22. Lululemon Athletica Inc., "Form 10-K for the Fiscal Year Ending February 2, 2025," US Securities and Exchange Commission, filed March 27, 2025, https://www.sec.gov/Archives/edgar/data/1397187/000139718725000013/lulu-20250202.htm; Lululemon Athletica Inc., "Lululemon Athletica Inc. Announces First Quarter Fiscal 2025 Results," press release, June 5, 2025, https://corporate.lululemon.com/media/press-releases/2025/06-05-2025-210525682.

23. Allbirds Inc., "Form 10-K for the Fiscal Year Ending December 31, 2024," US Securities and Exchange Commission, filed March 12, 2025, https://www.sec.gov/Archives/edgar/data/1653909/000162828025012130/bird-20241231.htm.

24. YETI Holdings Inc., "YETI Reports Fourth Quarter and Fiscal Year 2023 Results"; YETI Holdings Inc., "YETI Reports Fourth Quarter and Fiscal Year 2024 Results," news release, February 13, 2025, https://investors.yeti.com/news/news-details/2025/YETI-Reports-Fourth-Quarter-and-Fiscal-Year-2024-Results/default.aspx.

25. Savyata Mishra and Dietrich Knauth, "Tupperware Files for Bankruptcy as Its Colorful Containers Lose Relevance," Reuters, September 18, 2024, https://www.reuters.com/business/retail-consumer/tupperware-brands-files-chapter-11-bankruptcy-2024-09-18/.

26. Antenna, "2024 Top Subscription Insights," accessed April 27, 2026, https://www.antenna.live/reports/market-analysis-2023; Netflix, "Q3 2024 Shareholder Letter," October 17, 2024, https://s22.q4cdn.com/959853165/files/doc_financials/2024/q3/FINAL-Q3-24-Shareholder-Lettter.pdf.

27. Ashley Carman, "Subscription Podcast Company Luminary Cut Staff Salaries and Shows," Bloomberg, April 13, 2023, https://www.bloomberg.com/news/newsletters/2023-04-13/subscription-podcast-company-luminary-cut-staff-salaries-and-shows.

28. Antoine Gara and Eric Platt, "Luxury Gym Chain Equinox Raises $1.8bn to Avert Cash Crunch," *The Financial Times*, March 8, 2024, https://www.ft.com/content/be39a2d6-4757-402f-aa66-2d04761cabde?syn-25a6b1a6=1; Bloomberg Wire, "Gyms Face Tough Year as Key January Growth Screeches to Halt," Bloomberg, February 11, 2024, https://www.bloomberg.com/news/articles/2024-02-11/gyms-face-tough-year-as-key-january-growth-screeches-to-a-halt?embedded-checkout=true.

29. Weight Watchers, "WW International, Inc. Announces First Quarter 2024 Results," news release, May 2, 2024, https://corporate.ww.com/news/news-details/2024/WW-International-Inc--Announces-First-Quarter-2024-Results/; Weight Watchers,

"WW International, Inc. Announces First Quarter 2025 Results," news release, May 6, 2025, https://corporate.ww.com/news/news-details/2025/WW-International-Inc--Announces-First-Quarter-2025-Results/; Weight Watchers, "WW International, Inc. Announces Fourth Quarter and Full Year 2024 Results," news release, February 27, 2025, https://corporate.ww.com/news/news-details/2025/WW-International-Inc--Schedules-Fourth-Quarter-and-Full-Year-2024-Earnings-Conference-Call/default.aspx; Weight Watchers, "Form 10-K for the Fiscal Year Ended December 28, 2024," US Securities and Exchange Commission, filed February 28, 2025, https://www.sec.gov/Archives/edgar/data/105319/000095017025029511/ww-20241228.htm; Reuters, "WeightWatchers Files for Chapter 11 Bankruptcy to Cut Debt," May 6, 2025, https://www.reuters.com/business/weightwatchers-plans-file-bankruptcy-protection-2025-05-06/.

30. Cleveland Clinic, "State of the Clinic: In 2024, Cleveland Clinic Serves Most Patients in Its History," news release, January 27, 2025, https://newsroom.clevelandclinic.org/2025/01/27/state-of-the-clinic-in-2024-cleveland-clinic-serves-most-patients-in-its-history; *The World's Best Hospitals 2024* (*Newsweek*, 2024), https://rankings.newsweek.com/worlds-best-hospitals-2024.

31. "CVS Accelerates Pace of MinuteClinic Closures," *The Journal of Urgent Care Medicine*, December 20, 2024, https://www.jucm.com/cvs-accelerates-pace-of-minuteclinic-closures/; CVS Health Corp, "Form 10-K for the Fiscal Year Ended December 31, 2024," US Securities and Exchange Commission, filed February 12, 2025, https://www.sec.gov/Archives/edgar/data/64803/000006480325000007/cvs-20241231.htm.

32. Ron Miller, "Canva Introduces New Developer Tools and $50M Investment Fund," *TechCrunch*, June 14, 2023, https://techcrunch.com/2023/06/14/canva-introduces-new-developer-tools-and-50m-investment-fund/; Sankalp Phartiyal, "Canva Tests Low-Cost Plans in Emerging Markets After India Progress," Bloomberg, February 13, 2025, https://www.bloomberg.com/news/articles/2025-02-14/canva-tests-cheap-plans-in-emerging-markets-after-india-progress; "Top Art and Design Apps in the US—Q4 2024 Performance," Sensor Tower, January 2025, https://sensortower.com/blog/2024-q4-unified-top-5-art%20and%20design-units-us-60770ca2241bc16eb875665a.

33. Sarah Perez, "Evernote Pushes Users to Upgrade with Test of a Free Plan Limited to only 50 Notes," *TechCrunch*, November 27, 2023, https://techcrunch.com/2023/11/27/evernote-pushes-users-to-upgrade-with-test-of-a-free-plan-limited-to-only-50-notes/; David Pierce, "The Great Evernote Reboot," The Verge, September 15, 2024, https://www.theverge.com/2024/9/15/24242764/evernote-future-productivity-app-vergecast.

34. Ivan Zhao, "100 Million of You," *Notion HQ*, September 3, 2024, https://www.notion.com/blog/100-million-of-you; Frederic Lardinois, "Here Is Notion's Email Client," *TechCrunch*, October 24, 2024, https://techcrunch.com/2024/10/24/here-is-notions-email-client/.

35. Freshworks, "Freshworks Reports Fourth Quarter and Full Year 2024 Results," news release, February 11, 2025, https://ir.freshworks.com/news/news-details/2025/Freshworks-Reports-Fourth-Quarter-and-Full-Year-2024-Results-02-11-2025/default.aspx.

36. Duolingo, "Duolingo Achieves 54% DAU Growth and 40% Revenue Growth in Third Quarter 2024," news release, November 6, 2024, https://investors.duolingo.com/news-releases/news-release-details/duolingo-achieves-54-dau-growth-and-40-revenue-growth-third; Duolingo, "Form 8-K," US Securities and Exchange Commission, filed February 27, 2025, https://www.sec.gov/Archives/edgar/data/1562088/000156208825000039/duol-20250227.htm.

37. Chegg, "Chegg Reports 2024 Fourth Quarter and Full Year Financial Results," press release, February 24, 2025, https://investor.chegg.com/Press-Releases/press-release-details/2025/Chegg-Reports-2024-Fourth-Quarter-and-Full-Year-Financial-Results/default.aspx; Chegg, "Chegg Reports 2025 First Quarter Earnings," press release, May 12, 2025, https://investor.chegg.com/Press-Releases/press-release-details/2025/Chegg-Reports-2025-First-Quarter-Earnings/default.aspx.

38. "Sweetgreen," Apple App Store, accessed April 26, 2026, https://apps.apple.com/us/app/sweetgreen/id594329490; Sweetgreen, "Sweetgreen, Inc. Announces Fourth Quarter and Fiscal Year 2024 Financial Results," news release, February 26, 2025, https://s28.q4cdn.com/367108596/files/doc_news/Sweetgreen-Inc.-Announces-Fourth-Quarter-and-Fiscal-Year-2024-Financial-Results-2025.pdf.

39. Amelia Lucas and Gabrielle Fonrouge, "Red Lobster Files for Chapter 11 Bankruptcy Protection," CNBC, May 20, 2024, https://www.cnbc.com/2024/05/20/red-lobster-bankruptcy.html; Ramishah Maruf, "Red Lobster's Endless Shrimp Deal Was Too Popular, Company Says," CNN, November 29, 2023, https://www.cnn.com/2023/11/29/business/red-lobster-endless-shrimp-deal; Joe Guszkowski, "Red Lobster Could Close More Than 100 Additional Restaurants If It Can't Renogiate Leases," *Restaurant Business*, May 31, 2024, https://www.restaurantbusinessonline.com/financing/red-lobster-could-close-more-100-additional-restaurants-if-it-cant-renegotiate-leases; Bret Thorn, "Red Lobster Files for Chapter 11 Bankruptcy Protection," *Nation's Restaurant News*, May 19, 2024, https://www.nrn.com/casual-dining/red-lobster-files-for-chapter-11-bankruptcy-protection.

40. *Q4 2024 Shareholder Letter* (Airbnb, 2025), https://s26.q4cdn.com/656283129/files/doc_financials/2024/q4/Airbnb_Q4-2024-Shareholder-Letter_Final.pdf; *Q4*

2023 Shareholder Letter (Airbnb, 2024), https://s26.q4cdn.com/656283129/files/doc_financials/2023/q4/Airbnb_Q4-2023-Shareholder-Letter_Final.pdf.

41. US Department of Transportation, "DOT Penalizes Southwest Airlines $140 Million for 2022 Holiday Meltdown," news release, December 18, 2023, https://www.transportation.gov/briefing-room/dot-penalizes-southwest-airlines-140-million-2022-holiday-meltdown; David Shepardson, "Southwest Airlines Agrees to $140 Million Penalty over 2022 Holiday Meltdown," Reuters, December 18, 2023, https://www.reuters.com/business/aerospace-defense/southwest-airlines-agrees-140-million-penalty-over-2022-holiday-meltdown-2023-12-18/; David Shepardson, "Southwest Airlines Launches Compensation Program for Flight Delays," Reuters, April 29, 2024, https://www.reuters.com/business/aerospace-defense/southwest-airlines-launches-delay-compensation-program-2024-04-29/.

42. DoorDash, "DoorDash Announces Agreement to Acquire Deliveroo," news release, May 6, 2025, https://ir.doordash.com/news/news-details/2025/DoorDash-Announces-Agreement-to-Acquire-Deliveroo/default.aspx.

43. *TechCrunch*, "A Comprehensive Archive of 2024 Tech Layoffs," December 31, 2024, https://techcrunch.com/2024/12/31/a-comprehensive-archive-of-2024-tech-layoffs/.

44. *American Express 2024 Annual Report* (American Express, 2024), https://s26.q4cdn.com/747928648/files/doc_financials/2024/ar/v2/American-Express-2024-Annual-Report.pdf; American Express, "American Express Announces Record FY 2024 Revenue, Up 9%, or 10% on an FX-Adjusted Basis," news release, January 24, 2025, https://ir.americanexpress.com/news/investor-relations-news/investor-relations-news-details/2025/American-Express-Announces-Record-FY-2024-Revenue-Up-9-or-10-on-an-FX-Adjusted-Basis/default.aspx; JD Power, "Show Me the Money! Cashback and Value Credit Cards Grow in Popularity as Financial Health of Cardholders Declines, JD Power Finds," press release, August 15, 2024, https://www.jdpower.com/business/press-releases/2024-us-credit-card-satisfaction-study.

45. Robinhood, "Robinhood Reports Third Quarter 2023 Results," news release, November 7, 2023, https://investors.robinhood.com/news-releases/news-release-details/robinhood-reports-third-quarter-2023-results.

46. Miller, "Canva Introduces"; Phartiyal, "Canva Tests."

47. Rebecca Bellen, "From Graphic Design to Visual Workflows, Canva's New AI Core Is Changing Its Business," *TechCrunch*, December 28, 2023, https://techcrunch.com/2023/12/28/canva-ai-core-growth/; Phartiyal, "Canva Tests"; Jan-Erik Asplund, "Canva at $2.55B ARR," Sacra, December 11, 2024, https://sacra.com/research/canva-at-2-55b-arr/.

48. Chegg, "Chegg Reports 2024 Third Quarter Earnings," press release, November 12, 2024, https://investor.chegg.com/Press-Releases/press-release-details/2024/Chegg-Reports-2024-Third-Quarter-Earnings/default.aspx; Chegg, "Chegg Reports 2025 First Quarter Earnings."

49. Chegg, "Chegg Reports 2025 First Quarter Earnings."

50. Deborah Mary Sophia, "Chegg to Lay Off 22% of Workforce as AI Tools Shake Up Edtech Industry," Reuters, May 12, 2025, https://www.reuters.com/world/americas/chegg-lay-off-22-workforce-ai-tools-shake-up-edtech-industry-2025-05-12/.

51. Sabela Ojea, "Chegg to Initiate Business Review Amid AI-Shift in Education," *The Wall Street Journal*, February 24, 2025, https://www.wsj.com/tech/chegg-initiating-strategic-review-of-business-12857f34?.

CHAPTER 3: COMMUNICATIONS

1. Nidhi Arora et al., "The Value of Getting Personalization Right—or Wrong—Is Multiplying," McKinsey & Company, November 12, 2021, https://www.mckinsey.com/capabilities/growth-marketing-and-sales/our-insights/the-value-of-getting-personalization-right-or-wrong-is-multiplying.

2. Nielsen Norman Group, https://www.nngroup.com/; Baymard Institute, https://baymard.com/; industry analysis by category.

3. Christian Holst, "Top 1% E-Commerce UX Awards—2024 Winners," Baymard Institute, December 10, 2024, https://baymard.com/blog/ux-awards-2024.

4. SimilarWeb, "airbnb.com Website Analysis," accessed April 27, 2026, https://www.similarweb.com/website/airbnb.com/; Baymard Institute, "50 Cart Abandonment Rate Statistics 2026," 2026, https://baymard.com/lists/cart-abandonment-rate.

5. Baymard Institute, "Hotel & Property Rental Ecommerce UX Research," accessed April 27, 2026, https://baymard.com/research/travel-accommodations; Baymard Institute, "Cart & Checkout Usability Research," accessed April 27, 2026, https://baymard.com/research/checkout-usability.

6. Federal Trade Commission, "FTC, Illinois Attorney General Take Action Against Grubhub for Harming Diners, Workers, and Small Businesses," press release, December 17, 2024, https://www.ftc.gov/news-events/news/press-releases/2024/12/ftc-illinois-attorney-general-take-action-against-grubhub-harming-diners-workers-small-businesses; Jody Godoy, "Grubhub to Pay $25 Million for Misleading Customers, Restaurants, Drivers," Reuters, December 17, 2024, https://www.reuters.com/legal/grubhub-pay-25-million-misleading-customers-restaurants-drivers-2024-12-17/.

7. Federal Trade Commission, "FTC, Illinois Attorney."

8. Mailchimp, "Email Marketing Benchmarks," https://mailchimp.com/resources/email-marketing-benchmarks/; Sprout Social Index, https://sproutsocial.com/insights/index/; Litmus Email Analytics, https://www.litmus.com/email-analytics.

9. Krystal Hu, "ChatGPT Sets Record for Fastest-Growing User Base—Analyst Note," February 2, 2023, https://www.reuters.com/technology/chatgpt-sets-record-fastest-growing-user-base-analyst-note-2023-02-01/.

10. Aisha Malik, "OpenAI's ChatGPT Now Has 100 Million Weekly Active Users," *TechCrunch*, November 6, 2023, https://techcrunch.com/2023/11/06/openais-chatgpt-now-has-100-million-weekly-active-users/.

11. Shelley Kohan, "Wendy's Dynamic Pricing Announcement Puts New CEO Kirk Tanner in Spotlight," *Forbes*, March 2, 2024, https://www.forbes.com/sites/shelleykohan/2024/03/02/wendys-dynamic-pricing-announcement-puts-new-ceo-kirk-tanner-in-spotlight/.

12. Waylon Cunningham and Deborah Mary Sophia, "Wendy's, Burned by CEO Comment, Vows No Price Surges for Burgers," Reuters, February 28, 2024, https://www.reuters.com/business/retail-consumer/wendys-will-not-implement-surge-pricing-ceo-comment-causes-online-stir-2024-02-28/.

13. Aneurin Canham-Clyne, "Wendy's Backtracks on Dynamic Pricing," *Restaurant Dive*, February 28, 2024, https://www.restaurantdive.com/news/wendys-backtracks-on-dynamic-pricing-after-consumer-backlash/708799/.

14. Canham-Clyne, "Wendy's Backtracks."

15. *ACSI Restaurant and Food Delivery Study 2024* (ACSI, 2024), https://theacsi.org/wp-content/uploads/2024/06/24jun-restaurant-study-FINAL.pdf; *ACSI Restaurant and Food Delivery Study 2025* (ACSI, 2025), https://theacsi.org/wp-content/uploads/2025/06/25jun-Restaurant-Delivery-STUDY-FINAL.pdf.

16. Shmiruthaa Narayanan, "CSAT Benchmarks: What Is a Good Customer Satisfaction Score?" SurveySparrow, updated April 25, 2026, https://surveysparrow.com/blog/csat-benchmarks/.

17. ACSI, https://www.theacsi.org/; SurveySparrow, "CSAT Benchmarks," https://surveysparrow.com/blog/csat-benchmarks/; Sprout Social Index, https://sproutsocial.com/insights/index/.

18. JD Power, "Top Performing Airlines Set Themselves Apart with Friendly Staff, JD Power Finds," press release, May 8, 2024, https://www.jdpower.com/business/press-releases/2024-north-america-airline-satisfaction-study; ACSI, "The Definitive Measure of Passenger Satisfaction with Cause-and-Effect Analysis," accessed April 27, 2026, https://www.theacsi.org/industries/travel/airlines/.

19. *Air Travel Consumer Report* (The Office of Aviation Consumer Protection, July 2023, revised November 8, 2023), https://www.transportation.gov/sites/dot.gov/files/2023-11/July%202023%20ATCR_Revised%20110823.pdf.

20. Better Business Bureau, "Ticketmaster, LLC," accessed 2024–2025, https://www.bbb.org/us/ca/beverly-hills/profile/event-ticket-sales/ticketmaster-llc-1216-31068/complaints.

21. *S.Hrg. 118-31—That's the Ticket: Promoting Competition and Protecting Consumers in Live Entertainment*, 118th Congress (2023–2024), US Senate Judiciary Committee hearing, January 24, 2023, https://www.congress.gov/event/118th-congress/senate-event/333501/text; Alanna Durkin Richer and Wyatte Grantham-Philips, "Government Sues Ticketmaster Owner and Asks Court to Break Up Company's Monopoloy on Live Events," AP News, May 23, 2024, https://apnews.com/article/justice-department-live-nation-ticketmaster-antitrust-lawsuit-df9b552d127e1494db13e3cd625787a8.

22. Jarrett Renshaw, "Ticketmaster, Others Agree to Upfront, All-In Prices as Part of Biden War on Junk Fees," Reuters, June 15, 2023, https://www.reuters.com/world/us/ticketmaster-live-nation-agree-all-in-prices-part-biden-war-junk-fees-2023-06-15/; Federal Trade Commission, "Federal Trade Commission Announces Bipartisan Rule Banning Junk Ticket and Hotel Fees," press release, December 17, 2024, https://www.ftc.gov/news-events/news/press-releases/2024/12/federal-trade-commission-announces-bipartisan-rule-banning-junk-ticket-hotel-fees.

23. Nielsen Norman Group, https://www.nngroup.com/; Baymard Institute, https://baymard.com/; Mailchimp, "Email Marketing Benchmarks," https://mailchimp.com/resources/email-marketing-benchmarks/; ACSI, https://www.theacsi.org/; SurveySparrow, "CSAT Benchmarks," https://surveysparrow.com/blog/csat-benchmarks/.

24. Lululemon Athletica Inc., "Form 10-K for Fiscal Year Ending February 2, 2025," US Securities and Exchange Commission, filed March 27, 2025, https://www.sec.gov/Archives/edgar/data/1397187/000139718725000013/lulu-20250202.htm.

25. Jonathan Stempel, "Coach Sues Gap for Selling 'Coach' T-Shirts," Reuters, April 3, 2024, https://www.reuters.com/legal/coach-sues-gap-selling-coach-t-shirts-2024-04-03/; "Oldnavy," Trustpilot, accesed April 27, 2026, https://www.trustpilot.com/review/oldnavy.ca.

26. "Cannes Lions 2025: Media Winners," Contagious, June 18, 2025, https://www.contagious.com/en/article/news-and-views/cannes-lions-2025-media-winners; Cydney Lee, "Dove Wins Cannes Lions Media Grand Prix for Championing 'Real Beauty' in the Age of AI," *Adweek*, June 18, 2025, https://www.adweek.com/brand-marketing/dove-wins-media-grand-prix-real-beauty-ai/.

27. US Securities and Exchange Commission, "SEC Charges Keurig with Making Inaccurate Statements Regarding Recyclability of K-Cup Beverage Pod," press release, September 10, 2024, https://www.sec.gov/newsroom/press-releases/2024-122; Chris Prentice and Susan Heavey, "US SEC Hits Keurig with $1.5MLN Fine over Pod Recyclability," Reuters, September 10, 2025, https://www.reuters.com/business/retail-consumer/keurig-pay-15mln-fine-over-inaccurate-pod-recyclability-statements-sec-says-2024-09-10/.

28. Spotify, "Q4 2024 Earnings Call Prepared Remarks," press release, February 2025, https://s29.q4cdn.com/175625835/files/doc_financials/2024/q4/Q4-24-Earnings-Call-Prepared-Remarks-1.pdf.

29. Dan Primack, "Audio App Clubhouse Lays Off Half Its Employees," Axios, April 27, 2023, https://www.axios.com/2023/04/27/audio-app-clubhouse-layoffs; Amanda Silberling, "Clubhouse Is Trying to Make a Comeback," *TechCrunch*, September 6, 2023, https://techcrunch.com/2023/09/06/clubhouse-is-trying-to-make-a-comeback/.

30. "Strava," Apple App Store, accessed April 27, 2026, https://apps.apple.com/us/app/strava-run-bike-walk/id426826309; "Strava," Google Play Store, accessed April 27, 2026, https://play.google.com/store/apps/details?id=com.strava&hl=en_US.

31. Federal Trade Commission, "FTC to Ban BetterHelp from Revealing Consumers' Data, Including Sensitive Mental Health Information, to Facebook and Others for Targeted Advertising," press release, March 2, 2023, https://www.ftc.gov/news-events/news/press-releases/2023/03/ftc-ban-betterhelp-revealing-consumers-data-including-sensitive-mental-health-information-facebook.

32. "Mayo Clinic," Apple App Store, accessed April 27, 2026, https://apps.apple.com/us/app/mayo-clinic/id523220194; SimilarWeb, "mayoclinic.org Website Analysis," 2024, https://www.similarweb.com/website/mayoclinic.org/; *The World's Best Hospitals 2024* (*Newsweek*, 2024), https://rankings.newsweek.com/worlds-best-hospitals-2024.

33. Texas Commissioner of Insurance, "Official Order," no. 2024-8683, June 6, 2024, https://www.tdi.texas.gov/commissioner/disciplinary-orders/documents/20248683.pdf; Texas Commissioner of Insurance, "Official Order," no. 2024-9049, December 20, 2024, https://www.tdi.texas.gov/commissioner/disciplinary-orders/documents/20249049.pdf; *Report on Target Market Conduct Examination of Cigna Health and Life Insurance Company* (Bureau of Insurance, Commonwealth of Virginia, June 30, 2019), https://www.scc.virginia.gov/media/sccvirginiagov-home/regulated-industries/insurance/insurance-companies/for-companies/-market-conduct-examination-reports-/cigna-health-and-life-insurance-company.pdf.

34. *ACSI Wireless Phone Service and Cell Phone Study 2023–2024* (ACSI, 2024), https://theacsi.org/wp-content/uploads/2024/05/24may-cell-wireless-study-FINAL.pdf;

ACSI Telecommunications, Cell Phone, and Smartwatch Study 2025 (ACSI, 2025), https://theacsi.org/wp-content/uploads/2025/05/25may_ISP-Wireless-Cell-Smartwatch-Study-FINAL.pdf.

35. Richer and Grantham-Philips, "Government Sues Ticketmaster"; Renshaw, "Ticketmaster, Others Agree"; Dee-Ann Durbin, "As Biden-Era 'Junk Fee' Rule Takes Effect, Ticketmaster Says It Will Display Fees More Clearly," AP News, May 12, 2025, https://apnews.com/article/ticketmaster-concert-fees-tickets-79923046fbb8ad53583ff761aab7f1d2.

36. Palmer Houchins, "G2's 2024 Best Software Awards: Celebrating Winners & Uncovering Trends," G2, February 6, 2024, https://company.g2.com/news/g2s-2024-best-software-awards.

37. Realscape Group LLC v. Oracle America, Inc., Case No. 1:24-cv-00558-CEF, US District Court, Northern District of Ohio, Eastern Division, filed March 26, 2024, https://www.classaction.org/media/realscape-group-llc-v-oracle-america-inc.pdf.

38. Duolingo, "Duolingo Reports 62% DAU Growth, 44% Revenue Growth, and Stronger Profitability in Second Quarter 2023; Raises Full Year Guidance," news release, August 8, 2023, https://investors.duolingo.com/news-releases/news-release-details/duolingo-reports-62-dau-growth-44-revenue-growth-and-stronger; Duolingo, "Duolingo Achieves 54% DAU Growth and 40% Revenue Growth in Third Quarter 2024," news release, November 6, 2024, https://investors.duolingo.com/news-releases/news-release-details/duolingo-achieves-54-dau-growth-and-40-revenue-growth-third; Rebecca Stewart, "TikTok Fave Duolingo Boosts YouTube Shorts Viewership 430% in One Year," *Adweek*, April 11, 2025, https://www.adweek.com/brand-marketing/tiktok-fave-duolingo-boosts-youtube-shorts-viewership-430-in-one-year/.

39. Federal Trade Commission vs. Grand Canyon University, 2:23-cv-02711-JZB 2:23-02711-PHX-DWL (District of Arizona 2025), https://www.ftc.gov/legal-library/browse/cases-proceedings/grand-canyon-universitygrand-canyon-education.

40. "Sweetgreen," Apple App Store, accessed April 26, 2026, https://apps.apple.com/us/app/sweetgreen/id594329490.

41. *ACSI Restaurant and Food Delivery Study 2025*; Josh Kosman, "Subway Calls 'Emergency' Meeting with Franchisees as Sales Plummet: Sources," *New York Post*, August 14, 2024, https://nypost.com/2024/08/14/business/subway-calls-emergency-meeting-with-franchisees-as-sales-plummet-sources/; Carl Stoffers, "Subway Calls 'Essential' Franchisee Meeting Amid Plummeting Sales," *Entrepreneur*, August 15, 2024, https://www.entrepreneur.com/business-news/subway-holds-franchisee-conference-as-sales-plummet/478533.

42. Kimberly Inlander, "*Global Traveler* Announces 21st Annual GT Tested Reader Survey Awards," *Global Traveler*, December 2, 2024, https://www.globaltravelerusa.com/global-traveler-announces-21st-annual-gt-tested-reader-survey-awards/; Delta Air Lines, "Delta Air Lines Announces December Quarter and Full Year 2024 Financial Results," news release, January 10, 2025, https://ir.delta.com/news/news-details/2025/Delta-Air-Lines-Announces-December-Quarter-and-Full-Year-2024-Financial-Results/default.aspx; JD Power, "Top Performing Airlines"; Ed Bastian, "An Update to Delta Customers from CEO Ed Bastian," Delta, July 21, 2024, https://news.delta.com/update-delta-customers-ceo-ed-bastian.

43. *Air Travel Consumer Report* (The Office of Aviation Consumer Protection, July 2023, revised November 8, 2023), https://www.transportation.gov/sites/dot.gov/files/2023-11/July%202023%20ATCR_Revised%20110823.pdf; *ACSI Travel Study 2023–2024* (ACSI, April 23, 2024), https://theacsi.org/wp-content/uploads/2024/04/24apr_travel-study.pdf; *ACSI Travel Study 2023–2024* (ACSI, April 23, 2024), https://theacsi.org/wp-content/uploads/2024/04/24apr_travel-study.pdf; "Spirit Airlines," Trustpilot, accessed April 27, 2026, https://www.trustpilot.com/review/www.spirit.com.

44. "DoorDash," Apple App Store, accessed April 27, 2026, https://apps.apple.com/us/app/doordash-food-grocery-more/id719972451.

45. Federal Trade Commission, "FTC, Illinois Attorney General."

46. JD Power, "Customer Satisfaction with National Banks Improves as Trust Levels Rise, JD Power Finds," press release, December 12, 2024, https://www.jdpower.com/business/press-releases/2024-us-national-banking-satisfaction-study.

47. Hannah Lang and Manya Saini, "Robinhood to Pay $10MLN to Settle Operational Deficiency Charge," Reuters, April 6, 2023, https://www.reuters.com/legal/california-joins-multiple-states-10-mln-settlement-with-robinhood-2023-04-06/; FINRA, "FINRA Orders Robinhood Financial to Pay $3.75 Million in Restitution to Customers; Fines Robinhood Financial and Robinhood Securities for Anti-Money Laundering, Supervisory and Disclosure Violations," news release, March 7, 2025, https://www.finra.org/media-center/newsreleases/2025/finra-orders-robinhood-financial-pay-375-million-restitution.

48. Stewart, "TikTok Fave Duolingo."

49. Duolingo, "Duolingo Reports 62% DAU Growth."

50. Duolingo, "Shareholder Letter: Q4/FY2024," 2025, https://investors.duolingo.com/static-files/99006c40-d8cf-41ca-b5b1-c5cb1fa5ba88; Rebecca Stewart, "Hi! It's Duo: The Marketing Strategy Behind the Internet's Favorite Green Menace," *Adweek*, April 8, 2025, https://www.adweek.com/brand-marketing/duolingo-duo-owl-marketing-strategy/.

51. "Duolingo," Apple App Store, accessed April 27, 2026, https://apps.apple.com/us/app/duolingo-language-lessons/id570060128; "Duolingo," Google Play Store, https://play.google.com/store/apps/details?id=com.duolingo.

52. Benjamin Zhang, "Spirit Airlines Is Making a Bold New Push for Premium Customers," *Business Insider*, July 30, 2024, https://www.businessinsider.com/spirit-airlines-ticket-changes-bundled-fares-bags-snacks-premium-seats-2024-7.

53. Rajesh Kumar Singh, "Spirit Airlines Targets More Affluent Travelers After Emerging from Bankruptcy," Reuters, March 13, 2025, https://www.reuters.com/business/aerospace-defense/spirit-airlines-emerges-chapter-11-bankruptcy-2025-03-12/.

54. Megan Cerullo, "These Airlines Had the Most and Least Passenger Complaints in 2024," CBS, May 16, 2025, https://www.cbsnews.com/news/best-worst-airlines-complaints/.

55. *ACSI Travel Study 2025* (ACSI, 2025), https://theacsi.org/wp-content/uploads/2025/04/25apr_Travel-Study-FINAL-1.pdf.

CHAPTER 4: PSYCHOLOGY

1. Daniel Kahneman, *Thinking, Fast and Slow* (Farrar, Straus and Giroux, 2011).

2. Sheena Iyengar and Mark Lepper, "When Choice Is Demotivating: Can One Desire Too Much of a Good Thing?" *Journal of Personality and Social Psychology* 79, no. 6 (January 2001): 995–1006, https://www.researchgate.net/publication/12189991_When_Choice_is_Demotivating_Can_One_Desire_Too_Much_of_a_Good_Thing.

3. Dan Ariely, *Predictably Irrational: The Hidden Forces That Shape Our Decisions* (Harper, 2008).

4. Nidhi Arora et al., "The Value of Getting Personalization Right—or Wrong—Is Multiplying," McKinsey & Company, November 12, 2021, https://www.mckinsey.com/capabilities/growth-marketing-and-sales/our-insights/the-value-of-getting-personalization-right-or-wrong-is-multiplying.

5. Susan Farrell, "How Iterative Testing Decreased Support Calls by 70% on Mozilla's Support Website," Nielsen Norman Group, August 2, 2015, https://www.nngroup.com/articles/testing-decreased-support/; Kim Flaherty, "Minimize the Need for Customer Service to Improve the Omnichannel UX," Nielsen Norman Group, September 11, 2016, https://www.nngroup.com/articles/customer-service-omnichannel-ux/.

6. Epsilon, *The Power of Me: The Impact of Personalization on Marketing Performance* (Epsilon, 2022), https://www.slideshare.net/slideshow/the-power-of-me-the-impact-of-personalization-on-marketing-performance/85722934.

7. Marylène Gagné and Edward Deci, "Self-Determination Theory and Work Motivation," *Journal of Organizational Behavior* 26, no. 4 (2005): 331–62, https://selfdeterminationtheory.org/SDT/documents/2005_GagneDeci_JOB_SDTtheory.pdf.

8. *The Total Economic Impact of Figma Dev Mode* (Forrester Consulting, 2025), https://tei.forrester.com/go/Figma/DevMode/?lang=en-us.

9. Akash Sriram et al., "Adobe Shelves $20 Bln Figma Deal After Hitting Regulatory Roadblocks," Reuters, December 18, 2023, https://www.reuters.com/technology/adobe-figma-terminate-20-bln-deal-2023-12-18/.

10. Matt Alston, "Everyone Hates Workday," *Business Insider*, May 6, 2024, https://www.businessinsider.com/everyone-hates-workday-human-resources-customer-service-software-fortune-500-2024-5.

11. Alston, "Everyone Hates Workday."

12. "Workday," G2, accessed April 27, 2026, https://www.g2.com/sellers/workday.

13. Arora et al., "The Value of Getting Personalization Right."

14. Lucy Fuggle, "Your Email Engagement: 10 Ways to Get More People Clicking & Reading," HubSpot, updated July 24, 2025, https://blog.hubspot.com/marketing/increasing-email-engagement.

15. Spotify, "Spotify Reports Fourth Quarter 2023 Earnings," news release, February 6, 2024, https://newsroom.spotify.com/2024-02-06/spotify-reports-fourth-quarter-2023-earnings/; Spotify, "Spotify Reports First Quarter 2024 Earnings," news release, April 23, 2024, https://newsroom.spotify.com/2024-04-23/spotify-reports-first-quarter-2024-earnings/; Spotify, "Spotify Reports Second Quarter 2024 Earnings," news release, July 23, 2024, https://newsroom.spotify.com/2024-07-23/spotify-reports-second-quarter-2024-earnings/.

16. Spotify, "Q4 2024 Earnings Call Prepared Remarks," press release, February 2025, https://s29.q4cdn.com/175625835/files/doc_financials/2024/q4/Q4-24-Earnings-Call-Prepared-Remarks-1.pdf.

17. *2024 U.S. Auto Insurance Study* (JD Power, 2024), https://www.jdpower.com/business/insurance/auto-insurance-study.

18. "State Farm Seeks Rate Hikes in California to Offset Wildfire Payouts," Reuters, February 4, 2025, https://www.reuters.com/business/finance/state-farm-seeks-rate-hikes-california-offset-wildfire-payouts-2025-02-04/.

19. Zendesk, "Customer Service Metrics," accessed April 27, 2026, https://www.zendesk.com/blog/customer-service-metrics/; *Optimizing the Tradeoff: Cost vs. Quality in IT Support* (MetricNet, 2016), https://www.metricnet.com/wp-content/uploads/2016/07/MetricNets-Cost-vs.-Quality-in-IT-Service-and-Support_v1.pdf.

20. Gagné and Deci, self-determination theory research; *Optimizing the Tradeoff* (MetricNet).

21. Stripe, "Workbench Is Now Available to Everyone," Developer Digest, August 30, 2024, https://stripe.dev/blog/stripe-developer-digest-august-2024-workbench-is-now-available-to-everyone.

22. Stripe, "Stripe Named a Leader for Its Billing Product," February 6, 2025, https://stripe.com/newsroom/news/stripe-named-a-leader-by-forrester.

23. Ingrid Lunden, "Stripe, Doubling Down on Embedded Finance, De-Couples Payments from the Rest of Its Stack," *TechCrunch*, April 24, 2024, https://techcrunch.com/2024/04/24/stripe-doubling-down-on-embedded-finance-de-couples-payments-from-the-rest-of-its-stack/.

24. Harshita Mary Varghese, "T-Mobile Lifts Subscriber Addition Target on Demand for Premium Bundled Plans," Reuters, July 31, 2024, https://www.reuters.com/business/media-telecom/t-mobile-raises-annual-forecast-subscriber-additions-bundled-data-plans-demand-2024-07-31/; Jon Brodkin, "T-Mobile Users Thought They Had a Lifetime Price Lock—Guess What Happened Next," *Ars Technica*, June 11, 2024, https://arstechnica.com/tech-policy/2024/06/t-mobile-users-thought-they-had-a-lifetime-price-lock-guess-what-happened-next/.

25. "T-Mobile Sued for Breaking Lifetime Price Guarantees," MacRumors, July 26, 2024. https://www.macrumors.com/2024/07/26/t-mobile-price-guarantee-lawsuit/.

26. Based on conversion optimization research, UX benchmarks, behavioral economics studies, McKinsey personalization research, and self-service effectiveness research (2023–2024).

27. *ACSI Retail and Consumer Shipping Study 2025* (ACSI, 2025), https://theacsi.org/news-and-resources/press-releases/2025/01/28/press-release-retail-and-consumer-shipping-study-2025/; "Nordstrom Beats Holiday-Quarter Sales Estimates; CFO Jumps Ship to Starbucks," Reuters, March 4, 2025, https://www.reuters.com/business/retail-consumer/nordstrom-beats-holiday-quarter-sales-estimates-cfo-steps-down-2025-03-04/.

28. Stitch Fix, "Stitch Fix Announces Second Quarter of Fiscal Year 2025 Financial Results," news release, March 11, 2025, https://investors.stitchfix.com/news-events/press-releases/news-details/2025/Stitch-Fix-Announces-Second-Quarter-of-Fiscal-Year-2025-Financial-Results-03-11-2025/default.aspx; Stitch Fix, "Stitch Fix Announces Third Quarter of Fiscal Year 2025 Financial Results," news release, June 10, 2025, https://investors.stitchfix.com/news-events/press-releases/news-details/2025/Stitch-Fix-Announces-Third-Quarter-of-Fiscal-Year-2025-Financial-Results-06-10-2025/default.aspx; Daphne Howland, "Stitch Fix Ends Full-Time Work for Stylists, Lays off Some Leads," *Retail Dive*, January 18, 2024, https://www.retaildive.com/news/stitch-fix-ends-full-time-work-stylists-layoffs/704886/.

29. Hoang Nguyen, "A Look at How Liquid Death Is Cannibalizing the Beverage Industry," YouGov, May 30, 2024, https://yougov.com/en-us/articles/49562-a-look-at-how-liquid-death-is-cannibalizing-the-beverage-industry.

30. Ananya Rajesh, "Bud Light Loses Top US Beer Spot After Mulvaney Ad Boycott," Reuters, June 14, 2023, https://www.reuters.com/business/retail-consumer/bud-light-loses-top-us-beer-spot-after-mulvaney-ad-boycott-2023-06-14/; Nicholas Miller, "Bud Light Slips to No. 3 After Boycott Reshaped Beer Industry," *The Wall Street Journal*, July 18, 2024, https://www.wsj.com/business/bud-light-slips-to-no-3-after-boycott-reshaped-beer-industry-e4e9a102?; Hoang Nguyen, "Bud Light and Budweiser's Reputation under Fire—Are Other Ab-InBev Brands Weathering the Storm?" YouGov, May 26, 2023, https://yougov.com/en-us/articles/46696-bud-light-budweiser-anheuser-busch-brand-health-mulvaney-controversy.

31. Pinterest, "Pinterest Announces Fourth Quarter and Full Year 2024 Results, Delivers First Billion Dollar Revenue Quarter," press release, February 6, 2025, https://investor.pinterestinc.com/news-and-events/press-releases/press-releases-details/2025/Pinterest-Announces-Fourth-Quarter-and-Full-Year-2024-Results-Delivers-First-Billion-Dollar-Revenue-Quarter/default.aspx; "Pinterest," Apple App Store, accessed April 27, 2026, https://apps.apple.com/us/app/pinterest/id429047995.

32. *ACSI Telecommunications Study 2024* (ACSI, 2024), https://theacsi.org/wp-content/uploads/2024/05/24jun-telecom-study-FINAL.pdf; Federal Communications Commission, "All-In Pricing for Cable and Satellite Television Service," March 19, 2024, https://docs.fcc.gov/public/attachments/FCC-24-29A1.pdf; Federal Trade Commission, "Federal Trade Commission Proposes Rule Provision Making It Easier for Consumers to 'Click to Cancel' Recurring Subscriptions and Memberships," press release, March 23, 2023, https://www.ftc.gov/news-events/news/press-releases/2023/03/federal-trade-commission-proposes-rule-provision-making-it-easier-consumers-click-cancel-recurring.

33. Peloton, "Q3 FY2024 Shareholder Letter," May 2, 2024, https://investor.onepeloton.com/static-files/f17afda1-ef5e-4192-b0ed-2e8adfabad3d; Peloton Interactive, Inc., "Q2 FY2025 Shareholder Letter," February 6, 2025, https://investor.onepeloton.com/static-files/9404c038-4c2e-4652-8069-c6b5cd393b46.

34. Federal Trade Commission, "FTC to Ban BetterHelp from Revealing Consumers' Data, Including Sensitive Mental Health Information, to Facebook and Others for Targeted Advertising," press release, March 2, 2023, https://www.ftc.gov/news-events/news/press-releases/2023/03/ftc-ban-betterhelp-revealing-consumers-data-including-sensitive-mental-health-information-facebook.

35. PR Newswire, "Zocdoc Introduces Guided Search, Helping Patients More Confidently Connect with the Right Providers," Zocdoc, February 13, 2024, https://www.prnewswire.com/news-releases/zocdoc-introduces-guided-search-helping-patients-more-confidently-connect-with-the-right-providers-302060150.html; "Zocdoc," Apple App Store, accessed April 27, 2026, https://apps.apple.com/us/app/zocdoc-find-and-book-doctors/id391062219.

36. Brendan Pierson, "Lawsuit Claims UnitedHealth AI Wrongfully Denies Elderly Extended Care," Reuters, November 14, 2023, https://www.reuters.com/legal/lawsuit-claims-unitedhealth-ai-wrongfully-denies-elderly-extended-care-2023-11-14/; The Estate of Gene B. Lokken v. UnitedHealth Group, Inc. (0:23-cv-03514), US District Court, District of Minnesota, Court Listener, filed November 14, 2023, https://www.courtlistener.com/docket/68006832/estate-of-gene-b-lokken-the-v-unitedhealth-group-inc/.

37. "Grammarly," Apple App Store, accessed April 27, 2026, https://apps.apple.com/us/app/grammarly-ai-keyboard-notes/id1158877342; "Grammarly," Gartner Peer Insights, updated October 13, 2025, https://www.gartner.com/reviews/product/grammarly; Mark Sullivan, "How Grammarly's AI Is Writing the New Rules of Writing," *Fast Company*, March 19, 2024, https://www.fastcompany.com/91033463/grammarly-most-innovative-companies-2024.

38. Chris Welch, "Sonos Lays off 100 Employees as Its App Crisis Continues," The Verge, August 14, 2024, https://www.theverge.com/2024/8/14/24220357/sonos-layoffs-august-2024-app; Greg Bensinger, "Exclusive: Sonos CEO Promises Reform After May App Release 'Failure'; Leaders to Forgo Bonuses," Reuters, October 1, 2024, https://www.reuters.com/technology/sonos-ceo-promises-reforms-after-may-app-release-failure-leaders-forgo-bonuses-2024-10-01/; "Sonos CEO Patrick Spence Steps Down After App Update Debacle," Reuters, January 13, 2025, https://www.reuters.com/business/retail-consumer/sonos-ceo-patrick-spence-steps-down-after-app-update-debacle-2025-01-13/.

39. Aidan Kennedy, "Best Project Management Software for 2025," TrustRadius, December 2, 2024, https://solutions.trustradius.com/buyer-blog/top-10-project-management-software-and-tools/; "Best Software Products 2025," G2, 2025, https://www.g2.com/best-software-companies/2025/top-products; Asana, Inc., "Form 10-K for Year Ended January 31, 2025," US Securities and Exchange Commission, filed March 18, 2025, https://www.sec.gov/Archives/edgar/data/1477720/000147772025000045/asan-20250131.htm.

40. Homeland Security, "Cyber Safety Review Board Releases Report on Microsoft Online Exchange Incident from Summer 2023," news release, April 2, 2024, https://www.dhs.gov/archive/news/2024/04/02/cyber-safety-review-board-releases-report-microsoft-online-exchange-incident-summer; "Microsoft Teams Returns to Normalcy

After Outage," Reuters, January 26, 2024, https://www.reuters.com/technology/microsoft-teams-down-thousands-users-downdetector-2024-01-26/.

41. "Kahn Academy," Apple App Store, accessed March 15, 2026, https://apps.apple.com/us/app/khan-academy/id469863705; "Kahn Academy," Google Play, accessed March 15, 2026, https://play.google.com/store/apps/details?id=org.khanacademy.android&hl=en_US; Nishaal Bhaw et al., "A Study on the Impact of Khan Academy Videos: Enhancing Grade 11 Thermodynamics Learning in a Rural High School," *Science Education International* 35, no. 2 (2024): 163–72, https://files.eric.ed.gov/fulltext/EJ1428875.pdf; Nedim Slijepcevic and Ali Yaylali, "Leveraging 'Khanmigo' Generative AI-Powered Tool for Personalized Tutoring to Learn Scientific Concepts," *Journal of Teaching and Learning* 19, no. 4 (2025), https://jtl.uwindsor.ca/index.php/jtl/article/view/10052.

42. "CUNY and Missouri State Switch from Blackboard to Brightspace," EdScoop, June 28, 2023, https://edscoop.com/cuny-missouri-state-blackboard-brightspace/; "University at Buffalo Completes Transition to Brightspace LMS," EdScoop, August 22, 2023, https://edscoop.com/university-buffalo-completes-transition-brightspace-lms/; Phil Hill, "State of Higher Ed LMS Market for US and Canada: Year-End 2024 Edition," *On EdTech* newsletter, February 6, 2025, https://onedtech.philhillaa.com/p/state-of-higher-ed-lms-market-for-us-and-canada-year-end-2024-edition; "Blackboard," accessed March 15, 2026, Google Play, https://play.google.com/store/apps/details?id=com.blackboard.android.bbstudent&hl=en_US.

43. *ACSI Restaurant and Food Delivery Study 2025* (ACSI, 2025), https://theacsi.org/wp-content/uploads/2025/06/25jun-Restaurant-Delivery-STUDY-FINAL.pdf; Deborah Mary Sophia and Annett Mary Manoj, "Domino's Loyalty Program Revamp Boosts Results; to Lift Prices Modestly," Reuters, February 26, 2024, https://www.reuters.com/business/retail-consumer/dominos-pizza-beats-quarterly-sales-estimates-demand-bounces-back-2024-02-26/; Bryan Wassel, "Domino's Loyalty Program Fuels Carryout Growth," *Customer Experience Dive*, February 23, 2026, https://www.customerexperiencedive.com/news/dominos-loyalty-program-carryout-growth/812874/.

44. Waylon Cunningham and Deborah Mary Sophia, "Wendy's, Burned by CEO Comment, Vows No Price Surges for Burgers," Reuters, February 28, 2024, https://www.reuters.com/business/retail-consumer/wendys-will-not-implement-surge-pricing-ceo-comment-causes-online-stir-2024-02-28/; "Wendy's," Apple App Store, accessed April 27, 2026, https://apps.apple.com/us/app/wendys/id540518599.

45. "Booking.com," Apple App Store, accessed April 27, 2026, https://apps.apple.com/us/app/booking-com-hotels-travel/id367003839; *ACSI Travel Study 2025* (ACSI, 2025), https://theacsi.org/wp-content/uploads/2025/04/25apr_Travel-Study-FINAL-1.pdf; *ACSI Travel Study 2023–2024* (ACSI, April

23, 2024), https://theacsi.org/wp-content/uploads/2024/04/24apr_travel-study.pdf; Clifton Mark, "Which Travel Booking Sites Won the COVID Recovery?" YouGov, November 11, 2024, https://yougov.com/en-us/articles/50896-which-travel-booking-sites-won-the-covid-recovery.

46. *ACSI Travel Study 2025*; *ACSI Travel Study 2023–2024*; Utkarsh Shetti et al., "American Airlines Resumes Flights After Brief Grounding Ahead of Busy Christmas Travel," Reuters, December 24, 2024, https://www.reuters.com/business/aerospace-defense/american-airlines-says-experiencing-technical-issue-with-its-flights-2024-12-24/; "American Airlines Says Technology Issue Affecting Some Systems," Reuters, June 27, 2025, https://www.reuters.com/business/american-airlines-says-technology-issue-affecting-some-systems-2025-06-27/.

47. *ACSI Travel Study 2023–2024*; "Lyft," Apple App Store, accessed April 27, 2026, https://apps.apple.com/us/app/lyft/id529379082.

48. Federal Trade Commission, "FTC Finalizes Order with Online Alcohol Marketplace for Security Failures that Exposed Personal Data of 2.5 Million People," press release, January 10, 2023, https://www.ftc.gov/news-events/news/press-releases/2023/01/ftc-finalizes-order-online-alcohol-marketplace-security-failures-exposed-personal-data-25-million; Ivan Mehta, "Uber Is Closing Alcohol Delivery Service Drizly Three Years After Acquisition," *TechCrunch*, January 16, 2024, https://techcrunch.com/2024/01/16/uber-is-closing-alcohol-delivery-service-drizly-three-years-after-acquistion/.

49. JD Power, "Direct Banks Continue to Satisfy Customers by Supporting Them in Challenging Economic Times, JD Power Finds," press release, May 1, 2025, https://www.jdpower.com/business/press-releases/2025-us-direct-banking-satisfaction-study; "Marcus by Goldman Sachs," Apple App Store, accessed April 27, 2026, https://apps.apple.com/us/app/marcus-by-goldman-sachs/id1489511701.

50. *2024 U.S. Auto Insurance Study*.

51. Brett Day, "Asana Review: Features, Pros and Cons," Forbes Advisor, *Forbes*, December 5, 2024, https://www.forbes.com/advisor/business/software/asana-review/.

52. Kennedy, "Best Project Management Software for 2025."

53. "Best Software Products 2025," G2.

54. Asana, Inc., "Form 10-K."

55. *ACSI Telecommunications Study 2024*.

56. Federal Communications Commission, "All-In Pricing for Cable and Satellite Television Service."

57. *ACSI Telecommunications Study 2024.*

58. Federal Trade Commission, "Federal Trade Commission Proposes Rule Provision."

59. *2024 Communications Marketplace Report* (Federal Communications Commission, 2024), https://www.fcc.gov/document/fcc-releases-2024-communications-marketplace-report.

CHAPTER 5: SOCIOLOGY

1. Ipsos, "Ipsos Global Trends," accessed April 27, 2026, https://www.ipsos.com/en/global-trends.

2. Giusy Buonfantino, "New Research Shows Consumers More Interested in Brands' Values Than Ever," Google Cloud Blog, April 27, 2022, https://cloud.google.com/blog/topics/consumer-packaged-goods/data-shows-shoppers-prioritizing-sustainability-and-values.

3. Richard Edelman, "The New Normal: Your Brand, My Politics," Edelman, June 13, 2024, https://www.edelman.com/trust/2024/trust-barometer/special-report-brand/new-normal-your-brand-my-politics.

4. *Earth Day 2023* (Ipsos, 2023), https://www.ipsos.com/sites/default/files/ct/news/documents/2023-04/Ipsos%20Global%20Advisor%20-%20Earth%20Day%202023%20-%20Full%20Report%20-%20WEB.pdf.

5. Janice Fernandes, "Global: Are Consumers Mistrustful of Brands' Green Claims?" YouGov, February 10, 2023, https://yougov.com/articles/46193-global-are-consumers-mistrustful-of-brands-green-claims.

6. Edelman, "The New Normal."

7. Edelman, "The New Normal."

8. Ipsos, "Ipsos Global Trends."

9. *Most Trusted Brands 2024* (Morning Consult, 2024), https://pro.morningconsult.com/analyst-reports/most-trusted-brands-2024; *2024 Edelman Trust Barometer* (Edelman, 2024), https://www.edelman.com/trust/2024/trust-barometer; *Ipsos Global Trends* (Ipsos, 2024), https://www.ipsos.com/en/global-trends-2024; *Ipsos Global Trends* (Ipsos, 2023), https://www.ipsos.com/en/global-trends-2023.

10. "2023 Scorecard," REI Co-op, 2023, https://www.rei.com/dam/Scorecard.pdf.

11. "This Year's Most Innovative Companies in North America," *Fast Company*, March 19, 2024, https://www.fastcompany.com/91041293/north-america-most-innovative-companies-2024.

12. *REI Co-op Impact Report 2023* (REI, 2024), https://www.rei.com/dam/22055680_impact-report-2023.pdf.

13. US Securities and Exchange Commission, "In the Matter of Wells Fargo Clearing Services LLC and Wells Fargo Advisors Financial Network, LLC," administrative proceeding, updated September 29, 2023, https://www.sec.gov/enforcement-litigation/whistleblower-program/notice-covered-actions/award-claim-2023-123.

14. "Wells Fargo," Reuters, accessed April 27, 2026, https://www.reuters.com/company/wells-fargo-co/.

15. Chris Hydock et al., "Should Your Brand Pick a Side? How Market Share Determines the Impact of Corporate Political Advocacy," *Journal of Marketing Research* 57, no. 6 (September 2020), https://doi.org/10.1177/0022243720947682.

16. *Giving in Numbers* (Chief Executives for Corporate Purposes, 2024).

17. *FY25 Stakeholder Impact Report* (Salesforce, 2025), https://www.salesforce.com/en-us/wp-content/uploads/sites/4/documents/white-papers/salesforce-fy25-stakeholder-impact-report.pdf.

18. *FY25 Stakeholder Impact Report.*

19. *FY25 Stakeholder Impact Report.*

20. Susan Svrluga et al., "More Than 100 Arrested at Columbia as Police Clear Pro-Palestinian Protest," *The Washington Post*, April 18, 2024, https://www.washingtonpost.com/education/2024/04/18/columbia-student-gaza-protests-nypd/.

21. Apurva Chakravarthy, "Robert Kraft, CC '63, Trustee Emeritus, Announces He Is 'Not Comfortable' Supporting Columbia Until Protests End," *Columbia Spectator*, April 22, 2024, https://www.columbiaspectator.com/news/2024/04/22/robert-kraft-cc-63-trustee-emeritus-announces-he-is-not-comfortable-supporting-columbia-until-protests-end/.

22. The Russell Berrie Foundation, "The Russell Berrie Foundation Pauses Funding to Columbia University," news release, May 10, 2024, https://www.russellberriefoundation.org/news/2024/5/10/the-russell-berrie-foundation-pauses-funding-to-columbia-university.

23. Shea Vance, "Faculty of Arts and Sciences Passes Vote of No Confidence in Shafik," *Columbia Spectator*, May 16, 2024, https://www.columbiaspectator.com/news/2024/05/16/faculty-of-arts-and-sciences-passes-vote-of-no-confidence-in-shafik/.

24. Stefanie Wannow et al., "Is Brand Activism an Emotional Affair? The Role of Moral Emotions in Consumer Responses to Brand Activism," *Journal of Brand Management* 31 (May 24, 2023), 168–92, https://doi.org/10.1057/s41262-023-00326-9.

25. *The Sprout Social Index Edition XIX* (Sprout Social, 2023), https://media.sproutsocial.com/uploads/Sprout-Social-Index-Report-2023.pdf.

26. Marketing Arm Cultural Resonance Score, https://wearetma.com/crs/; Morning Consult community engagement tracking, https://start.morningconsult.com; Kantar BrandZ cultural relevance data, https://discover.kantar.com/ marketplace.

27. Stine Jacobsen, "Lego Outplays Wobbly Game Market," Reuters, March 12, 2024, https://www.reuters.com/markets/europe/lego-outplays-wobbly-game-market-2024-03-12/; Helen Reid, "Lego Sales Rise as Bricks Click with More Shoppers," Reuters, March 11, 2025, https://www.reuters.com/business/retail-consumer/lego-sales-rise-bricks-click-with-more-shoppers-2025-03-11/.

28. Siddharth Cavale, "Target Removing Some LGBTQ Merchandise Following Customer Backlash," Reuters, May 24, 2023, https://www.reuters.com/business/retail-consumer/target-remove-some-lbgtq-merchandise-after-facing-customer-backlash-2023-05-23/; "Why Is Target Pulling Some Pride Merch? The Retailer's Response to Hostile Backlash, Explained," AP News, May 24, 2023, https://apnews.com/article/target-pride-collection-lgbtq-merchandise-backlash-cf4a19844579e6041c6938b13568e17c.

29. Target, "Target Corporation Reports Second Quarter Earnings," press release, August 16, 2023, https://corporate.target.com/press/release/2023/08/target-corporation-reports-second-quarter-earnings; Ananya Mariam Rajesh, "Target Sees Profit Boost on Fewer Discounts, Pride Backlash Hurt Sales," Reuters, August 16, 2023, https://www.reuters.com/business/retail-consumer/target-cuts-annual-forecasts-americans-hold-back-non-essential-spending-2023-08-16/; Anne D'Innocenzio, "Target Q2 Sales Fall on Muted Spending, Pride Month Backlash, and It Cuts Profit Outlook for 2023," AP News, August 16, 2023, https://apnews.com/article/target-second-quarter-earnings-inflation-pride-ab2aba86d83a23431eeb00e30eba37a5.

30. "Target to Cut LGBTQ Pride Month Products from Some Stores After Backlash, Bloomberg Reports," Reuters, May 9, 2024, https://www.reuters.com/business/retail-consumer/target-pull-lgbtq-themed-items-some-stores-during-pride-month-bloomberg-news-2024-05-09/; Anne D'Innocenzio, "Target to Reduce Number of Stores Carrying Pride-Themed Merchandise After Last Year's Backlash," AP News, May 11, 2024, https://apnews.com/article/target-lgbtq-pride-667ab2f6545645f5f86ca76394e531d6.

31. Reuters, coverage of Target REACH initiative, 2023–2024, https://www.reuters.com/.

32. "Patagonia," B Lab, accessed April 27, 2026, https://www.bcorporation.net/en-us/find-a-b-corp/company/patagonia-inc/; "The 2023 Axios Harris Poll 100 Reputation Rankings," Axios, May 23, 2023, https://www.axios.com/2023/05/23/corporate-brands-reputation-america; Oliver Balch, "Brand Watch: Patagonia Pioneers New Grassroots Approach to Corporate Giving," Reuters, June 4, 2024, https://www.reuters.com/sustainability/boards-policy-regulation/brand-watch-patagonia-pioneers-new-grassroots-approach-corporate-giving-2024-06-04/.

33. *Fashion Accountability Report 2024* (Remake, 2024), https://remake.world/wp-content/uploads/2024/03/Remake-Fashion-Accountability-Report-2024-Updated3.18.24.pdf; Dorit Zimand-Sheiner and Sabina Lissitsa, "Generation Z—Factors Predicting Decline in Purchase Intentions After Receiving Negative Environmental Information: Fast Fashion Brand SHEIN as a Case Study," *Journal of Retailing and Consumer Services* 81 (November 2024), https://www.sciencedirect.com/science/article/abs/pii/S0969698924002959; Elisa Anzolin and Helen Reid, "Italy Opens Greenwashing Probe into Shein Website," Reuters, September 25, 2024, https://www.reuters.com/business/retail-consumer/italys-antitrust-opens-probe-into-shein-over-environmental-claims-2024-09-25/.

34. "The 2024 Axios Harris Poll," Axios, May 22, 2024, https://www.axios.com/2024/05/22/axios-harris-poll-company-reputation-ranking-data-source; Naomi Rovnick and Harry Robertson, "Tranquility Reigns over Markets Still Awash with Cash, for Now," Reuters, June 14, 2023, https://www.reuters.com/markets/global-markets-liquidity-2023-06-14/.

35. Doyinsola Oladipo and Philip Blenkinsop, "As Bud Slips, Heineken Plots Further Shake-Up of U.S. Light Beer," Reuters, May 23, 2023, https://www.reuters.com/business/retail-consumer/bud-slips-heineken-plots-further-shake-up-us-light-beer-2023-05-23/; Dee-Ann Durbin, "Bud Light Is No Longer America's Top Beer Following Anti-LGBTQ+ Pushback," AP News, June 14, 2023, https://apnews.com/article/bud-light-beer-modelo-sales-35db706836ca38d5fe194c93a3f641ff; Clifton Mark, "Evaluating Bud Light's Dylan Mulvaney Sponsorship," YouGov, May 4, 2023, https://yougov.com/en-us/articles/46590-evaluating-bud-lights-dylan-mulvaney-sponsorship; Hoang Nguyen, "Bud Light and Budweiser's Reputation Under Fire—Are Other AB-InBev Brands Weathering the Storm?" YouGov, May 26, 2023, https://yougov.com/en-us/articles/46696-bud-light-budweiser-anheuser-busch-brand-health-mulvaney-controversy.

36. Taylor Orth and Carl Bialik, "Trust in Media 2025: Which News Sources Americans Use and Trust," YouGov, May 30, 2025, https://yougov.com/en-us/articles/52272-trust-in-media-2025-which-news-sources-americans-use-and-trust.

37. *Media Reactions 2024 U.S. Insights* (Kantar, 2025), https://www.kantar.com/north-america/campaigns/media-reactions-us; "Musk's X Ineffective Against Surge in US Election Misinformation, Report Says," Reuters, October 31, 2024, https://www.reuters.com/world/us/musks-x-ineffective-against-surge-us-election-misinformation-report-says-2024-10-31/.

38. Jennifer Maloney, "Planet Fitness's New Chief Steps Into a Culture-War Storm," *The Wall Street Journal*, May 19, 2024, https://www.wsj.com/business/planet-fitness-ceo-colleen-keating-culture-war-5433fbec?; Boys & Girls Clubs of America, "Boys & Girls Clubs of America Opens the Door to Enhanced Youth Wellness Resources with Help from a Village of Partners," press release, May 20, 2025, https://www.bgca.org/news-stories/2025/May/boys-girls-clubs-of-america-opens-the-door-to-enhanced-youth-wellness-resources-with-help-from-a-village-of-partners/.

39. "Safety and Procedural Changes After the 2024 CrossFit Games," CrossFit, November 20, 2024, https://games.crossfit.com/article/safety-and-procedural-changes-after-2024-crossfit-games; Jamie Stengle and Josh Kelety, "A Serbian Competitor in the CrossFit Games Dies During a Swimming Event at a Texas Lake," AP News, August 8, 2024, https://apnews.com/article/crossfit-competition-death-texas-lake-74b2aaac5962ce35dc40a3838a9a4076.

40. *Most Trusted Nonprofits 2024* (Morning Consult, 2024), https://pro.morningconsult.com/analyst-reports/most-trusted-nonprofits-2024; "Brands That Matter 2023," *Fast Company*, accessed April 27, 2026, https://www.fastcompany.com/section/brands-that-matter-2023; "St. Jude Children's Research Hospital Rated Most Trusted Nonprofit for Third Year Running; Achieves Highest Trust Score Across All Nonprofit and For-Profit Brands," *Business Wire*, July 30, 2024, https://www.businesswire.com/news/home/20240730872134/en/St.-Jude-Childrens-Research-Hospital-rated-most-trusted-nonprofit-for-third-year-running-achieves-highest-trust-score-across-all-nonprofit-and-for-profit-brands.

41. John Kruzel, "US Supreme Court Blocks Purdue Pharma Bankruptcy Settlement," Reuters, June 27, 2024, https://www.reuters.com/legal/us-supreme-court-blocks-purdue-pharma-bankruptcy-settlement-2024-06-27/; Dietrich Knauth, "Purdue Pharma, Sacklers Reach $7.4 Billion National Opiod Settlement," Reuters, January 23, 2025, https://www.reuters.com/business/healthcare-pharmaceuticals/purdue-pharma-sacklers-reach-74-bln-national-opioid-settlement-2025-01-23/; Jonathan Stempel, "Purdue Pharma $7.4 Billion Opioid Settlement Wins Broad Support from US States," Reuters, June 16, 2025, https://www.reuters.com/business/healthcare-pharmaceuticals/all-us-state-attorneys-general-agree-74-billion-purdue-pharma-settlement-2025-06-16/.

42. "Canva Surpasses 60 Million Education Users as Partnerships Surge with Schools Eager for Cutting-Edge Learning Tools," *Business Wire*, February 15, 2024, https://www.businesswire.com/news/home/20240215492485/en/

Canva-Surpasses-60-Million-Education-Users-as-Partnerships-Surge-With-Schools-Eager-for-Cutting-Edge-Learning-Tools.

43. "The 2025 Axios Harris Poll," Axios, May 20, 2025, https://www.axios.com/2025/05/20/axios-harris-poll-company-reputation-ranking; Dan Primack, "Tesla, SpaceX Reputations Crater in New Axios Harris Poll 100," Axios, May 20, 2025, https://www.axios.com/2025/05/20/axios-harris-poll-tesla-spacex-elon-musk.

44. "The 2025 Axios Harris Poll"; David Hood, "Apple, Microsoft Defend DEI as Big Tech Rivals Back Down," Bloomberg Law, January 20, 2025, https://news.bloomberglaw.com/esg/apple-microsoft-defend-dei-as-big-tech-rivals-back-down; *Annual Report 2024* (Microsoft, 2024), https://www.microsoft.com/investor/reports/ar24/index.html.

45. USAspending.gov, "Contract Summary," Contract to Palantir Technologies Inc, accessed April 27, 2026, https://www.usaspending.gov/award/CONT_AWD_70CTD022FR0000170_7012_GS35F0086U_4730; Caroline Haskins, "ICE Is Paying Palantir $30 Million to Build 'ImmigrationOS' Surveillance Platform," *WIRED*, April 18, 2025, https://www.wired.com/story/ice-palantir-immigrationos/.

46. *Merit America 2024 Impact Report* (Merit America, 2025), https://meritamerica.org/2024-impact-report/.

47. Federal Trade Commission, "FTC Action Leads U.S. Dept. of Education to Forgive Nearly $37 Million in Loans for Students Deceived by University of Phoenix," press release, September 20, 2023, https://www.ftc.gov/news-events/news/press-releases/2023/09/ftc-action-leads-us-dept-education-forgive-nearly-37-million-loans-students-deceived-university.

48. *2023 Responsibility Update* (Panera Bread, 2023), https://www.panerabread.com/content/dam/panerabread/integrated-web-content/documents/press/2024/panera-bread-2023-responsibility-update.pdf; "Panera Bread," YouGov, accessed April 27, 2026, https://yougov.com/en-us/topics/brand/Panera_Bread.

49. Hilary Russ, "Barista Union to Ask Starbucks Shareholders to Back Labor Review," Reuters, March 10, 2023, https://www.reuters.com/business/retail-consumer/barista-union-ask-starbucks-shareholders-back-labor-review-2023-03-10/; Reuters, Starbucks NLRB and strike coverage, 2023–2024, https://www.reuters.com/; Jonathan Stempel, "Starbucks Largely Loses Appeal over Baristas' Firing in NLRB Case," Reuters, December 27, 2024, https://www.reuters.com/legal/starbucks-largely-loses-appeal-over-baristas-firing-nlrb-case-2024-12-27/.

50. Marriott International, Inc., "Form 10-K for the Fiscal Year Ended December 31, 2023," US Securities and Exchange Commission, filed February 6, 2024, https://marriott.gcs-web.com/static-files/e15046a3-f3e5-413a-bb4b-51238b71cb95; *Environmental, Social & Governance Global Progress* (Serve360

and Marriott International, 2024), https://serve360.marriott.com/wp-content/uploads/2024/07/2024ESGProgress.pdf.

51. David Shepardson et al., "Boeing to Withdraw MAX 7 Exemption Request as Safety Scrutiny Intensifies," Reuters, January 30, 2024, https://www.reuters.com/business/aerospace-defense/boeing-under-microscope-safety-issues-it-reports-results-2024-01-29/; David Shepardson and Allison Lampert, "Boeing CEO to Tell US Congress Planemaker's Culture Is 'Far from Perfect,'" Reuters, June 17, 2024, https://www.reuters.com/business/aerospace-defense/boeing-ceo-tell-congress-planemaker-culture-far-perfect-2024-06-17/; Chris Prentice et al., "Boeing to Plead Guilty to Fraud in US Probe of Fatal 737 MAX Crashes," Reuters, July 8, 2024, https://www.reuters.com/business/aerospace-defense/boeing-plead-guilty-us-probe-fatal-737-max-crashes-says-doj-official-2024-07-08/.

52. *America's Best Online Platforms* (*Newsweek* and Statista, 2025), https://rankings.newsweek.com/americas-best-online-platforms-2025.

53. Tom Singleton and Imran Rahman-Jones, "Grindr Sued for Allegedly Revealing Users' HIV Status," BBC, April 22, 2024, https://www.bbc.com/news/articles/cj7mxnvz42no.

54. Stripe, "Stripe Launches Climate Orders, Enabling Businesses to Pre-Order Carbon Removal Tons," news release, November 30, 2023, https://stripe.com/newsroom/news/climate-orders; Peter Henderson, "Climate Tech Firms Get $80 Million to Pull Carbon from Paper Mills, Sewage Plant," Reuters, December 17, 2024, https://www.reuters.com/sustainability/climate-tech-firms-get-80-million-pull-carbon-paper-mills-sewage-plant-2024-12-17/.

55. Federal Trade Commission, "FTC Reaches Settlement with Crypto Platform Celsius Network; Charges Former Executives with Duping Consumers into Transferring Cryptocurrency into their Platform and then Squandering Billions in User Deposits," press release, July 13, 2023, https://www.ftc.gov/news-events/news/press-releases/2023/07/ftc-reaches-settlement-crypto-platform-celsius-network-charges-former-executives-duping-consumers; U.S. Securities and Exchange Commission, "SEC Charges Celsius Network Limited and Founder Alex Mashinsky with Fraud and Unregistered Offer and Sale of Securities," press release, July 13, 2023, https://www.sec.gov/newsroom/press-releases/2023-133; Dietrich Knauth, "Crypto Lender Celsius Network Cleared to Exit Bankruptcy," Reuters, November 9, 2023, https://www.reuters.com/markets/deals/crypto-lender-celsius-network-cleared-exit-bankruptcy-2023-11-09/.

56. Oliver Balch, "Ryan Gellert: 'At Patagonia We Have to Be Greener Than Green—and Make a Profit,'" Reuters, April 11, 2023, https://www.reuters.com/business/sustainable-business/ryan-gellert-patagonia-we-have-be-greener-than-green-make-profit-2023-04-11/.

57. "Patagonia," B Lab.

58. "The 2023 Axios Harris Poll."

59. Eleanor Hawkins, "Corporate Reputations with Staying Power," Axios, May 30, 2024, https://www.axios.com/2024/05/30/corporate-reputations-with-staying-power-communicators.

60. "The 2025 Axios Harris Poll"; Eleanor Hawkins, "Companies That Kept DEI Commitments Saw Higher Reputation Scores in 2025, "Axios, May 29, 2025, https://www.axios.com/2025/05/29/dei-patagonia-costco-microsoft-reputation-surge.

61. KPMG, "Empathy and AI Shape Today's Leading Customer Experiences—New KPMG Report," news release, December 4, 2024, https://kpmg.com/us/en/media/news/customer-experience-excellence-2024.html.

62. Balch, "Brand Watch: Patagonia."

63. *Fashion Accountability Report 2022* (Remake, 2023), https://remake.world/wp-content/uploads/2023/01/Remake_AccountabilityReport_2022.pdf.

64. Remake, *Fashion Accountability Report 2024.*

65. "UK Human Rights Group Launches Campaign to Stop Shein's Potential IPO," Reuters, June 27, 2024, https://www.reuters.com/business/retail-consumer/uk-human-rights-group-launches-campaign-stop-sheins-potential-london-ipo-2024-06-26/; Sanvi Bangalore, "Shein's Mounting Ethical Concerns May Be Pushing Some of Its Gen Z Consumers Away," CBS News, August 11, 2023, https://www.cbsnews.com/news/shein-controversy-why-is-it-so-popular/.

66. Zimand-Sheiner and Lissitsa, "Generation Z."

CHAPTER 6: ECONOMICS

1. *The Top 20 Reasons Startups Fail* (CB Insights), https://s3-us-west-2.amazonaws.com/cbi-content/research-reports/The-20-Reasons-Startups-Fail.pdf.

2. Helen Reid, "IKEA Reports Higher Profit Despite Revenue Hit from Price Cuts," Reuters, November 8, 2024, https://www.reuters.com/business/retail-consumer/ikea-reports-higher-profit-despite-revenue-hit-price-cuts-2024-11-08/.

3. Nate Berg, "How IKEA Turned Flat-Pack Furniture into a Business Worth Billions," *Fast Company*, April 17, 2025, https://www.fastcompany.com/91315449/how-ikea-turned-flat-pack-furniture-into-business-worth-billions; Reuters, IKEA cost discipline coverage, 2023–2024, reuters.com.

4. Jonathan Maze, "Subway Says Its Sales Grew Again Last Year," *Restaurant Business*, February 2, 2023, https://www.restaurantbusinessonline.com/financing/

subway-says-its-sales-grew-again-last-year; Jordan Valinsky, "Subway Announces a New Price for Footlongs as It Enters the Value Menu Wars," CNN, August 23, 2024, https://www.cnn.com/2024/08/23/food/subway-footlongs-deal.

5. "Subway Aims for a Resurgence as Decades of Popularity Fade," YouGov, August 18, 2023, https://yougov.com/en-us/articles/47198-subway-aims-for-a-resurgence-as-decades-of-popularity-fade.

6. *ACSI Restaurant and Food Delivery Study 2024* (ACSI, 2024), https://theacsi.org/wp-content/uploads/2024/06/24jun-restaurant-study-FINAL.pdf; *ACSI Restaurant and Food Delivery Study 2025* (ACSI, 2025), https://theacsi.org/wp-content/uploads/2025/06/25jun-Restaurant-Delivery-STUDY-FINAL.pdf.

7. Jonathan Maze, "Subway Is Ending Its Latest Value Offer After Poor Performance," *Restaurant Business*, November 22, 2024, https://www.restaurantbusinessonline.com/marketing/subway-ending-its-latest-value-offer-after-poor-performance.

8. Amy Gallo, "The Value of Keeping the Right Customers," *Harvard Business Review*, October 29, 2014, https://hbr.org/2014/10/the-value-of-keeping-the-right-customers.

9. *Customer Revenue Leadership Study* (ChurnZero, 2024), https://churnzero.com/customer-success-leadership-study/; Stripe Revenue Retention benchmarks, stripe.com; SaaS Capital surveys, https://www.saas-capital.com/.

10. Dawn Chmielewski, "Netflix Hits Fourth-Quarter Subscriber Record, Fueled by 'The Crown' and 'The Killer,'" Reuters, January 24, 2024, https://www.reuters.com/business/netflix-reports-record-fourth-quarter-subscriber-gains-falls-shy-per-share-2024-01-23/.

11. "Netflix Says Ad-Supported Service Has 94 Million Subscribers," Reuters, May 14, 2025, https://www.reuters.com/technology/netflix-says-ad-supported-service-has-94-million-subscribers-2025-05-14/.

12. Lisa Richwine and Dawn Chmielewski, "Netflix Raises Prices and Adds Subscribers, Despite Strikes," Reuters, October 19, 2023, https://www.reuters.com/technology/netflix-raises-prices-it-adds-9-million-subscribers-2023-10-18/.

13. Stitch Fix, Inc., "Form 10-K for the Fiscal Year Ended July 31, 2021," US Securities and Exchange Commission, filed September 27, 2021, https://s21.q4cdn.com/158972969/files/doc_financials/2021/ar/Stitch-Fix-10K-FY21_FINAL.pdf; Stitch Fix, Inc., "Form 10-K for the Fiscal Year Ended August 3, 2024," US Securities and Exchange Commission, filed September 25, 2024, https://www.sec.gov/Archives/edgar/data/1576942/000157694224000099/sfix-20240803.htm.

14. Daphne Howland, "Can Stitch Fix's New Transformation Team Prove Its Model at Last?," *Retail Dive*, January 30, 2024, https://www.retaildive.com/news/stitch-fix-transformation-strategy/705657/.

15. Stitch Fix, "Form 10-K for the Fiscal Year Ended August 3, 2024."

16. SaaS Capital benchmarks, https://www.saas-capital.com/; *2024 B2B SaaS Performance Metrics Benchmark Report* (Benchmarkit, 2024), https://www.benchmarkit.ai/2024benchmarks.

17. Duolingo, "Form 10-K for the Fiscal Year Ended December 31, 2024," US Securities and Exchange Commission, filed February 28, 2025, https://www.sec.gov/Archives/edgar/data/1562088/000156208825000042/duol-20241231.htm.

18. Rebecca Stewart, "Hi! It's Duo: The Marketing Strategy Behind the Internet's Favorite Green Menace," *Adweek*, April 8, 2025, https://www.adweek.com/brand-marketing/duolingo-duo-owl-marketing-strategy/.

19. Rebecca Stewart, "TikTok Fave Duolingo Boosts YouTube Shorts Viewership 430% in One Year," *Adweek*, April 11, 2025, https://www.adweek.com/brand-marketing/tiktok-fave-duolingo-boosts-youtube-shorts-viewership-430-in-one-year/.

20. Duolingo, "Q4 & FY 2024 Shareholder Letter," Form 8-K exhibit, February 27, 2025, https://investors.duolingo.com/static-files/d0adccff-bfe0-4d10-a5bc-f116d746afd2.

21. Rent the Runway, "Form 10-K for the Fiscal Year Ended January 31, 2025," US Securities and Exchange Commission, filed April 15, 2025, https://investors.renttherunway.com/node/10376/html.

22. SEC, "Rent the Runway, Inc. Announces Fourth Quarter and Full Year 2022 Results," April 12, 2023, https://www.sec.gov/Archives/edgar/data/1468327/000146832723000047/fy22earningsrelease.htm.

23. Savyata Mishra, "Ralph Lauren Raises Sales Target on Strong Holiday Demand for Sweaters, Shirts," Reuters, November 7, 2024, https://www.reuters.com/business/retail-consumer/ralph-lauren-posts-quarterly-sales-beat-2024-11-07/; Ananya Mariam Rajesh, "Ralph Lauren's Dresses, Polo Shirts Drive Sales Forecast Raise," Reuters, February 6, 2025, https://www.reuters.com/business/retail-consumer/ralph-lauren-raises-annual-revenue-forecast-strong-apparel-demand-2025-02-06/; Ralph Lauren, "Ralph Lauren Reports Fourth Quarter and Full Year Fiscal 2024 Results Ahead of Expectations; Provides Initial Outlook for Fiscal 2025," news release, May 23, 2024, https://corporate.ralphlauren.com/pr_240523_Q4FY24_EarningsResults.html.

24. Under Armour, "Under Armour Reports Fourth Quarter and Full-Year Fiscal 2024 Results; Provides Initial Fiscal 2025 Outlook," press release, May 16, 2024, https://about.underarmour.com/en/stories/press-releases/release.24181.html; PR Newswire, "Under Armour Reports Third Quarter 2025 Results; Raises Fiscal 2025 Outlook," news release, February 6, 2025, http://prnewswire.com/news-releases/under-armour-reports-third-quarter-2025-results-raises-fiscal-2025-outlook-302369503.

html; "Under Armour to Pay $434 Million to Settle Lawsuit over Sales Disclosures," Reuters, June 21, 2024, https://www.reuters.com/legal/under-armour-pay-434-million-settle-2017-lawsuit-2024-06-21/; "Under Armour Warns Restructuring May Cost More Than Previously Expected," Reuters, September 9, 2024, https://www.reuters.com/business/retail-consumer/under-armour-sees-bigger-fiscal-2025-loss-restructuring-charges-2024-09-09/.

25. YETI Holdings Inc., "YETI Reports Fourth Quarter and Fiscal Year 2024 Results," news release, February 13, 2025, https://investors.yeti.com/news/news-details/2025/YETI-Reports-Fourth-Quarter-and-Fiscal-Year-2024-Results/default.aspx.

26. "Red Lobster Seeks Bankruptcy Protection with $100 Million in Financing Commitments," Reuters, May 20, 2024, https://www.reuters.com/legal/litigation/red-lobster-seeks-bankruptcy-protection-with-100-mln-financing-commitments-2024-05-20/; Aimee Picchi and Khristopher Brooks, "Red Lobster Files for Chapter 11 Bankruptcy Protection," CBS News, May 20, 2024, https://www.cbsnews.com/news/red-lobster-bankruptcy-chapter-11-sale-restaurants/; Soma Biswas and P. R. Venkat, "Red Lobster Files for Bankruptcy With Plan to Sell Business and Reduce Locations," *The Wall Street Journal*, May 20, 2024, https://www.wsj.com/articles/red-lobster-files-for-bankruptcy-plans-to-sell-business-88e710fe?.

27. Fox, "Tubi Surpasses 97 Million Monthly Active Users and 10 Billion Streaming Hours in 2024," news release, January 6, 2025, https://investor.foxcorporation.com/news/business/2025/tubi-surpasses-97-million-monthly-active-users-and-10-billion-streaming-hours-in-2024/; "Fox Corporation (FOX) Q2 2025 Earnings Call Transcript," Seeking Alpha, February 4, 2025, https://seekingalpha.com/article/4754671-fox-corporation-fox-q2-2025-earnings-call-transcript; "Fox Corporation Conference Transcript," Fox Corporation, May 14, 2025, https://media.investor.foxcorporation.com/wp-content/uploads/2025/05/16232715/FOX-MoffettNathanson-Conference-Transcript.pdf.

28. Sarah Perez, "Advertiser Exodus Expected to Deeply Impact X Ad Revenue, Analysis Indicates," *TechCrunch*, November 20, 2023, https://techcrunch.com/2023/11/20/advertiser-exodus-expected-to-deeply-impact-x-ad-revenue-analysis-indicates/; Aisha Malik, "X Will Soon Let Advertisers Run Ads Next to a 'Curated List' of Creators," *TechCrunch*, February 12, 2024, https://techcrunch.com/2024/02/12/x-will-soon-let-advertisers-run-ads-next-to-a-curated-list-of-creators/; Ivan Mehta, "Fidelity Marks Down X Valuation by 71.5%," *TechCrunch*, January 2, 2024, https://techcrunch.com/2024/01/02/fidelity-marks-down-x-to-almost-a-third-of-the-investment-price/.

29. Antoine Gara and Eric Platt, "Luxury Gym Chain Equinox Raises $1.8bn to Avert Cash Crunch," *The Financial Times*, March 8, 2024, https://www.ft.com/content/be39a2d6-4757-402f-aa66-2d04761cabde?syn-25a6b1a6=1; Reshmi Basu, "Fitness Company Equinox Gets $1.8 Billion to Refinance Debt," Bloomberg, March 8, 2024, https://www.bloomberg.com/news/articles/2024-03-08/

fitness-company-equinox-gets-1-8-billion-to-refinance-debt-as-loans-come-due?embedded-checkout=true.

30. Lululemon Athletica Inc., "Form 10-K for the Fiscal Year Ended January 28, 2024," US Securities and Exchange Commission, filed March 2024, 64–66, https://www.sec.gov/Archives/edgar/data/1397187/000139718724000010/lulu-20240128.htm.

31. *Annual Report 2024* (Novo Nordisk, 2024), https://www.novonordisk.com/content/dam/nncorp/global/en/investors/irmaterial/annual_report/2025/novo-nordisk-annual-report-2024.pdf; Novo Nordisk, "2024 Performance and 2025 Outlook," *Annual Report 2024*, https://annualreport.novonordisk.com/2024/strategic-aspirations/financials.html.

32. US Securities and Exchange Commission, "23andMe Reports Third Quarter Fiscal Year 2025 Financial Results," news release, January 28, 2025, https://www.sec.gov/Archives/edgar/data/1804591/000180459125000005/me-20250128x8kxexx991.htm; 23andMe, "23andMe Reports Third Quarter Fiscal Year 2025 Financial Results," press release, January 28, 2025, https://mediacenter.23andme.com/press-releases/23andme-reports-third-quarter-fiscal-year-2025-financial-results/; United States Bankruptcy Court Eastern District of Missouri Eastern Division, "Chapter 11 Memorandum Opinion 23andMe Holding Co. et al.," Case No. 25-40976, June 27, 2025, https://www.moeb.uscourts.gov/sites/moeb/files/opinions/25-40976_BK_01_23andMe.pdf; Bhanvi Satija et al., "DNA Testing Firm 23andMe Files for Bankruptcy as Demand Dries Up," Reuters, March 24, 2025, https://www.reuters.com/business/healthcare-pharmaceuticals/dna-testing-firm-23andme-files-chapter-11-bankruptcy-sell-itself-2025-03-24/.

33. Apple, "Form 10-K for the Fiscal Year Ended September 28, 2024," US Securities and Exchange Commission, filed October 31, 2024, https://www.sec.gov/Archives/edgar/data/320193/000032019324000123/aapl-20240928.htm.

34. Jaspreet Singh, "Match Forecasts Lackluster Revenue as Tinder Turnaround Takes Longer," Reuters, November 6, 2024, https://www.reuters.com/technology/match-group-forecasts-quarterly-revenue-below-estimates-2024-11-06/; "Q4 2024 Executive Commentary," MatchGroup, 2025, https://s203.q4cdn.com/993464185/files/doc_financials/2024/q4/Q4-2024-Executive-Commentary_vF.pdf.

35. Salesforce, "Salesforce Announces Fourth Quarter and Fiscal Year 2025 Results," press release, February 26, 2025, https://www.salesforce.com/news/press-releases/2025/02/26/fy25-q4-earnings/.

36. WeWork Inc., "Quarterly Report for Three and Nine Months Ended September 30, 2023," US Securities and Exchange Commission, 2023, https://www.sec.gov/Archives/edgar/data/1813756/000181375623000067/wework2023q310q.htm; United States Bankruptcy Court, District of New Jersey, "WeWork Inc. (23-19865-JKS)," accessed April 27, 2026, https://www.njb.uscourts.gov/wework;

Medha Singh, "WeWork Shares Sink to Record Low on Reports Bankruptcy Filing Imminent," Reuters, November 1, 2023, https://www.reuters.com/business/wework-shares-sink-reports-imminent-plans-bankruptcy-filing-2023-11-01/.

37. *Annual Report* (Coursera, 2024), https://www.sec.gov/Archives/edgar/data/1651562/000165156225000029/a2024annualreportdraftfina.pdf; Coursera, "Coursera Reports Fourth Quarter and Full Year 2024 Financial Results," news release, January 30, 2025, https://investor.coursera.com/news/news-details/2025/Coursera-Reports-Fourth-Quarter-and-Full-Year-2024-Financial-Results/default.aspx; Coursera, "Coursera Reports First Quarter 2024 Financial Results," news release, April 29, 2024, https://investor.coursera.com/news/news-details/2024/Coursera-Reports-First-Quarter-2024-Financial-Results/default.aspx.

38. Federal Trade Commission, "FTC Action Leads U.S. Dept. of Education to Forgive Nearly $37 Million in Loans for Students Deceived by University of Phoenix," press release, September 20, 2023, https://www.ftc.gov/news-events/news/press-releases/2023/09/ftc-action-leads-us-dept-education-forgive-nearly-37-million-loans-students-deceived-university.

39. Leigh Anne Zinsmeister, "Meet the 2025 Top 500: The Biggest Restaurant Chains in America," *Nation's Restaurant News*, June 12, 2025, https://www.nrn.com/top-500-restaurants/meet-the-2025-top-500-the-biggest-restaurant-chains-in-america.

40. Jonathan Maze, "Boston Market Is Down to 27 Restaurants," *Restaurant Business*, March 11, 2024, https://www.restaurantbusinessonline.com/financing/boston-market-down-27-restaurants; "New Jersey Shutters 27 Boston Market Restaurants over Unpaid Wages, Related Worker Issues," AP News, August 17, 2023, http://apnews.com/article/boston-market-restaurants-closed-unpaid-wages-cf0f98b7662c02284df59d1c5e91f4ca; Julie Littman, "Boston Market Owner Jay Pandya Files for Bankruptcy a Second Time," *Restaurant Dive*, 2024, https://www.restaurantdive.com/news/boston-market-owner-jay-pandya-files-bankruptcy-second-time/707482/.

41. *Q4 2023 Shareholder Letter* (Airbnb, 2024), https://s26.q4cdn.com/656283129/files/doc_financials/2023/q4/Airbnb_Q4-2023-Shareholder-Letter_Final.pdf; *Q4 2024 Shareholder Letter* (Airbnb, 2025), https://s26.q4cdn.com/656283129/files/doc_financials/2024/q4/Airbnb_Q4-2024-Shareholder-Letter_Final.pdf; Airbnb, "Form 10-K for the Year Ended December 31, 2024," US Securities and Exchange Commission, filed February 13, 2025, https://www.sec.gov/Archives/edgar/data/1559720/000155972025000010/abnb-20241231.htm.

42. Rajesh Kumar Singh, "Southwest Air's Lackluster Profit Fuels Pressure to Revamp Business Model," Reuters, September 25, 2024, https://www.reuters.com/business/aerospace-defense/southwest-airs-lackluster-profit-fuels-pressure-revamp-business-model-2024-09-25/; Southwest Airlines, "Southwest Airlines Reports Fourth

Quarter and Full Year 2024 Results," press release, January 30, 2025, https://www.southwestairlinesinvestorrelations.com/news-events/press-releases/detail/7/southwest-airlines-reports-fourth-quarter-and-full-year-2024-results; Rajesh Kumar Singh and Nathan Gomes, "Activist Investor Elliott Calls for Southwest Airlines Leadership, Board Changes," Reuters, June 10, 2024, https://www.reuters.com/business/aerospace-defense/southwest-airlines-jumps-after-report-elliotts-2-bln-stake-2024-06-10/; Rajesh Kumar Singh and Shivansh Tiwary, "Southwest Airlines' Open Seating to End as It Looks to Lift Earnings," Reuters, July 25, 2024, https://www.reuters.com/business/aerospace-defense/southwest-airlines-beats-q2-profit-expectations-marks-shift-premium-seating-2024-07-25/; U.S. Department of Transportation, "DOT Penalizes Southwest Airlines $140 Million for 2022 Holiday Meltdown," news release, December 18, 2023, https://www.transportation.gov/briefing-room/dot-penalizes-southwest-airlines-140-million-2022-holiday-meltdown.

43. Uber Technologies, Inc., "Form 10-K for the Year Ended December 31, 2023," US Securities and Exchange Commission, filed February 21, 2024, https://www.sec.gov/Archives/edgar/data/1543151/000154315124000012/uber-20231231.htm.

44. Paul Sawers, "Electric Scooter Company Bird Files for Bankruptcy," *TechCrunch*, December 20, 2023, https://techcrunch.com/2023/12/20/bird-bankruptcy/.

45. *The Progressive Corporation 2024 Annual Report* (Progressive, 2024), https://s202.q4cdn.com/605347829/files/doc_financials/2024/q4/interactive/pdfs/Progressive-2024-AR.pdf; Progressive, "Progressive Reports December 2024 Results," news release, January 29, 2025, https://investors.progressive.com/financials/financial-news-releases/news-details/2025/Progressive-Reports-December-2024-Results/default.aspx.

46. Elliot Smith, "Credit Suisse Logged Asset Outflows of More Than $68 Billion During First-Quarter Collapse," CNBC, April 24, 2023, https://www.cnbc.com/2023/04/24/credit-suisse-earnings-q1-2023.html; "Bank of England Welcomes Credit Suisse–UBS Merger," Reuters, March 19, 2023, https://www.reuters.com/business/finance/bank-england-welcomes-credit-suisse-ubs-merger-2023-03-19/; Pablo Mayo Cerqueiro et al., "Credit Suisse Says $17 Billion Debt Worthless, Angering Bondholders," Reuters, March 19, 2023, https://www.reuters.com/business/finance/credit-suisse-writes-down-17-bln-bonds-zero-angering-holders-2023-03-19/.

47. Apple Inc., "Apple Reports Fourth Quarter Results," press release, October 31, 2024, https://www.apple.com/newsroom/2024/10/apple-reports-fourth-quarter-results/.

48. Apple Inc., "Form 10-K for the Year Ended September 28, 2024," US Securities and Exchange Commission, filed November 1, 2024, https://www.sec.gov/Archives/edgar/data/320193/000032019324000123/aapl-20240928.htm.

49. "Apple (AAPL) Q1 2025 Earnings Call Transcript," The Motley Fool, January 30, 2025, https://www.fool.com/earnings/call-transcripts/2025/01/30/apple-aapl-q1-2025-earnings-call-transcript/.

50. WeWork Inc., "Quarterly Report for Three and Nine Months Ended September 30, 2023."

51. US Securities and Exchange Commission, "WeWork Reports Second Quarter 2023 Results," news release, August 8, 2023, https://www.sec.gov/Archives/edgar/data/1813756/000181375623000061/wework2023q2pressrelease.htm.

52. Singh, "WeWork Shares Sink"; United States Bankruptcy Court, District of New Jersey, "WeWork Inc. (23-19865-JKS)."

CHAPTER 7: THE VALEDICTORIANS

1. Granth Vanaik, "Lululemon Says Third Quarter off to 'Solid Start' as North America Improves," Reuters, August 31, 2023, https://www.reuters.com/business/retail-consumer/lululemon-raises-annual-forecasts-second-time-buoyant-demand-2023-08-31/.

2. Christian Holtz, "Top 1% E-Commerce UX Winners—2024 Winners," Baymard Institute, December 10, 2024, https://baymard.com/blog/ux-awards-2024.

3. Savyata Mishra, "Lululemon Tops Quarterly Estimates on Solid China Demand; to Buy Back More Shares," Reuters, June 5, 2024, https://www.reuters.com/business/retail-consumer/lululemon-beats-quarterly-revenue-estimate-2024-06-05/.

4. Casey Hall, "In China, a Search for Identity Boosts Lululemon, Premium Sportswear Brands," Reuters, June 10, 2024, https://www.reuters.com/business/retail-consumer/china-search-identity-boosts-lululemon-premium-sportswear-brands-2024-06-11/.

5. Mishra, "Lululemon Tops Quarterly"; Lululemon Athletica Inc., "Lululemon Athletica Inc. Announces First Quarter Fiscal 2025 Results," press release, June 5, 2025, https://corporate.lululemon.com/media/press-relea ses/2025/06-05-2025-210525682.

6. Lululemon Athletica Inc., "Form 10-K for the Year Ended February 2, 2025," US Securities and Exchange Commission, filed March 27, 2025, https://www.sec.gov/Archives/edgar/data/1397187/000139718725000013/lulu-20250202.htm.

7. Under Armour, "Under Armour Reports Fourth Quarter and Full-Year Fiscal 2024 Results; Provides Initial Fiscal 2025 Outlook," press release, May 16, 2024, https://about.underarmour.com/en/stories/press-releases/release.24181.html; PR Newswire, "Under Armour Reports Third Quarter 2025 Results; Raises Fiscal 2025 Outlook," news release, February 6, 2025, http://prnewswire.com/news-releases/under-armour-reports-third-quarter-2025-results-raises-fiscal-2025-outlook-302369503.html

8. "Retail Trends to Watch in 2025," Placer.ai, November 18, 2024, https://www.placer.ai/anchor/reports/retail-trends-to-watch-in-2025?gated=true.

9. Bill Wilson, "Trader Joe's Continues to Crank Out Store Openings," *Supermarket News*, July 21, 2025, https://www.supermarketnews.com/new-stores/trader-joe-s-continues-to-crank-out-store-openings; "Largest Private Companies," *Los Angeles Business Journal*, October 6, 2025, https://labusinessjournal.com/wp-content/uploads/2025/10/20251006_labj_021-23_LPC-LIST.pdf.

10. "Retail Trends to Watch in 2025"; Bracha Arnold, "Trader Joe's and Aldi's Continued Success," Placer.ai., March 25, 2025, https://www.placer.ai/anchor/articles/trader-joes-and-aldis-continued-success.

11. *Raising the Bar: Wellness Bars, Trends and the Future of Functional Snacking* (SPINS, November 2024), https://www.spins.com/wp-content/uploads/2024/11/FFT-Wellness-Snack-Bars-Nov2024.pdf; Jenni Spinner, "Lifting the Bars," *Snack Food & Wholesale Bakery*, February 27, 2024, https://digitaledition.snackandbakery.com/february-2024/category-focus/; Caleb Wilson, "Better-for-You Brand Launches Cookie Line," *Food Business News*, April 11, 2023, https://www.foodbusinessnews.net/articles/23586-protein-brands-gain-as-nutrition-bars-struggle.

12. Fox, "Tubi Releases New Findings on Streaming TV Trends in Its Annual Report, The Stream 2023: Actionable Audience Insights for Brands," news release, February 14, 2023, https://www.foxcorporation.com/news/business/2023/tubi-releases-new-findings-on-streaming-tv-trends-in-its-annual-report-the-stream-2023-actionable-audience-insights-for-brands/; Tubi, "Tubi Unveils Insights on How Marketers Can Reach Cord-Cutters and Cord-Nevers in The Stream 2024," press release, March 12, 2024, https://corporate.tubitv.com/press/tubi-unveils-insights-on-how-marketers-can-reach-cord-cutters-and-cord-nevers-in-the-stream-2024/; Tubi, "Tubi Surpasses 97 Million Monthly Active Users and 10 Billion Streaming Hours in 2024," press release, January 6, 2025, https://corporate.tubitv.com/press/tubi-surpasses-97-million-monthly-active-users-and-10-billion-streaming-hours-in-2024/.

13. Tubi, "Tubi Releases New Findings on Streaming TV Trends in Its Annual Report, *The Stream 2023: Actionable Audience Insights for Brands*," press release, February 14, 2023, https://corporate.tubitv.com/press/tubi-releases-new-findings-on-streaming-tv-trends-in-its-annual-report-the-stream-2023-actionable-audience-insights-for-brands/.

14. Fox, "Super Bowl LIX on FOX and Tubi Generates More Than $800 Million in Gross Advertising Revenue," press release, February 12, 2025, https://www.foxcorporation.com/news/business/2025/super-bowl-lix-on-fox-and-tubi-generates-more-than-800-million-in-gross-advertising-revenue/; Daniel Frankel, "Fox Delivers Solid Super Bowl Livestream, This Time Through Tubi," StreamTV Insider, February 12, 2025, https://www.streamtvinsider.com/video/fox-delivers-solid-super-bowl-livestream-time-through-tubi; Stephen Battaglio, "Super Bowl LIX Scores a Record 127.7 Million Viewers Despite Blowout," *Los Angeles Times*, February 10, 2025, https://www.latimes.com/entertainment-arts/business/story/2025-02-10/

super-bowl-lix-scores-126-million-viewers-despite-blowout; Rick Porter, "Super Bowl Sets All-Time Ratings Record for Second Straight Year," *The Hollywood Reporter*, February 10, 2025, https://www.hollywoodreporter.com/tv/tv-news/super-bowl-lix-tv-ratings-record-feb-9-2025-1236132107/.

15. SEC, "Fox Reports Third Quarter Fiscal 2023," SEC Form 8-K, Exhibit 99.1, May 9, 2023, https://www.sec.gov/Archives/edgar/data/1754301/000119312523138936/d370789dex991.htm; Fox Corporation, "Fox Corporation Reports First Quarter Fiscal 2025 Financial Results," press release, November 4, 2024, https://investor.foxcorporation.com/news/corp-press-releases/2024/fox-corporation-reports-first-quarter-fiscal-2025-financial-results/; SEC, "Fox Reports Third Quarter Fiscal 2025," SEC Form 8-K, Exhibit 99.1, May 12, 2025, https://www.sec.gov/Archives/edgar/data/1754301/000162828025024454/foxearningsreleaseq325.htm.

16. "*Washington Post*'s Bezos Defends Decision to End Presidential Endorsements," Reuters, October 28, 2024, https://www.reuters.com/world/us/over-200000-subscribers-flee-washington-post-after-it-blocks-harris-endorsement-2024-10-28/.

17. David Bauder, "Sally Buzbee Steps Down as Executive Editor of *The Washington Post*," AP News, June 3, 2024, https://apnews.com/article/washington-post-buzbee-resign-editor-705e69a42fe8022ce46205bb06932fb8; David Folkenflik, "A Pulitzer Winner Quits 'Washington Post' After a Cartoon on Bezos Is Killed," NPR, January 4, 2025, https://www.npr.org/2025/01/04/nx-s1-5248299/cartoonist-quits-wapo-over-bezos-trump-cartoon-washingtonpost; David Bauder, "Washington Post Columnist Quits After Her Opinion Piece Criticizing Owner Jeff Bezos Is Rejected," AP News, March 10, 2025, https://apnews.com/article/washington-post-resignation-marcus-bezos-8d6ce32b27f5c965fc972d73d0f95aac.

18. "Washington Post Will Offer Buyouts to Employees to Reduce Staff," Reuters, October 10, 2023, https://www.reuters.com/markets/us/washington-post-will-offer-buyouts-employees-reduce-staff-2023-10-10/; "Washington Post to Lay Off 4% of Staff to Cut Costs," Reuters, January 7, 2025, https://www.reuters.com/business/media-telecom/washington-post-lay-off-4-staff-cut-costs-2025-01-07/.

19. Antoine Gara and Eric Platt, "Luxury Gym Chain Equinox Raises $1.8bn to Avert Cash Crunch," *The Financial Times*, March 8, 2024, https://www.ft.com/content/be39a2d6-4757-402f-aa66-2d04761cabde?syn-25a6b1a6=1.

20. Bloomberg Wire, "Gyms Face Tough Year as Key January Growth Screeches to Halt," Bloomberg, February 11, 2024, https://www.bloomberg.com/news/articles/2024-02-11/gyms-face-tough-year-as-key-january-growth-screeches-to-a-halt?embedded-checkout=true.

21. Gara and Platt, "Luxury Gym Chain Equinox."

22. Weight Watchers, "WW International, Inc. Announces Fourth Quarter and Full Year 2024 Results," news release, February 27, 2025, https://corporate.ww.com/news/

news-details/2025/WW-International-Inc--Announces-Fourth-Quarter-and-Full-Year-2024-Results/default.aspx.

23. "WeightWatchers Files for Chapter 11 Bankruptcy to Cut Debt," Reuters, May 6, 2025, https://www.reuters.com/business/weightwatchers-plans-file-bankruptcy-protection-2025-05-06/.

24. "Facts & Figures," Cleveland Clinic, accessed April 27, 2026, https://my.clevelandclinic.org/about/overview/who-we-are/facts-figures.

25. "Treatment Oucomes," Cleveland Clinic, https://my.clevelandclinic.org/departments/patient-experience/depts/quality-patient-safety/treatment-outcomes/736-patient-experience-outpatient-office-visit-survey.

26. "Financial Information & Annual Reports," Cleveland Clinic, accessed April 27, 2026, https://my.clevelandclinic.org/about/overview/financial-information.

27. *Consolidated Financial Statements and Supplementary Information: Years Ended December 31, 2024 and 2023* (Cleveland Clinic Foundation, 2025), https://my.clevelandclinic.org/-/scassets/files/org/about/financial-statements/cchs-2024-w-ob-nonob.pdf.

28. Lorenzo Franceschi-Bicchierai, "23andMe Confirms Hackers Stole Ancestry Data on 6.9 Million Users," *TechCrunch*, December 4, 2023, https://techcrunch.com/2023/12/04/23andme-confirms-hackers-stole-ancestry-data-on-6-9-million-users/.

29. SEC, "23andMe Reports First Quarter Fiscal 2025 Financial Results," SEC Form 8-K, Exhibit 99.1, August 8, 2024, https://www.sec.gov/Archives/edgar/data/1804591/000180459124000045/me-20240808x8kxexx991.htm; SEC, "23andMe Reports Third Quarter Fiscal Year 2025 Financial Results," SEC Form 8-K, Exhibit 99.1, January 28, 2025, https://www.sec.gov/Archives/edgar/data/1804591/000180459125000005/me-20250128x8kxexx991.htm; 23andMe, "23andMe Reports First Quarter Fiscal 2025 Financial Results," press release, August 8, 2024, https://mediacenter.23andme.com/press-releases/23andme-reports-first-quarter-fiscal-2025-financial-results/.

30. 23andMe, "23andMe Reports Third Quarter Fiscal Year 2025 Financial Results," press release, January 28, 2025, https://mediacenter.23andme.com/press-releases/23andme-reports-third-quarter-fiscal-year-2025-financial-results/; United States Bankruptcy Court Eastern District of Missouri Eastern Division, "Chapter 11 Memorandum Opinion 23andMe Holding Co. et al.," Case No. 25-40976, June 27, 2025, https://www.moeb.uscourts.gov/sites/moeb/files/opinions/25-40976_BK_01_23andMe.pdf.

31. Connie Loizos, "T. Rowe Price Has Marked Down Its Stake in Canva by 67.6%," *TechCrunch*, June 2, 2023, https://techcrunch.com/2023/06/02/t-rowe-price-has-marked-down-its-stake-in-canva-by-67-6/; Sankalp Phartiyal, "Canva Tests Low-Cost Plans in Emerging Markets After India Progress," Bloomberg, February 13, 2025, https://www.bloomberg.com/news/articles/2025-02-14/canva-tests-cheap-plans-in-emerging-markets-after-india-progress

32. "Canva Surpasses 60 Million Education Users as Partnerships Surge with Schools Eager for Cutting-Edge Learning Tools," *Business Wire*, February 15, 2024, https://www.businesswire.com/news/home/20240215492485/en/Canva-Surpasses-60-Million-Education-Users-as-Partnerships-Surge-With-Schools-Eager-for-Cutting-Edge-Learning-Tools.

33. Rebecca Bellen, "From Graphic Design to Visual Workflows, Canva's New AI Core Is Changing Its Business," *TechCrunch*, December 28, 2023, https://techcrunch.com/2023/12/28/canva-ai-core-growth/; Phartiyal, "Canva Tests Low-Cost"; "Canva," Sacra, December 11, 2024, https://sacra.com/c/canva/.

34. Chris Welch, "Sonos Lays off 100 Employees as Its App Crisis Continues," The Verge, August 14, 2024, https://www.theverge.com/2024/8/14/24220357/sonos-layoffs-august-2024-app.

35. Greg Bensinger, "Exclusive: Sonos CEO Promises Reform After May App Release 'Failure'; Leaders to Forgo Bonuses," Reuters, October 1, 2024, https://www.reuters.com/technology/sonos-ceo-promises-reforms-after-may-app-release-failure-leaders-forgo-bonuses-2024-10-01/; "Sonos CEO Patrick Spence Steps Down After App Update Debacle," Reuters, January 13, 2025, https://www.reuters.com/business/retail-consumer/sonos-ceo-patrick-spence-steps-down-after-app-update-debacle-2025-01-13/.

36. Connie Loizos, "T. Rowe Price Has Marked Down Its Stake in Canva by 67.6%," *TechCrunch*, June 2, 2023, https://techcrunch.com/2023/06/02/t-rowe-price-has-marked-down-its-stake-in-canva-by-67-6/; Sankalp Phartiyal, "Canva Tests Low-Cost Plans in Emerging Markets After India Progress," Bloomberg, February 13, 2025, https://www.bloomberg.com/news/articles/2025-02-14/canva-tests-cheap-plans-in-emerging-markets-after-india-progress

37. "Canva Surpasses 60 Million Education Users as Partnerships Surge with Schools Eager for Cutting-Edge Learning Tools," *Business Wire*, February 15, 2024, https://www.businesswire.com/news/home/20240215492485/en/Canva-Surpasses-60-Million-Education-Users-as-Partnerships-Surge-With-Schools-Eager-for-Cutting-Edge-Learning-Tools.

38. Rebecca Bellen, "From Graphic Design to Visual Workflows, Canva's New AI Core Is Changing Its Business," *TechCrunch*, December 28, 2023, https://techcrunch.

com/2023/12/28/canva-ai-core-growth/; Phartiyal, "Canva Tests Low-Cost"; "Canva," Sacra, December 11, 2024, https://sacra.com/c/canva/.

39. Chris Welch, "Sonos Lays off 100 Employees as Its App Crisis Continues," The Verge, August 14, 2024, https://www.theverge.com/2024/8/14/24220357/sonos-layoffs-august-2024-app.

40. Greg Bensinger, "Exclusive: Sonos CEO Promises Reform After May App Release 'Failure'; Leaders to Forgo Bonuses," Reuters, October 1, 2024, https://www.reuters.com/technology/sonos-ceo-promises-reforms-after-may-app-release-failure-leaders-forgo-bonuses-2024-10-01/; "Sonos CEO Patrick Spence Steps Down After App Update Debacle," Reuters, January 13, 2025, https://www.reuters.com/business/retail-consumer/sonos-ceo-patrick-spence-steps-down-after-app-update-debacle-2025-01-13/.

41. Salesforce, "Salesforce Announces Strong Fourth Quarter Fiscal 2024 Results," news release, February 28, 2024, https://www.salesforce.com/news/press-releases/2024/02/28/fy24-q4-earnings/.

42. Anna Huddleston, "Field Report: 10 Things We Loved at Dreamforce 2024," Event Marketer, September 27, 2024, https://www.eventmarketer.com/article/field-report-10-things-we-loved-at-dreamforce-2024/.

43. "Gartner Magic Quadrant for Customer Data Platforms," Gartner, February 14, 2024, https://www.gartner.com/en/documents/5197463; "Gartner Magic Quadrant for Multichannel Marketing Hubs," Gartner, October 23, 2024, https://www.gartner.com/en/documents/5861279.

44. *FY25 Stakeholder Impact Report* (Salesforce, 2025), https://www.salesforce.com/en-us/wp-content/uploads/sites/4/documents/white-papers/salesforce-fy25-stakeholder-impact-report.pdf.

45. Salesforce, "Salesforce Announces Fourth Quarter and Fiscal Year 2025 Results," news release, February 26, 2025, https://www.salesforce.com/news/press-releases/2025/02/26/fy25-q4-earnings/.

46. Zoom Video Communications, Inc., "Form 8-K," US Securities and Exchange Commission, May 22, 2023, https://investors.zoom.us/static-files/ef22d1e9-dadc-4141-849e-dffb70bce3ef; Zoom, "Zoom Communications Reports Fourth Quarter and Fiscal Year 2025 Financial Results," February 24, 2025, https://investors.zoom.us/node/13246/pdf.

47. *Annual Report: Fiscal 2025* (Zoom, 2025), https://investors.zoom.us/static-files/f5b92b93-5af9-42cb-ab0d-931c309417a9.

48. Zoom Video Communications, Inc., "Form 8-K," US Securities and Exchange Commission, June 1, 2023, https://ir.zoominfo.com/static-files/45e49117-1f21-4769-bea9-7bb8549336c0; *Annual Report: Fiscal 2025* (Zoom).

49. Duolingo, "Duolingo Achieves 54% DAU Growth and 40% Revenue Growth in Third Quarter 2024," news release, November 6, 2024, https://investors.duolingo.com/news-releases/news-release-details/duolingo-achieves-54-dau-growth-and-40-revenue-growth-third; Nishaal Bhaw et al., "A Study on the Impact of Khan Academy Videos: Enhancing Grade 11 Thermodynamics Learning in a Rural High School," *Science Education International* 35, no. 2 (2024): 163–72, https://files.eric.ed.gov/fulltext/EJ1428875.pdf.

50. *Shareholder Letter: Q4/FY 2024* (Duolingo, 2025), https://investors.duolingo.com/static-files/99006c40-d8cf-41ca-b5b1-c5cb1fa5ba88.

51. Rebecca Stewart, "TikTok Fave Duolingo Boosts YouTube Shorts Viewership 430% in One Year," *Adweek*, April 11, 2025, https://www.adweek.com/brand-marketing/tiktok-fave-duolingo-boosts-youtube-shorts-viewership-430-in-one-year/.

52. Duolingo, "Duolingo Achives 54%"; *Shareholder Letter: Q4/FY 2024* (Duolingo).

53. Chegg, "Chegg Reports 2025 First Quarter Earnings," US Securities and Exchange Commission, May 12, 2025, https://www.sec.gov/Archives/edgar/data/1364954/000136495425000049/a9901-financialresultsq120.htm.

54. Alex Wilhelm and Natasha Mascarenhas, "OpenAI's ChatGPT Is Shaking Up the Edtech Markets," *TechCrunch*, May 5, 2023, https://techcrunch.com/2023/05/05/openai-chatgpt-chegg-edtech/.

55. Kyle Wiggers, "Chegg Sues Google Over AI Search Summaries," *TechCrunch*, February 24, 2025, https://techcrunch.com/2025/02/24/chegg-sues-google-over-ai-search-summaries/.

56. Chegg, "Chegg Reports 2025 First Quarter Earnings."

57. Leigh Anne Zinsmeister, "Meet the 2025 Top 500: The Biggest Restaurant Chains in America," *Nation's Restaurant News*, June 12, 2025, https://www.nrn.com/top-500-restaurants/meet-the-2025-top-500-the-biggest-restaurant-chains-in-america.

58. "Support/Corporate Employment," In-N-Out Burger, accessed April 27, 2026, https://www.in-n-out.com/employment/corporate/full-time-benefits.

59. PR Newswire, "Datassential Unveils the 2025 Datassential 500 Awards, Honoring the Most Beloved and Innovative Restaurant Chains," news release, June 12, 2025, https://www.prnewswire.com/news-releases/datassential-unveils-the-2025-datassential-500-awards-honoring-the-most-beloved-and-innovative-restaurant-chains-302479866.html.

60. Jonathan Maze, "Boston Market Is Down to 27 Restaurants," *Restaurant Business*, March 11, 2024, https://www.restaurantbusinessonline.com/financing/boston-market-down-27-restaurants.

61. Aneurin Canham-Clyne, "New Jersey DOL issues stop-work orders at 27 Boston Markets over wage complaints," *Restaurant Dive*, August 17, 2023, https://www.restaurantdive.com/news/boston-market-27-stop-work-orders-njdol-new-jersey-department-of-labor/691036/.

62. Aneurin Canham-Clyne, "U.S. Foods Wins $11.9 Million Suit Against Boston Market by Default," *Restaurant Dive*, February 1, 2024, https://www.restaurantdive.com/news/judge-grants-us-foods-default-judgement-against-boston-market/706288/.

63. *Q4 2023 Shareholder Letter* (Airbnb, 2024), https://s26.q4cdn.com/656283129/files/doc_financials/2023/q4/Airbnb_Q4-2023-Shareholder-Letter_Final.pdf; *Q4 2024 Shareholder Letter* (Airbnb, 2025), https://s26.q4cdn.com/656283129/files/doc_financials/2024/q4/Airbnb_Q4-2024-Shareholder-Letter_Final.pdf; *Q1 2025 Shareholder Letter* (Airbnb, 2025), https://s26.q4cdn.com/656283129/files/doc_financials/2025/q1/Airbnb_Q1-2025-Shareholder-Letter_Final.pdf.

64. *Q4 2023 Shareholder Letter* (Airbnb); *Q4 2024 Shareholder Letter* (Airbnb).

65. Airbnb, "Form 10-Q for the Quarter Ended September 30, 2023," US Securities and Exchange Commission, filed November 2, 2023, https://www.sec.gov/Archives/edgar/data/1559720/000155972023000020/abnb-20230930.htm.

66. *Q1 2025 Shareholder Letter* (Airbnb); *Q4 2024 Shareholder Letter* (Airbnb).

67. *Q4 2024 Shareholder Letter* (Airbnb); *Q4 2023 Shareholder Letter* (Airbnb).

68. Carnival, "Form 10-K for the year ended November 30, 2024," US Securities and Exchange Commission, January 27, 2025, https://www.sec.gov/Archives/edgar/data/815097/000081509725000007/pdfofform10k.pdf.

69. Michael Kaczmarski, "Which Company Is Winning the Restaurant Food Delivery War?" Bloomberg Second Measure, April 15, 2024, https://secondmeasure.com/datapoints/food-delivery-services-grubhub-uber-eats-doordash-postmates/.

70. DoorDash, "DoorDash Releases Fourth Quarter and Full Year 2023 Results," news release, February 15, 2024, https://ir.doordash.com/news/news-details/2024/DoorDash-Releases-Fourth-Quarter-and-Full-Year-2023-Financial-Results/default.aspx.

71. DoorDash, "DoorDash Announces Agreement to Acquire Deliveroo," news release, May 6, 2025, https://ir.doordash.com/news/news-details/2025/DoorDash-Announces-Agreement-to-Acquire-Deliveroo/default.aspx.

72. Sarah Perez, "The FTC Orders HomeAdvisor to Pay Up to $7.2M for Lying About Lead Quality and Other Matters," *TechCrunch*, January 23, 2023, https://techcrunch.com/2023/01/23/the-ftc-fines-homeadvisor-up-to-7-2m-for-lying-about-lead-quality-and-other-matters/.

73. *Vanguard 500 Index Fund* (Vanguard, 2023), https://fund-docs.vanguard.com/q400.pdf; *Annual Shareholder Report* (Vanguard, 2024), https://workplace.vanguard.com/assets/corp/fund_communications/pdf_publish/us-products/tsr/AR857.pdf.

74. *Global Fund Flows—2024 in Review* (Morningstar, 2024), https://www.morningstar.com/business/insights/research/global-asset-flows-report; Joe Morris, "Vanguard Wins US 2024 ETF Flows Crown," *Financial Times*, January 8, 2025, https://www.ft.com/etf-hub.

75. Vanguard, "Vanguard Announces Largest Ever Expense Ratio Reduction," news release, February 3, 2025, https://corporate.vanguard.com/content/corporatesite/us/en/corp/who-we-are/pressroom/press-release-vanguard-announces-largest-ever-expense-ratio-reduction-020325.html.

76. Charles Schwab, "Schwab Reports Fourth Quarter and Full Year Results," January 21, 2025, https://content.schwab.com/web/retail/public/about-schwab/schwab_q4_2024_earnings_release.pdf.

77. Lemonade, "Form 10-K for the Year Ended December 31, 2024," US Securities and Exchange Commission, filed February 26, 2025, https://www.sec.gov/Archives/edgar/data/1691421/000169142125000031/lmnd-20241231.htm.

78. Texas Department of Insurance, "Consent Order No. 2024-8780," August 13, 2024, https://www.tdi.texas.gov/commissioner/disciplinary-orders/documents/20248780.pdf; David Jones, "Lemonade Says Applicant Driver's License Numbers Exposed," *Cybersecurity Dive*, April 18, 2025, https://www.cybersecuritydive.com/news/lemonade-drivers-license-exposed/745762/.

79. On, "On Announces Fourth Quarter and Full Year Results, and the Filing of its Annual Report on Form 20-F for 2023," news release, March 12, 2024, https://investors.on-running.com/news/news-details/2024/On-Announces-Fourth-Quarter-and-Full-Year-Results-and-the-Filing-of-its-Annual-Report-on-Form-20-F-for-2023/default.aspx; On, "On Announces Fourth Quarter and Full Year Results, and the Filing of its Annual Report on Form 20-F for 2025," financials, accessed April 27, 2026, https://investors.on-running.com/financials/default.aspx"; Ananya Mariam Rajesh, "On Holding Raises Annual Sales Forecast on Strong Running Shoes Demand," Reuters, May 14, 2024, https://www.reuters.com/business/retail-consumer/holding-raises-annual-sales-forecast-strong-running-shoes-demand-2024-05-14/.

80. YETI Holdings Inc., "YETI Reports Fourth Quarter and Fiscal Year 2023 Results," news release, February 15, 2024, https://investors.yeti.com/news/news-details/2024/YETI-Reports-Fourth-Quarter-and-Fiscal-Year-2023-Results/; YETI Holdings Inc., "YETI Reports Fourth Quarter and Fiscal Year 2024 Results," news release, February 13, 2025, https://investors.yeti.com/news/news-details/2025/YETI-Reports-Fourth-Quarter-and-Fiscal-Year-2024-Results/default.aspx.

81. Reddit, "Reddit Announces First Quarter 2024 Results," news release, May 7, 2024, https://investor.redditinc.com/news-events/news-releases/news-details/2024/Reddit-Announces-First-Quarter-2024-Results/; Reddit, "Reddit Announces Second Quarter 2024 Results," news release, August 6, 2024, https://investor.redditinc.com/news-events/news-releases/news-details/2024/Reddit-Announces-Second-Quarter-2024-Results/; Reddit, "Reddit Announces Third Quarter 2024 Results," news release, October 29, 2024, https://investor.redditinc.com/news-events/news-releases/news-details/2024/Reddit-Announces-Third-Quarter-2024-Results/; Reddit, "Reddit Announces Fourth Quarter and Full Year 2024 Results," news release, February 12, 2025, https://investor.redditinc.com/news-events/news-releases/news-details/2025/Reddit-Announces-Fourth-Quarter-and-Full-Year-2024-Results/; Reddit, "Form 10-Q for the Quarterly Period Ended March 31, 2025," US Securities and Exchange Commission, https://s203.q4cdn.com/380862485/files/doc_financials/2025/q1/80fd347c-6d90-4264-8bac-b8ff9f56cb02.pdf; Echo Wang and Anirban Sen, "Reddit Prices IPO at Top of Indicated Range to Raise $748 Million," Reuters, March 21, 2024, https://www.reuters.com/markets/deals/reddit-prices-ipo-top-indicated-range-sources-say-2024-03-20/; Yuvraj Malik, "Reddit Stock Jumps After OpenAI Partnership," Reuters, May 17, 2024, https://www.reuters.com/technology/reddit-stock-jumps-after-openai-partnership-2024-05-17/.

82. "The Future of Smart Rings," IDC, October 23, 2024, https://www.idc.com/resource-center/blog/the-future-of-smart-rings/; "Oura," Apple App Store, accessed April 27, 2026, https://apps.apple.com/us/app/oura/id1043837948.

83. Hims & Hers, "Hims & Hers Health, Inc. Reports Fourth Quarter and Full Year 2025 Financial Results," news release, February 23, 2026, https://investors.hims.com/news/news-details/2026/Hims--Hers-Health-Inc--Reports-Fourth-Quarter-and-Full-Year-2025-Financial-Results/default.aspx.

84. Sony Group Corporation, "Form 6-K for the Month of May 2024," US Securities and Exchange Commission, May 14, 2024, https://www.sec.gov/Archives/edgar/data/313838/000110465924060824/tm2414161d1_6k.htm; Donovan Erskine, "PlayStation Network Had 118 Million Monthly Active Users in Q4 2023," Shacknews, May 14, 2024, https://www.shacknews.com/article/139872/playstation-network-mau-q4-2023; Sony Group Corporation, "Corporate Strategy Presentation 2025," news release, May 14, 2025, https://www.sony.com/en/SonyInfo/News/Press/202505/25-014E/.

85. ServiceNow, "ServiceNow Reports First Quarter 2023 Financial Results," press release, April 26, 2023, https://newsroom.servicenow.com/press-releases/details/2023/ServiceNow-Reports-First-Quarter-2023-Financial-Results-04-26-2023-traffic/default.aspx; ServiceNow, "ServiceNow Reports Fourth Quarter and Full-Year 2024 Financial Results," press release, January 29, 2025, https://newsroom.servicenow.com/press-releases/details/2025/ServiceNow-Reports-Fourth-Quarter-and-Full-Year-2024-Financial-Results-01-29-2025-traffic/default.aspx; Melody Brue,

"ServiceNow Challenges Traditional CRM at Knowledge 2025 Conference," *Forbes*, May 14, 2025, https://www.forbes.com/sites/moorinsights/2025/05/14/servicenow-challenges-traditional-crm-at-knowledge-2025-conference/; Gartner, "Invest Implications: Magic Quadrant for Artificial Intelligence Applications in IT Service Management," October 15, 2024, https://www.gartner.com/en/documents/5841247; Gartner, "Gartner Magic Quadrant for the CRM Customer Engagement Center," December 11, 2024, https://www.gartner.com/en/documents/6006703.

86. QS Quacquarelli Symonds, "Rankings Released! QS World University Rankings 2025," June 4, 2024, https://www.qs.com/insights/rankings-released-qs-world-university-rankings-2025; U.S. News and World Report, "U.S. News Releases 2025 Best Colleges Rankings," news release, September 23, 2024, https://s24.q4cdn.com/538403808/files/doc_news/U.S.-News-Releases-2025-Best-Colleges-Rankings-2024.pdf; "Times Higher Education World University Rankings 2025 Released," *Times Higher Education*, October 9, 2024, https://www.timeshighereducation.com/press-releases/times-higher-education-world-university-rankings-2025-released; *Higher Education Research and Development (HERD) Survey* (National Center for Science and Engineering Statistics, 2024), https://ncses.nsf.gov/surveys/higher-education-research-development/2024; QS Quacquarelli Symonds, "Massachusetts Institute of Technology (MIT)," accessed April 27, 2026, https://www.topuniversities.com/universities/massachusetts-institute-technology-mit.

87. Texas Roadhouse, "Texas Roadhouse, Inc. Announces First Quarter 2024 Results," news release, May 2, 2024, https://investor.texasroadhouse.com/news/news-details/2024/Texas-RoadhouseInc--Announces-First-Quarter-2024-Results/default.aspx; Texas Roadhouse, "Texas Roadhouse, Inc. Announces Second Quarter 2024 Results," news release, July 5, 2024, https://investor.texasroadhouse.com/news/news-details/2024/Texas-Roadhouse-Inc--Announces-Second-Quarter-2024-Results/default.aspx; Texas Roadhouse, "Texas Roadhouse, Inc. Announces Third Quarter 2024 Results," news release, October 24, 2024, https://investor.texasroadhouse.com/news/news-details/2024/Texas-RoadhouseInc--Announces-Third-Quarter-2024-Results/default.aspx; Texas Roadhouse, "Texas Roadhouse, Inc. Announces Fourth Quarter 2024 Results," news release, February 20, 2025, https://investor.texasroadhouse.com/news/news-details/2025/Texas-RoadhouseInc--Announces-Fourth-Quarter-2024-Results/default.aspx; Alicia Kelso, "How Texas Roadhouse Is Managing Higher Volumes," *Nation's Restaurant News*, February 21, 2025, https://www.nrn.com/casual-dining/how-texas-roadhouse-is-managing-higher-volumes.

88. Emirates Airline, "Emirates Group Announces 2023–24 Results," news release, May 13, 2024, https://www.emirates.com/media-centre/emirates-group-zannounces-2023-24-results/.

89. Kirsten Korosec, "Waymo Has Doubled Its Weekly Robotaxi Rides in Less Than A Year," *TechCrunch*, February 27, 2025, https://techcrunch.com/2025/02/27/waymo-has-doubled-its-weekly-robotaxi-rides-in-less-than-a-year/; Brad

Templeton, "Waymo's New Safety Data Is Impressive and Teaches a Lesson," *Forbes*, September 5, 2024, https://www.forbes.com/sites/bradtempleton/2024/09/05/waymos-new-safety-data-is-impressive-and-teaches-a-lesson/; Steven Aquino, "For Many Disabled San Franciscans, a No-Waitlist Waymo Means More Agency, Autonomy in Transportation," *Forbes*, June 28, 2024, https://www.forbes.com/sites/stevenaquino/2024/06/28/for-many-disabled-san-franciscans-a-no-waitlist-waymo-means-more-agency-autonomy-in-transportation/; Waymo, "Advice letter 0002 (Tier 2) to the Public Utilities Commission of the State of California," January 19, 2024, https://www.cpuc.ca.gov/-/media/cpuc-website/divisions/consumer-protection-and-enforcement-division/documents/tlab/av-programs/waymo-llc-cpuc-advice-letter-0002-tier-2--january-2024-passenger-safety-plan-update-january-192024.pdf; Alphabet Inc., "Form 10-K for the Fiscal Year Ended December 31, 2024," US Securities and Exchange Commission, filed February 4, 2025, https://s206.q4cdn.com/479360582/files/doc_financials/2024/q4/goog-10-k-2024.pdf; "Waymo," Apple App Store, accessed April 27, 2026, https://apps.apple.com/us/app/waymo/id1343524838.

90. NerdWallet, "NerdWallet Announces Winners of Its 2025 Best-Of Awards," news release, January 2, 2025, https://investors.nerdwallet.com/news-releases/news-release-details/nerdwallet-announces-winners-its-2025-best-awards; June Sham, "Wealthfront Review 2026: Our Editorial Team's Honest Take," NerdWallet, January 21, 2026, https://www.nerdwallet.com/investing/reviews/wealthfront-2026.

91. Watermark Consulting, "The Customer Experience ROI Study," August 20, 2024, https://watermarkconsult.net/blog/2024/08/20/customer-experience-roi-study/; "Retaining Customers Is the Real Challenge," Bain & Company, January 2006, https://www.bain.com/insights/retaining-customers-is-the-real-challenge/.

CHAPTER 8: THE COMEBACK KIDS

1. U.S. Equal Employment Opportunity Commission, "EEOC Agrees to Landmark Resolution of Discrimination Case Against Abercrombie & Fitch," press release, November 18, 2024, https://www.eeoc.gov/newsroom/eeoc-agrees-landmark-resolution-discrimination-case-against-abercrombie-fitch-0.

2. US Securities and Exchange Commission, "Abercrombie & Fitch Co. Reports Fourth Quarter and Full Year Results," March 2, 2021, https://www.sec.gov/Archives/edgar/data/1018840/000101884021000014/q42020pressrelease.htm.

3. "Abercrombie & Fitch Names Merchandising Head as New CEO," Reuters, February 1, 2017, https://www.reuters.com/article/business/abercrombie-fitch-names-merchandising-head-as-new-ceo-idUSL4N1FM47F/.

4. "Abercrombie & Fitch," YouGov, BrandIndex, https://yougov.com/en-us/topics/brand/Abercrombie_Fitch.

5. Abercrombie & Fitch Co., "Abercrombie & Fitch Co. Reports Fourth Quarter and Full Year Results," news release, March 6, 2025, https://corporate.abercrombie.com/blog/abercrombie-fitch-co-reports-fourth-quarter-and-full-year-results/.

6. Ellen Hammett, "Polaroid Unveils New Identity to Bring More Clarity to Brand," *MarketingWeek*, March 26, 2020, https://www.marketingweek.com/polaroid-rebrand-2020/.

7. Markets & Data, "Global Instant Print Camera Market Assessment, By Type [Analog, Digital], By Exposure [Automatic, Manual], By Film [Polaroid, Instax], By Price Range [Below USD 80, USD 81—USD 160, USD 161—USD 240, Above USD 240], By Connectivity Type [Micro USB Type, Bluetooth Type], By End-user [Professionals, Individuals], By Distribution Channel [Online, Offline], By Region, Opportunities and Forecast, 2017-2031F," January 2026, https://www.marketsandata.com/industry-reports/instant-print-camera-market.

8. FUJIFILM Corporation, "instax™ Cumulative Sales Exceeds 100 Million Units," news release, April 8, 2025, https://www.fujifilm.com/jp/en/news/hq/12295.

9. Markets & Data, "Global Instant Print Camera Market Assessment."

10. Hammett, "Polaroid Unveils New Identity."

11. "Polaroid x Basquiat Camera & Film Have Eye-Popping Action Scribbled All Over," DesignTAXI, March 8, 2024, https://community.designtaxi.com/topic/2690-polaroid-x-basquiat-camera-film-have-eye-popping-action-scribbled-all-over/; Jeremy Gray, "Polaroid and MoMA Collab on Bright Blue Instant Camera and Vibrant Film," PetaPixel, May 20, 2025, https://petapixel.com/2025/05/20/polaroid-and-moma-collab-on-bright-blue-instant-camera-and-vibrant-film/.

12. Beau Hayhoe, "Polaroid Debuts Arty Camera Inspired by Jean-Michel Basquiat" Maxim, March 7, 2024, https://www.maxim.com/gear/polaroid-debuts-arty-camera-inspired-by-jean-michel-basquiat/.

13. Markets & Data, "Global Instant Print Camera Market Assessment."

14. Fujifilm Holdings Corporation, "Fujifilm Announces Global Cumulative Shipments of 'instax' Series Surpass 100 Million Units," March 2024, https://www.fujifilm.com/jp/en/news/list/2024/0313_01.

15. Suzanne Vranica, "America's Newest Hit Candy Is Gummy, Crunchy and Printing Money," *The Wall Street Journal*, October 26, 2024, https://www.wsj.com/business/media/nerds-gummy-clusters-candy-halloween-35ae2e2a?.

16. Julia Waldow, "How Gummy Clusters Became Nerds' Hero Product," Modern Retail, March 5, 2024, https://www.modernretail.co/marketing/how-gummy-clusters-became-nerds-hero-product/.

17. Vranica, "America's Newest Hit Candy."

18. Christopher Doering, "How Nerds Gummy Clusters Became the Candy Aisle's Biggest Hit," *Food Dive*, June 9, 2025, https://www.fooddive.com/news/how-nerds-gummy-clusters-became-the-candy-aisles-biggest-hit/748865/.

19. "NCA Announces Winners of the 2021 Most Innovative New Product Awards," Snack Food & Wholesale Bakery, June 22, 2021, https://www.snackandbakery.com/articles/105961-nca-announces-winners-of-the-2021-most-innovative-new-product-awards.

20. Alyse Thompson-Richards, "State of the Industry: Non-Chocolate Novelty Sees Double-Digit Growth," Candy Industry, July 21, 2022, https://www.snackandbakery.com/articles/106387-state-of-the-industry-non-chocolate-novelty-sees-double-digit-growth.

21. "Ferrara Debuts Very Berry Nerds Gummy Clusters," Snack Food & Wholesale Bakery, May 25, 2022, https://www.snackandbakery.com/articles/104350-ferrara-debuts-very-berry-nerds-gummy-clusters.

22. Waldow, "How Gummy Clusters."

23. Liz Parker Kuhn, "State of the Industry 2024: Gummies Shine with Innovation," Snack Food & Wholesale Bakery, September 25, 2024, https://www.snackandbakery.com/articles/112171-state-of-the-industry-2024-gummies-shine-with-innovation.

24. Doering, "How Nerds Gummy Clusters."

25. Kuhn, "State of the Industry 2024."

26. Christopher Doering, "Confection Giants Find Gummy Sales Anything but Soft," *Food Dive*, July 9, 2024, https://www.fooddive.com/news/confection-giants-hershey-mars-wrigley-gummies-chocolate-snacking/715481/.

27. Doering, "Confection Giants Find Gummy Sales."

28. Echo Wang, "Triller Says Made $20 Bln Bid with Centricus for TikTok Assets," Reuters, August 28, 2020, https://www.reuters.com/world/americas/corrected-update-1-triller-says-made-20-bln-bid-with-centricus-tiktok-assets-2020-08-29/; Tim Baysinger, "Instagram Adds Advertising to Instagram Stories," Reuters, January 11, 2017, https://www.reuters.com/article/facebook-advertising-instagram/corrected-instagram-adds-advertising-to-instagram-stories-idUKL1N1F01YY/.

29. Snap Inc., "Q4 2020 Earnings Slides," February 4, 2021, https://s25.q4cdn.com/442043304/files/doc_financials/2020/q4/Snap-Inc.-Q4-2020-Earnings-Slides.pdf.

30. Snap Inc., "Snap Inc. Announces Third Quarter 2024 Financial Results," press release, October 29, 2024, https://investor.snap.com/news/news-details/2024/

Snap-Inc.-Announces-Third-Quarter-2024-Financial-Results/default.aspx; Snap Inc., "Snap Inc. Announces Fourth Quarter and Full Year 2022 Financial Results," press release, January 31, 2023, https://investor.snap.com/news/news-details/2023/Snap-Inc.-Announces-Fourth-Quarter-and-Full-Year-2022-Financial-Results/default.aspx.

31. Snap Engineering, "Don't Rewrite Your App, Unless You Have To," May 7, 2020, https://eng.snap.com/dont-rewrite-your-app-unless-you-have-to.

32. Snap Inc., "Snap Inc. Announces Fourth Quarter and Full Year 2020 Financial Results," February 4, 2021, https://investor.snap.com/news/news-details/2021/Snap-Inc.-Announces-Fourth-Quarter-and-Full-Year-2020-Financial-Results/default.aspx; Snap Inc., "Snap Inc. Announces Fourth Quarter and Full Year 2021 Financial Results," February 3, 2022, https://investor.snap.com/news/news-details/2022/Snap-Inc.-Announces-Fourth-Quarter-and-Full-Year-2021-Financial-Results/default.aspx; Snap Inc., "Snap Inc. Announces Fourth Quarter and Full Year 2022 Financial Results"; Snap Inc., "Snap Inc. Announces Third Quarter 2024 Financial Results."

33. Snap Inc., "Snap Inc. Announces Second Quarter 2024 Financial Results," August 1, 2024, https://investor.snap.com/news/news-details/2024/Snap-Inc.-Announces-Second-Quarter-2024-Financial-Results/default.aspx.

34. Snap Inc., "Snap Inc. Announces Fourth Quarter and Full Year 2020 Financial Results"; Snap Inc., "Snap Inc. Announces Fourth Quarter and Full Year 2021 Financial Results"; Snap Inc., "Snap Inc. Announces Fourth Quarter and Full Year 2022 Financial Results."

35. Amber van der Wal et al., "Diverse Platforms, Diverse Effects: Evidence from a 100-Day Study on Social Media and Adolescent Mental Health," *Current Psychology* 45, no. 1 (December 2025), https://pmc.ncbi.nlm.nih.gov/articles/PMC12717229/.

36. Emily Vogels et al., "Teens, Social Media and Technology 2022," Pew Research Center, August 10, 2022, https://www.pewresearch.org/internet/2022/08/10/teens-social-media-and-technology-2022/; Michelle Faverio and Olivia Sidoti, "Teens, Social Media and Technology 2024," Pew Research Center, December 12, 2024, https://www.pewresearch.org/internet/2024/12/12/teens-social-media-and-technology-2024/.

37. Faverio and Sidoti, "Teens, Social Media and Technology 2024"; Snap Inc., "Snap Inc. Investor Letter Q3 2022," October 20, 2022, https://s25.q4cdn.com/442043304/files/doc_financials/2022/q3/Snap-Inc.-Q3-2022-Investor-Letter-(10.20.2022).pdf.

38. "Snap Launches Paid Version of Snapchat App," Reuters, June 29, 2022, https://www.reuters.com/technology/snap-launches-paid-version-snapchat-app-2022-06-29/.

39. Snap Inc., "Snap Inc. Announces Fourth Quarter and Full Year 2023 Financial Results," February 6, 2024, https://investor.snap.com/news/news-details/2024/

Snap-Inc.-Announces-Fourth-Quarter-and-Full-Year-2023-Financial-Results/default.aspx; Snap Inc., "Snap Inc. Announces Third Quarter 2024 Financial Results"; Snap Inc., "Snap Inc. Investor Letter Q4 2024," February 2025, https://s25.q4cdn.com/442043304/files/doc_financials/2024/q4/Q4-2024-Investor-Letter.pdf.

40. Sheila Dang, "Snap to Cut 20% of Staff, Cancel Projects in Cost-Cutting Effort," Reuters, August 31, 2022, https://www.reuters.com/technology/snap-restructures-ad-business-amid-worst-sales-growth-rate-its-history-2022-08-31/; Snap Inc., "Snap Inc. Announces Fourth Quarter and Full Year 2020 Financial Results"; Snap Inc., "Snap Inc. Announces Fourth Quarter and Full Year 2021 Financial Results," Snap Inc., "Snap Inc. Announces Fourth Quarter and Full Year 2023 Financial Results."

41. Life Time Group Holdings, Inc., "Quarterly Report on Form 10-Q for the Quarter Ended September 30, 2021," US Securities and Exchange Commission, filed October 12, 2021, https://ir.lifetime.life/sec-filings/all-sec-filings/content/0001869198-23-000063/lth-20230930.htm; Life Time Group Holdings, Inc., "Form 10-K for the Fiscal Year Ended December 31, 2021," US Securities and Exchange Commission, filed March 10, 2022, https://www.sec.gov/Archives/edgar/data/1869198/000186919822000010/lth-20211231.htm.

42. Life Time Group Holdings, Inc., "Form 10-K for the Fiscal Year Ended December 31, 2021."

43. Life Time Group Holdings, Inc., "Quarterly Report on Form 10-Q for the Quarter Ended September 30, 2021."

44. Life Time Group Holdings, Inc., "Form 10-K for the Fiscal Year Ended December 31, 2024."

45. Life Time Group Holdings, Inc., "Form 424B4," October 8, 2021, https://ir.lifetime.life/sec-filings/all-sec-filings/content/0001193125-21-294420/d157859d424b4.htm; Life Time Group Holdings, Inc., "Form 10-K for the Fiscal Year Ended December 31, 2024," US Securities and Exchange Commission, filed February 27, 2025, https://ir.lifetime.life/sec-filings/all-sec-filings/content/0001869198-25-000009/lth-20241231.htm.

46. Life Time Group Holdings, Inc., "Form 10-K for the Fiscal Year Ended December 31, 2021"; Life Time Group Holdings, Inc., "Form 10-K for the Fiscal Year Ended December 31, 2023," US Securities and Exchange Commission, filed February 28, 2024, https://ir.lifetime.life/sec-filings/all-sec-filings/content/0001869198-24-000008/lth-20231231.htm; Life Time Group Holdings, Inc., "Form 10-K for the Fiscal Year Ended December 31, 2024."

47. Life Time Group Holdings, Inc., "Form 10-K for the Fiscal Year ended December 31, 2023"; Life Time Group Holdings, Inc., "Form 10-K for the Fiscal Year Ended December 31, 2024."

48. Life Time Group Holdings, Inc., "10-K for the Fiscal Year Ended December 31, 2021"; Life Time Group Holdings, Inc., "Form 10-K for the Fiscal Year Ended December 31, 2023"; Life Time Group Holdings, Inc., "Form 10-K for the Fiscal Year Ended December 31, 2024."

49. Life Time Group Holdings, Inc., "Form 10-K for the Fiscal Year Ended December 31, 2023"; Life Time Group Holdings, Inc., "Form 10-K for the Year Ended December 31, 2024"; Life Time Group Holdings, Inc., "10-K for the Fiscal Year Ended December 31, 2021."

50. Life Time Group Holdings, Inc., "Form 10-K for the Year Ended December 31, 2024."

51. Life Time Group Holdings, Inc., "10-K for the Fiscal Year Ended December 31, 2021"; Life Time Group Holdings, Inc., "Form 10-K for the Year Ended December 31, 2024."

52. Life Time Group Holdings, Inc., "10-K for the Fiscal Year Ended December 31, 2021"; Life Time Group Holdings, Inc., "Form 10-K for the Year Ended December 31, 2024."

53. Life Time Group Holdings, Inc., "Form 10-K for the Year Ended December 31, 2024"; Life Time Group Holdings, Inc., "10-K for the Fiscal Year Ended December 31, 2021."

54. Oscar Health, Inc, "Form 10-K for the Fiscal Year Ended December 31, 2021," US Securities and Exchange Commission, filed March 1, 2022, https://www.sec.gov/Archives/edgar/data/1568651/000156865122000011/oscr-20211231.htm; Alex Wilhelm, "Oscar Health Prices IPO at $39 and Secures a $9.5B Valuation," *TechCrunch*, March 3, 2021, https://techcrunch.com/2021/03/03/oscar-health-prices-ipo-at-39-and-secures-a-9-5b-valuation/; Oscar Health, Inc., "Form 10-K for the Fiscal Year Ended December 31, 2022," US Securities and Exchange Commission, filed February 24, 2023, https://www.sec.gov/Archives/edgar/data/1568651/000156865123000017/oscr-20221231.htm; Oscar Health, "Oscar Health Announces Results for Third Quarter 2022," US Securities and Echange Commission, November 8, 2022, https://www.sec.gov/Archives/edgar/data/1568651/000156865122000054/oscr-3q22xpressrelease.htm.

55. Oscar Health, Inc., "Form 10-K for the Fiscal Year Ended December 31, 2021."

56. Oscar Health, Inc., "Form 10-K for the Fiscal Year Ended December 31, 2024," US Securities and Exchange Commission, filed February 27, 2025, https://www.sec.gov/Archives/edgar/data/1568651/000156865125000008/oscr-20241231.htm; Nona Tepper, "Oscar Health Leaves Two States Amid Regulatory, Commercial Challenges," Modern Healthcare, May 10, 2022, https://www.modernhealthcare.com/insurance/oscar-health-leaves-two-states-amid-regulatory-commercial-challenges/.

57. Oscar Health, Inc., "Form 10-K for the Fiscal Year Ended December 31, 2024."

58. "Oscar Health, Inc. (OSCR) Historical Prices," Yahoo Finance, accessed March 2026, https://finance.yahoo.com/quote/OSCR/history/; Rebecca Parduhn, "Oscar Health Reports First Profitable Year," *Healthcare Dive*, February 5, 2025, https://www.healthcaredive.com/news/oscar-health-first-profitable-year-aca/739269/.

59. Oscar Health, Inc., "Form 10-K for the Fiscal Year Ended December 31, 2024."

60. Oscar Health, Inc., "Form 10-K for the Fiscal Year Ended December 31, 2024."

61. Oscar Health, Inc., "Form 10-K for the Fiscal Year Ended December 31, 2024."

62. Centers for Medicare & Medicaid Services, "Health Insurance Exchanges Quality Rating System (QRS) for Plan Year (PY) 2023: Results at a Glance," October 2023, https://www.cms.gov/files/document/qrs-results-glance-py2023.pdf.

63. Oscar Health, Inc., "Form 10-K for the Fiscal Year Ended December 31, 2023," US Securities and Exchange Commission, filed February 28, 2024, https://www.sec.gov/Archives/edgar/data/1568651/000156865124000006/oscr-20231231.htm.

64. Oscar Health, Inc., "Form 10-K for the Fiscal Year Ended December 31, 2023."

65. Oscar Health, Inc., "Form 10-K for the Fiscal Year Ended December 31, 2024."

66. Oscar Health, Inc., "Form 10-K for the Fiscal Year Ended December 31, 2024."

67. Oscar Health, Inc., "Form 10-K for the Fiscal Year Ended December 31, 2024."

68. "Oscar Health, Inc. (OSCR) Historical Prices"; Parduhn, "Oscar Health Reports."

69. Atlassian, "Our Q4 FY24 Letter"; Atlassian, "Atlassian Announces Third Quarter Fiscal Year 2025 Results"; Atlassian, "Atlassian Announces Fourth Quarter and Fiscal Year 2024 Results," news release, August 1, 2024, https://s206.q4cdn.com/270053503/files/doc_financials/2024/q4/TEAM-Q4-2024-Earnings-Release.pdf.

70. Rosalie Chan, "The Co-CEO of $47 Billion Atlassian Explains Why It Plans to Stop Selling Its Server Product Lineup Starting in February: 'The Cloud Is the Natural Future,'" *Business Insider*, October 16, 2020, https://www.businessinsider.com/atlassian-server-support-sales-ending-data-center-cloud-2020-10.

71. "Cloud Migration Guide," Atlassian, accessed March 2026, https://www.atlassian.com/migration/plan/cloud-guide; "Migrate Your Atlassian Server to Cloud," Atlassian Support, accessed March 2026, https://support.atlassian.com/migration/resources/; Atlassian, "Cloud Roadmap," accessed March 2026, https://www.atlassian.com/roadmap/cloud; Atlassian, "The Ultimate Guide to Migrating at Scale," June 10, 2021, https://www.atlassian.com/whitepapers/ultimate-guide-to-cloud-migrations.

72. Disha Rustogi, "100 Days to Go: Get to Cloud Before Server Support Ends," Atlassian, November 7, 2023, https://www.atlassian.com/blog/announcements/server-support-100-day-countdown; Disha Rustogi, "Migrate Now: Server Support Ends on Feb. 15," Atlassian, January 22, 2024, https://www.atlassian.com/blog/announcements/server-support-30-day-countdown.

73. Molly Bronstein, "Atlassian Recognized as Visionary in the 2021 Gartner Magic Quadrant for IT Service Management Tools," Atlassian, September 3, 2021, https://www.atlassian.com/blog/it-service-management/2021-gartner-mq-itsm-atlassian; *Business Wire*, "Atlassian Named a Leader in the 2022 Gartner® Magic Quadrant™ for IT Service Management Platforms," news release, November 3, 2022, https://www.businesswire.com/news/home/20221103006331/en/Atlassian-Named-a-Leader-in-the-2022-Gartner-Magic-Quadrant-for-IT-Service-Management-Platforms.

74. Atlassian, "Service Level Agreement for Atlassian Cloud Apps," accessed April 27, 2026, https://support.atlassian.com/subscriptions-and-billing/docs/service-level-agreement-for-atlassian-cloud-products/.

75. Gartner Peer Insights, "Jira Service Management Reviews & Ratings," accessed March 13, 2026, https://www.gartner.com/reviews/product/jira-service-management.

76. Atlassian, "Our Q4 FY25 Letter to Shareholders," August 8, 2025, https://www.atlassian.com/blog/announcements/shareholder-letter-q4fy25.

77. Tom Tsao, "The Atlassian Marketplace Picks Up Momentum," Atlassian, December 9, 2021, https://www.atlassian.com/blog/add-ons/marketplace-momentum; Fede Baronti-Deiser, "Things You Might Not Know About the Atlassian Marketplace," Atlassian Community, April 10, 2023, https://community.atlassian.com/forums/App-Central-articles/Things-you-might-not-know-about-the-Atlassian-Marketplace/ba-p/2326712.

78. Christa Nitchals, "Hy-Vee Advanced ITSM and Saved 100+ Downtime Hours per Year with Jira Service Management Cloud," Atlassian, https://www.atlassian.com/customers/hy-vee.

79. Atlassian, "Our Q4 FY24 Letter"; Atlassian, "Atlassian Announces Third Quarter Fiscal Year 2025 Results"; Atlassian, "Atlassian Announces Fourth Quarter and Fiscal Year 2024 Results."

80. Atlassian, "Atlassian Announces Third Quarter Fiscal Year 2024 Results and CEO Transition," news release, April 25, 2024, https://s206.q4cdn.com/270053503/files/doc_financials/2024/q3/TEAM-Q3-2024-Earnings-Release.pdf.

81. Karishma Vanjani, "Atlassian Stock Surges on Big Cloud Beat. AI Could Be Its Next Growth Driver," *Barron's*, January 31, 2025, https://www.barrons.com/articles/atlassian-stock-earnings-reaction-0142307e?.

82. Vincent Woo, "Lambda Coding Boot Camp Claims 86 Percent of Students Get Tech Jobs. They Don't," *New York Magazine*, February 19, 2020, https://nymag.com/intelligencer/tags/coding/.

83. Consumer Financial Protection Bureau, "Consent Order," file no. 2024-CFPB-0001, BloomTech Inc., filed April 17, 2024, https://files.consumerfinance.gov/f/documents/cfpb_bloomtech-inc-consent-order_2024-04.pdf.

84. California Bureau for Private Postsecondary Education, "Order of Abatement: Lambda School," issued March 20, 2019, https://www.bppe.ca.gov/enforcement/actions/lamba_ord.pdf; California Bureau for Private Postsecondary Education, "Citation Affirmed/Modified Citation: Assessment of Fine and Order of Abatement," July 24, 2019, https://www.bppe.ca.gov/enforcement/actions/1819150_lambda_affirmed.pdf.

85. Natalie Schwartz, "For-Profit Coding School BloomTech Sued Over Alleged Misrepresented Job Placements," *Higher Ed Dive*, April 18, 2022, https://www.highereddive.com/news/for-profit-coding-school-bloomtech-sued-over-alleged-misrepresented-job-pla/622253/; Sean Hollister, "Coding Bootcamp Lambda School—now BloomTech—Is Finally Getting Punished," The Verge, April 17, 2024, https://www.theverge.com/2024/4/17/24133577/lambda-school-bloomtech-loan-ban-student-debt.

86. Natasha Mascarenhas, "BloomTech, Previously Lambda School, Cuts Half of Staff," *TechCrunch*, December 1, 2022, https://techcrunch.com/2022/12/01/bloomtech-previously-lambda-school-cuts-half-of-staff/; Consumer Financial Protection Bureau, "BloomTech Inc., d/b/a Bloom Institute of Technology or BloomTech, and Austen Allred," April 17, 2024, https://www.consumerfinance.gov/enforcement/actions/bloomtech-inc-and-austen-allred/; Consumer Financial Protection Bureau, "CFPB Takes Action Against Coding Boot Camp BloomTech and CEO Austen Allred for Deceiving Students and Hiding Loan Costs," news release, April 17, 2024, https://www.consumerfinance.gov/about-us/newsroom/cfpb-takes-action-against-coding-boot-camp-bloomtech-and-ceo-austen-allred-for-deceiving-students-and-hiding-loan-costs/.

87. Natasha Mascarenhas, "Lambda School Shakes Off Its Brand with New Name," *TechCrunch*, November 16, 2021, https://techcrunch.com/2021/11/16/lambda-school-rebrand-bloom-institute-of-technology/."

88. California Bureau for Private Postsecondary Education, "School Performance Fact Sheet, Calendar Years 2021 & 2022," November 29, 2023, https://www.bppe.ca.gov/webapplications/annualReports/2022/document/9ef0a67c-5a26-414a-8bf7-4c98827619f5.

89. California Bureau for Private Postsecondary Education, "Bloom Institute of Technology Course Catalog," November 1, 2022, https://www.bppe.ca.gov/

webapplications/annualReports/2022/document/4781b16a-0161-48de-a637-759704338f93.

90. Consumer Financial Protection Bureau, "Consent Order."

91. *Bloom Institute of Technology 2021 Outcomes Report* (Bloom Institute of Technology, 2021), https://www.bloomtech.com/reports/outcomes-report; *Bloom Institute of Technology 2022 Outcomes Report* (Bloom Institute of Technology, 2022), https://www.bloomtech.com/reports/outcomes-report-2022; Bloom Institute of Technology, "Tuition Refund Guarantee," accessed March 2026, https://www.bloomtech.com/tuition/tuition-refund-guarantee; Consumer Financial Protection Bureau, "Consent Order."

92. Consumer Financial Protection Bureau, "Consent Order"; Bloom Institute of Technology, "Tuition Refund Guarantee."

93. Hollister, "Coding Bootcamp Lambda School."

94. Consumer Financial Protection Bureau, "BloomTech Inc., d/b/a Bloom Institute of Technology or BloomTech, and Austen Allred"; Consumer Financial Protection Bureau, "CFPB Takes Action."

95. Bloom Institute of Technology, "Tuition Refund Guarantee"; Consumer Financial Protection Bureau, "Consent Order."

96. California Bureau for Private Postsecondary Education, "Bloom Institute of Technology Course Catalog."

97. Chipotle Mexican Grill, "Chipotle Announces Fourth Quarter and Full Year 2021 Results," news release, February 8, 2022, https://ir.chipotle.com/2022-02-08-CHIPOTLE-ANNOUNCES-FOURTH-QUARTER-AND-FULL-YEAR-2021-RESULTS; Chipotle Mexican Grill, "Chipotle Announces Fourth Quarter and Full Year 2022 Results," news release, February 7, 2023, https://ir.chipotle.com/2023-02-07-CHIPOTLE-ANNOUNCES-FOURTH-QUARTER-AND-FULL-YEAR-2022-RESULTS; Chipotle Mexican Grill, "Chipotle Announces Fourth Quarter and Full Year 2023 Results," news release, February 6, 2024, https://ir.chipotle.com/2024-02-06-CHIPOTLE-ANNOUNCES-FOURTH-QUARTER-AND-FULL-YEAR-2023-RESULTS.

98. Chipotle Mexican Grill, "Form 10-K for the Fiscal Year Ended December 31, 2021," US Securities and Exchange Commission, filed February 15, 2022, https://www.sec.gov/Archives/edgar/data/1058090/000105809022000011/cmg-20211231x10k.htm; Chipotle Mexican Grill, "Form 10-K for the Year Ended December 31, 2023," US Securities and Exchange Commission, filed February 15, 2024, https://www.sec.gov/Archives/edgar/data/1058090/000156276224000023/cmg-20231231x10k.htm; Chipotle Mexican Grill, "Form 10-K for the Year Ended December 31, 2024,"

US Securities and Exchange Commission, filed February 2025, https://www.sec.gov/Archives/edgar/data/1058090/000105809025000014/cmg-20241231.htm.

99. Joe Guszkowski, "Chipotle to Focus on Portion Sizes at Some 'Outlier' Restaurants," *Restaurant Business*, July 25, 2024, https://www.restaurantbusinessonline.com/operations/chipotle-focus-portion-sizes-some-outlier-restaurants.

100. Chipotle Mexican Grill, "Chipotle Adds Chicken al Pastor to Menus in the U.S., Canada, and Europe," news release, March 14, 2023, https://ir.chipotle.com/2023-03-14-CHIPOTLE-ADDS-CHICKEN-AL-PASTOR-TO-MENUS-IN-THE-U-S-,-CANADA,-AND-EUROPE; Patricia Cobe, "Chipotle Brings Back Chicken al Pastor, Answering Pleas from Fans," *Restaurant Business*, March 11, 2024, https://www.restaurantbusinessonline.com/food/chipotle-brings-back-chicken-al-pastor-answering-pleas-fans.

101. Chipotle Mexican Grill, "Chipotle Announces Fourth Quarter and Full Year 2024 Results," news release, February 4, 2025, https://ir.chipotle.com/2025-02-04-CHIPOTLE-ANNOUNCES-FOURTH-QUARTER-AND-FULL-YEAR-2024-RESULTS; Chipotle Mexican Grill, "Chipotle Announces Fourth Quarter and Full Year 2023 Results."

102. "Chipotle," Apple App Store, accessed April 27, 2026, https://apps.apple.com/us/app/chipotle/id327228455.

103. Chipotle Mexican Grill, "Chipotle Announces Fourth Quarter and Full Year 2024 Results"; Alicia Kelso, "Chipotle Adds Free Food Incentives to Its Loyalty Program," *Nation's Restaurant News*, January 9, 2023, https://www.nrn.com/marketing-branding/chipotle-adds-free-food-incentives-to-its-loyalty-program.

104. Chipotle Mexican Grill, "Form 10-K for the Year Ended December 31, 2024."

105. Chipotle Mexican Grill, "Form 10-K for the Year Ended December 31, 2024."

106. Chipotle Mexican Grill, "Chipotle Introduces Its First-Ever Creator Class, Gives One Fan the Chance to Join the Exclusive Group," news release, September 9, 2021, https://ir.chipotle.com/2021-09-09-Chipotle-Introduces-Its-First-Ever-Creator-Class,-Gives-One-Fan-The-Chance-To-Join-The-Exclusive-Group.

107. Chipotle Mexican Grill, "Chipotle Announces Fourth Quarter and Full Year 2023 Results"; Chipotle Mexican Grill, "Chipotle Announces Fourth Quarter and Full Year 2024 Results."

108. Chipotle Mexican Grill, "Form 10-K for the Year Ended December 31, 2024"; Chipotle Mexican Grill, "Chipotle Announces Fourth Quarter and Full Year 2023 Results"; Chipotle Mexican Grill, "Chipotle Announces Fourth Quarter and Full Year 2024 Results."

109. Daniela Sirtori and Jeran Wittenstein, "Chipotle to Seek 50-to-1 Stock Split at Annual Meeting," Bloomberg, March 19, 2024, https://www.bloomberg.com/news/articles/2024-03-19/chipotle-to-seek-50-to-1-stock-split-at-june-6-annual-meeting?embedded-checkout=true; "Chipotle Mexican Grill, Inc. (CMG)," Yahoo Finance historical price data, accessed March 2026, https://finance.yahoo.com/quote/CMG/history/.

110. Norwegian Cruise Line Holdings Ltd., "Form 10-K for the Year Ended December 31, 2021," US Securities and Exchange Commission, filed February 2022, https://www.sec.gov/Archives/edgar/data/1513761/000155837022002516/nclh-20211231x10k.htm; Norwegian Cruise Line Holdings Ltd., "Form 10-Q for the Quarter Ended September 30, 2022," US Securities and Exchange Commission, filed November 2022, https://content.bsx.com/CompanyDocuments/1099939847/NCLH%20Q3%202022%20Form%2010-Q%20(As%20filed).pdf.

111. Doyinsola Oladipo, "Norwegian Cruise Line Posts Strong Bookings as Demand Rebounds," Reuters, November 2023, https://www.reuters.com/business/norwegian-cruise-line-posts-strong-bookings-demand-rebounds-2023-11-01/.

112. Norwegian Cruise Line Holdings Ltd., "Form 10-K for the Year Ended December 31, 2024," US Securities and Exchange Commission, filed February 27, 2025, https://www.sec.gov/Archives/edgar/data/1513761/000155837025001743/nclh-20241231x10k.htm.

113. Norwegian Cruise Line, "Norwegian Cruise Line Unveils 'More at Sea'—A New, Elevated Guest Experience," October 2024, https://www.nclhltd.com/investors/news-events/press-releases/detail/419/norwegian-cruise-line-unveils-more-at-sea.

114. SEC, "Norwegian Cruise Line Holdings Reports Strong Third Quarter 2023 Financial Results," SEC Form 8-K, Exhibit 99.1, November 1, 2023, https://www.sec.gov/Archives/edgar/data/1513761/000117184323006578/exh_991.htm.

115. SEC, "S&P Upgrades NCL Corporation Ltd.'s Credit Ratings," SEC Form 8-K, Exhibit 99.1, March 12, 2024, https://www.sec.gov/Archives/edgar/data/1513761/000110465924033277/tm248194d1_ex99-1.htm.

116. Norwegian Cruise Line Holdings Ltd., "Form 10-K for the Fiscal Year Ended December 31, 2024."

117. *State of the Cruise Industry Report* (Cruise Lines International Association, 2024), https://cruising.org/sites/default/files/2025-03/2024%20State%20of%20the%20Cruise%20Industry%20Report_updated%20050824_Web.pdf.

118. Norwegian Cruise Line Holdings Ltd., "Form 10-Q for the Quarter Ended September 30, 2022"; Norwegian Cruise Line Holdings Ltd., "Form 10-K for the Fiscal Year Ended December 31, 2021."

119. Norwegian Cruise Line Holdings Ltd., "Form 10-K for the Fiscal Year Ended December 31, 2024."

120. Norwegian Cruise Line Holdings Ltd., "Form 10-K for the Fiscal Year Ended December 31, 2024."

121. Maplebear Inc. (Instacart), "Form 10-K for the Fiscal Year Ended December 31, 2024," US Securities and Exchange Commission, filed February 26, 2025, https://investors.instacart.com/sec-filings/sec-filing/10-k/0001579091-25-000015.

122. Echo Wang, "Instacart Valued at $9.9 Bln as IPO Market Rebounds," Reuters, September 18, 2023, https://www.reuters.com/markets/deals/instacart-valued-99-billion-ipo-2023-09-18/.

123. Maplebear Inc., "Amendment No. 1 to Form S-1," US Securities and Exchange Commission, filed September 11, 2023, https://www.sec.gov/Archives/edgar/data/1579091/000119312523231909/d55348ds1a.htm; Maplebear Inc. (Instacart), "Form 10-K for the Fiscal Year Ended December 31, 2024."

124. Instacart, "Instacart Announces Fourth Quarter and Full Year 2024 Financial Results," news release, February 25, 2025, https://investors.instacart.com/news-releases/news-release-details/instacart-announces-fourth-quarter-and-full-year-2024-financial.

125. Instacart, "Instacart Announces Fourth Quarter and Full Year 2024."

126. Instacart, "Q3 2025 Letter to Shareholders," November 10, 2025, https://investors.instacart.com/static-files/b38c311a-f792-4829-ae79-191d179c615e.

127. Maplebear Inc. (Instacart), "Form 10-K for the Fiscal Year Ended December 31, 2024."

128. Instacart, "Instacart Announces Fourth Quarter and Full Year 2024"; Instacart, "Q3 2025."

129. Instacart, "Instacart Announces Fourth Quarter and Full Year 2024."

130. Ally Financial Inc., "Ally Financial Reports Second Quarter 2020 Financial Results," press release, July 17, 2020, https://media.ally.com/2020-07-17-Ally-Financial-Reports-Second-Quarter-2020-Financial-Results.

131. Arasu Kannagi Basil, "Ally Financial Warns of 'Intensifying' Credit Challenges, Shares Slump," Reuters, September 10, 2024, https://www.reuters.com/business/finance/ally-financial-flags-intensifying-credit-challenges-shares-slump-2024-09-10/.

132. Ally Financial Inc., "Form 10-K for the Fiscal Year Ended December 31, 2023," US Securities and Exchange Commission, filed February 21, 2024, https://www.sec.gov/ix?doc=/Archives/edgar/data/0000040729/000004072924000004/ally-20231231.htm.

133. Ally Financial Inc., "Form 10-K for the Fiscal Year Ended December 31, 2024," US Securities and Exchange Commission, filed February 19, 2025, https://www.sec.gov/Archives/edgar/data/40729/000004072925000006/ally-20241231.htm; Ally Financial Inc., 2024 Proxy Statement, April 5, 2024, https://www.ally.com/content/dam/pdf/investor-relations/2024-proxy.pdf.

134. Ally Bank, "High-Yield Savings Account Rate Disclosures," September 2024, https://www.ally.com/bank/view-rates/.

135. *Ally Corporate Social Responsibility Report* (Ally Financial, 2023), https://filecache.mediaroom.com/mr5mr_ally/186176/2023%20Ally%20CSR%20report%20Final%20v3.pdf; "Home Page," Thurgood Marshall College Fund, accessed April 27, 2026, https://tmcf.org/; "Moguls in the Making," Ally Financial Inc., accessed April 27, 2026, https://www.ally.com/go/moguls/.

136. Ally Financial Inc., "Form 10-K for the Fiscal Year Ended December 31, 2024."

137. Ally Financial Inc., "Ally Financial Reports Fourth Quarter and Full Year 2024 Financial Results," press release, January 22, 2025, https://media.ally.com/2025-01-22-Ally-Financial-reports-fourth-quarter-and-full-year-2024-financial-results; "Ally Financial Inc. (ALLY) Q4 FY2025 Earnings Call Transcript," Yahoo Finance, January 21, 2026, https://finance.yahoo.com/quote/ALLY/earnings/ALLY-Q4-2025-earnings_call-396518.html.

138. Basil, "Ally Financial Warns."

139. Ally Financial Inc., "Form 10-K for the Fiscal Year Ended December 31, 2024"; Ally Financial Inc., "Form 10-K for the Fiscal Year Ended December 31, 2023."

CHAPTER 9: CLASS SUMMARY

1. Jim Lecinski, "Are you simply asking #AI to just do things you are already doing but faster, cheaper, easier?" LinkedIn, 2024, linkedin.com/posts/jimlecinski_ai-ai-transformational-activity-7271552972612874240-pY8Q.

2. *State of the Connected Customer* (Salesforce, 2024), https://www.salesforce.com/eu/resources/research-reports/state-of-the-connected-customer-sa/.

3. "Experience Is Everything. Get It Right," PwC, https://www.pwc.com/us/en/services/consulting/library/consumer-intelligence-series/future-of-customer-experience.html; Zendesk, "AI Ushers in Era of Intelligent CX, Fuels Massive Industry Transformation," press release, January 17, 2024, https://www.zendesk.com/newsroom/press-releases/cx-trends-2024/.

ABOUT THE AUTHOR

JOSH GRAU HAS SPENT HIS CAREER AT COMPANIES that weren't riding waves—they were making them. As a four-time CMO and former executive at Twitter, YouTube, Wealthfront, and Yext, he helped build the marketing foundations for the defining technologies—online video, social media, fintech, and AI—that fundamentally changed how people interact with brands.

At the same time, he's watched even the world's most iconic brands struggle to connect with the people who matter most: their customers. After two decades helping brands find the plot, he translated those experiences into *The Brand GPA: Making the Grade with Your Customers*—a guide for leaders who want to move their brands to the top of the class.

He has taught marketing and storytelling at Northwestern and Stanford, coached NCAA Division I volleyball, and advises companies at all stages of growth. He writes *Shades of Grau* on Substack, where brands, technology, and popular culture intersect—and sometimes collide. He splits his time between Austin and San Francisco.